PRODUCING
POLITICS

PRODUCING POLITICS

INSIDE THE EXCLUSIVE CAMPAIGN WORLD WHERE THE PRIVILEGED FEW SHAPE POLITICS FOR ALL OF US

DANIEL LAURISON

Beacon Press · Boston

BEACON PRESS
Boston, Massachusetts
www.beacon.org

Beacon Press books
are published under the auspices of
the Unitarian Universalist Association of Congregations.

25 24 23 22   8 7 6 5 4 3 2 1

This book is printed on acid-free paper that meets the uncoated paper
ANSI/NISO specifications for permanence as revised in 1992.

Text design and composition by Kim Arney

Library of Congress Cataloguing in Publication Data is available for this title.
Library of Congress Control Number: 2022001571
Hardcover ISBN: 978-0-8070-2506-2
Ebook ISBN: 978-0-8070-2507-9

For my mom, Jenny Hover,
who couldn't make politics her job but insisted that working
for economic and racial justice was her true "career."
And for my partner, Hannah Laurison,
and for everyone who works to make our democracy more
representative and our country more just.

CONTENTS

INTRODUCTION

On November 4, 2008, I was crammed into the Oakland Convention Center alongside other Obama campaign staff, volunteers, and voters, all thrilled to celebrate the election of our nation's first Black president, Barack Obama. My partner, Hannah, and our thirteen-month-old baby were there with me, but Hannah was—in retrospect, entirely justifiably—furious with me. She nearly skipped the victory party altogether.

For months I'd been consumed by my role in Obama's campaign. When every action could in theory tip the balance toward our candidate, and with a firm end-date in sight, it had been all too easy to prioritize the election over friends, family, sleep, and nutrition. I remained proud, however, that I made it home for family dinner and my daughter's bedtime almost every night (unlike my boss, who also had children). Sure, I'd return to the campaign office afterward or stay up into the wee hours generating call sheets and emailing with the other campaign staff, and, yes, I'd put out salt instead of sugar for the guests' coffee at my daughter's first-birthday celebration, but I thought I was keeping an acceptable balance. I wasn't. By election night in 2008, Hannah was sick of handling every other aspect of our lives while I fanatically logged hours in the campaign office.

To top off my consistent absence in late summer and fall, I spent the final four days and nights of the election out of the house and unavailable to my family. Hannah and I both knew I was a low-level volunteer staffer in a noncompetitive state—my job was mostly managing volunteer field organizers, who were mostly organizing other volunteers to make phone calls into one battleground state or another. Still, I was frustrated that Hannah wasn't on the same page as I was. She couldn't understand why

I was needed so urgently and totally for a campaign in a notoriously blue state in an election that polls had all but called for the Democrats before the voting began. My family needed me, and I was so tired I couldn't be the spouse and co-parent my partner deserved. And I couldn't understand why she couldn't understand. All I could tell her was, "This is such an important election, and I have to do everything I can to make sure Obama wins."

I couldn't have imagined that night eight years earlier, when I was twenty-three and the presidential contest was between George W. Bush and Al Gore. I voted that year, but I wasn't at all sure that the distinctions between the candidates mattered for the issues I cared about. By 2004, however, after 9/11 and the wars in Iraq and Afghanistan, I understood the contest between George W. Bush and John Kerry as deeply consequential. I was certain the world and the country would be better off if Bush lost his reelection bid. So I wanted to get involved, to do more than vote to help ensure a Kerry victory.

In the early fall of 2004, I'd just moved to Berkeley, California, to start graduate school in sociology. With four years' experience working at a small nonprofit in Philadelphia, I knew how to raise money, recruit and manage volunteers, and organize and publicize events. I figured I could make a real contribution to the Bay Area portion of the Kerry effort, and so I headed down to the local campaign office in an out-of-the-way office park. Though I told anyone who looked like they were in charge about my relevant experience, I was relegated to phone-banking. Calling my way through pages and pages of potential voters in swing states, my ardor dimmed. Was this really the best use of my time and talents?

That year, I spent Election Day in Nevada, the nearest swing state, with a group of grad students I'd recruited to come along to help get out the vote with the group America Coming Together. When we arrived in Reno, there were so many out-of-state volunteers that I found myself stationed outside a polling place with three other volunteers, with nothing to do other than double-check and report voter tallies every few hours. When Kerry lost, I was both deeply disappointed and frustrated. I had the passion, skills, and availability to really help, and I felt I hadn't been able to do so. That's what first piqued my sociological interest: How did campaigns actually work? Who gets the access and influence to make decisions, implement strategies, and work directly with candidates?

The 2006 midterms provided an opening, I thought. Early in the summer I found a newly competitive House race nearby and showed up at every volunteer opportunity I could. I told campaign staff that I could dedicate an entire day every week to the effort, a time commitment substantial enough, I hoped, to get me really involved in the campaign. Instead, I spent a single afternoon inflating helium balloons and attaching them to a decorative arch for a one-off event. No one called me again until it was time for phone-banking and canvassing, which I showed up for every time I could. Still, that was the extent of my involvement. The *next* election cycle, in May of 2008, I again attempted to find meaningful work on the same House candidate's reelection campaign. This time I got a callback. Excitedly, I outlined my experience and said I could work four half-days a week, after my grad school job ended at noon, and all day on Fridays—twenty-eight hours a week, for free. I was told that if I could work sixty to seventy hours a week, there might be a staff position for me. They couldn't use a part-time volunteer. I couldn't quit my summer grading job, so I passed.

Later in the summer of 2008, I'd wrapped up my grading commitment and secured funding through my graduate program that would pay my bills. I set out to work on the Obama campaign full-time. I had begun learning the lay of the land. Clearly, I'd been naïve in my earlier attempts to contribute meaningfully to a campaign: no one was going to give any substantial responsibilities to an unknown volunteer, no matter their on-paper skills. So this time I started by showing up at each and every volunteer event I could find. I offered to staff the campaign's newly opened Oakland office full-time. Still, I met resistance: I remained a newcomer, and the long-standing volunteers who had been active since the primary were reluctant to hand over any decision-making power or authority. Even at the local level, in a firmly blue state, clout was closely guarded. It took an acquaintance being hired as the Bay Area field director and tapping me as a "regional field organizer" to find my way in. Finally, I became a real, if unpaid, campaign staffer, on the hierarchy's lowest level.

As soon as I had a title, I craved deeper involvement and access to the "inner circle" meetings. I didn't want to leave the office, though I was already there full-time. And I joined in the campaign staff tradition of complaining about volunteers who unreasonably believed they could walk in, announce competencies and capabilities developed in other fields, and be given responsibility within our campaign's world. We scoffed at their sense of entitlement and assigned the eager walk-ins to data entry and phone-banking, treating them just the way earlier campaign staffers had treated me.

That's how, on the night Obama won, I ended up in the Convention Center after spending ninety-six hours straight with my campaign co-workers. I'd spent the prior three months working well beyond full-time, staffing the local campaign office and managing a team of volunteer leaders who in turn were organizing even more volunteers, who dialed their way through long lists of potential supporters, undecided voters, and people who didn't always make it to the polls on Election Day.

When I had set out, back in 2004, to help the candidate who I thought was better for the country to win the presidency, I thought of campaigns as the collective efforts of interested people to bring every like-minded person into the fold. Instead, I was kept out by closed doors, closed meetings, and closed networks. When I gained access, I knew I was just one of many, yet the work felt urgent and all-consuming. I was socialized into my role, as well as the organizational structure and its approach to politics. On election night, with people in the streets of Oakland honking their horns and cheering, I was utterly exhausted and entirely thrilled to have played my small part in helping Barack Obama become president.

Through that campaign experience, I learned that getting even a low-level unpaid job in politics takes persistence and knowing someone on the inside. I learned that the job requires nearly unlimited working hours and being willing to ignore most responsibilities outside the campaign (I promised Hannah I'd never work on a campaign again). I also came away with a renewed commitment to making sense of what I'd been through and understanding how campaigns work.

Obama's campaign was in many ways markedly different from previous presidential contests. The campaign worked with the longtime activist and social movement scholar Marshall Ganz to incorporate organizing training for its volunteers and staff, and empowered individual volunteers to organize phone banks and other efforts on their own initiative using the tools at My.BarackObama.com. Obama's candidacy inspired artists like Shepard Fairey to contribute their creative talents to the campaign. Neighbors walked in off the street to volunteer in our Oakland office, and often came back day after day. Many observers and scholars thought Obama's campaign was the beginning of a new era of "more fluid" twenty-first-century campaigning that used "ideas, direction, and support from grassroots" activists.[1] But subsequent campaigns, for both Democrats and Republicans, did not take up many of the innovations of Obama '08. And in important ways Obama's campaigns were not so different from those that have come before or since. Potential voters were subjected to a deluge of advertising from both sides on television, the radio, and the internet. Campaign strategists identified the segments of the population they thought key to victory, and sought to sway them with carefully crafted messaging. Volunteers were used primarily to make phone calls, knock on doors, and do data entry. Key campaign decisions were made by an exclusive group: David Axelrod, David Plouffe, Robert Gibbs, and Anita Dunn were widely reported to be the innermost inner circle.[2] All four of them are White and grew up in college-educated, upper-middle-class homes; three of the four are men.[3] That exclusivity might not be surprising for those who understand the foundations of the United States as inextricably linked to White supremacy, patriarchy, and the interests of the wealthy, but it is at odds with the principles of democracy most of us would like to believe in.[4]

· · ·

I got involved with the campaign primarily because I knew the outcome was so important, but I have come to believe that even beyond who gets elected, the activities, culture, and organization of campaigns are essential aspects of American democracy.

Campaigns should matter to all of us. The candidates who ultimately win elected offices wield enormous power, through the laws they pass and the executive orders they issue, the judges they appoint, and the norms they promote or discard. Political decisions touch every aspect of our lives, from the most personal outwards. I'm a transgender man, and my marriage to Hannah in 2006 would not have been recognized by the state if I hadn't yet transitioned; now, two people of any gender can legally wed across the country. Most public schools in Philadelphia, where my kids go to school, are overcrowded and poorly maintained because the laws that govern school funding are relics of White people's flight from cities and integration. Many people in Philadelphia and around the country were able to stay in their homes despite losing jobs during the Covid-19 pandemic because of stimulus checks, expanded unemployment benefits, and an eviction moratorium; some will lose their homes as those resources dry up. The Biden administration's dedication to promoting and distributing vaccines helped stem the pandemic; the politicization of masks, vaccination, and public health by Trump and other Republicans did the opposite. Every one of these outcomes is the result of elections.

But campaigns and the people who work in them are at least as important because of how their actions define our democracy. During federal election contests, it's hard to miss hearing the campaigns' attempts to win votes. By late summer 2016, nearly half of registered voters had been contacted directly by a campaign; in 2020, federal, state, and local campaigns combined bought 9.3 million television advertisements.[5] Campaign communications try to convince us that we should be hopeful or fearful, that government can help solve problems or that it creates them, that politicians are on our side or that they are out-of-touch elites. Political ads and speeches often play on racism, sexism, xenophobia, or homophobia, but they can challenge these as well.

The sociologist C. Wright Mills famously wrote, "It is the political task of the social scientist . . . continually to translate personal troubles into public issues, and public issues into the terms of their human meaning for a variety of individuals." He called this the use of the "sociological imagination"; if done successfully, he thought, it could work to "secure reason and individuality, and to make these the predominant values of a democratic society."[6]

This is a role many social scientists aspire to play, but in reality most people don't get their understanding of the relationship between their private experiences of hardship (let alone privilege) and broader social issues from scholars. Instead, when people learn how to connect their experiences to larger trends outside their direct perception, they get those insights from their community, from media commentary, and to some substantial extent from campaign messages.

Political campaigns actively try in their communications to get people to link the struggles in their personal lives to larger issues. Can't find a well-paying job? Republican campaigns and politicians will tell you it's probably because of undocumented immigrants or Democrats' "anti-business" policies, and promise to change those policies once they win. Democratic campaigns and politicians might instead promise infrastructure programs or an increase in the minimum wage. Campaigns rarely offer anything approaching Mills's sociological imagination, genuinely helping people to understand the forces shaping their lives. Instead, they try to figure out the message that will most likely connect people's underlying concerns and desires for change (or to fend off threatening change) with a particular candidate's election.

The professionals who run campaigns craft and target these communications. They decide which potential voters should be contacted and what messages we should receive and what candidates should emphasize as they seek office, and they even influence how politicians govern once they get into office.

To understand campaigns, then, we need to understand the people whose work builds them: the political consultants and political operatives who make their living working for parties, campaigns, and allied partisan organizations. Just as the decision-makers at Netflix, HBO, and ABC determine what kinds of entertainment to provide, these campaign professionals curate our political options. The ways they shape the system and its offerings for voters come out of their perceptions of what is politically possible, which persuasion strategies are effective, how the electorate operates, and what will make sense to and be rewarded by the rest of the political world. Politicos' beliefs about how politics ought to work and how regular people see politics shape the decisions, strategies, and public messaging of the party leaders, presidents, legislators, and governors they advise. To make sense of a political landscape that's often baffling to outsiders, we need to know how and why campaign professionals do what they do.

Why should we care about the people who run campaigns or about the way they think and feel about their work? One of my mentors, a political scientist, asked me that at the outset of this project. No matter what, she argued, these professionals will of necessity do the same thing: whatever it takes to win. On the basis of what we know about election laws, voter behavior, and the factors that predict electoral success, she told me, we can also know why the people running campaigns do what they do—and it doesn't matter who is making those decisions. My mentor is very smart, and a lot of other political scientists agree with her assessment. But it's wrong.

Scholars and politicos do have access to a treasure trove of data and sophisticated statistical analyses of voters and their behavior. Contemporary polling, modeling, and targeting techniques can provide guidance about messaging, ad placement, and other aspects of campaign strategy. But no amount of technology can predict what potential voters will actually do, especially in the complicated tumult of an election, when competing campaigns are trying to leverage the same information to different ends. Our country has a free press. About 160 million voters turned out for the 2020 presidential election.[7] Even if the data available to campaigns were perfectly accurate (which voter databases and polls rarely are), algorithms alone could not decide the best ways to influence the requisite number of voters on Election Day.[8]

In fact, if you assume that politicos are simply rational strategic actors trying to win elections, many campaign decisions don't make much sense, as some political scientists have observed.[9] Political professionals are undoubtedly experts in campaigning. But they are not, nor could they be, the rational-actor wonks some scholars imagine, making dispassionate, whatever-it-takes-to-win strategy decisions. Even with the increasing power of data-driven politicking extolled in books like Sasha Issenberg's *The Victory Lab*, even when research is clear about more and less effective strategies, campaigns do not reliably do what scholarship says they should.[10] Campaign professionals' perspectives and priorities are therefore necessary to understanding the forces that construct politics in the United States.

Whether they serve as intermediaries or firewalls, political professionals stand between regular people and the politicians who make life-or-death, poverty-or-comfort decisions about our lives. In the hidden world of campaigns, the field director, the fundraiser, the communications consultant, and the pollster all have roles to play in producing political priorities and outcomes. Their decisions, their approaches to politics and to voters, affect not only the likelihood that people will vote for a particular candidate but our very understanding of what politics is about. Campaigns and the people who run them are some of the most important, yet poorly understood, parts of American politics.

The people in these positions are different from ordinary Americans in many ways, beyond the peculiarities of their daily work lives, even beyond their political passions and power over the country's political discourse.

They are a relatively homogenous group: mostly White, mostly men, and mostly from middle- to upper-middle-class backgrounds. They spend most of their time with other people who work in politics, in political hubs like Washington, DC. Yet they create the political environment of our democracy.

Reasonable readers might object here: Do we really need another book about campaigns? There are countless tomes authored by well-known political operatives such as David Axelrod and Karl Rove, not to mention all those talking heads chatting politics on cable news shows and social networks.[11] But, as we see across so many areas of civic life, what people say publicly, on the record, tends to be just the bits that make them look best.

It is quite difficult for an outsider to know what it is like to be part of a major national campaign, let alone exactly how those in the inner circle make their strategic and creative decisions. Campaigns are usually very reluctant, if not entirely unwilling, to let people from outside the campaign into their war rooms. While the contest is under way, most information about internal campaign dynamics comes from leaks, whether comments from disgruntled or occasionally careless staffers or calculated communications with journalists. After the fact, though, postelection accounts tend to come from insiders interested in preserving their reputations for the next election season.

That's where my experience as a participant observer in campaigns, my in-depth interviews with politicos, and my extensive database of campaign professionals' careers come in. With these data, we can get an inside look at how campaign professionals understand, experience, and explain the love and sacrifices that go into the "war," or "game," of electoral politics.

Teams of undergraduate research assistants, at UC Berkeley and then at Swarthmore College, worked with me to collect the names and positions of over 4,400 people who held posts on presidential or Senate campaigns from 2004 through 2020. We found and organized as much information as we could on these politicos: whether and where they went to college, their race and gender, and what other jobs they held before and after the campaign we found them in.[12]

I also talked at length with seventy-two politicos for this book—thirty-one Republicans, forty Democrats, and one Independent.[13] What they told me in anonymous interviews revealed much about US politics—the kind of information that doesn't make it onto CNN. All had worked as either a campaign staffer or consultant on at least one presidential, Senate, or House race; many had played key roles in numerous national races.

I found people to talk with through personal connections I developed on the Obama campaign and in grad school, as well as my partner's family. I also cold-emailed people who I knew had held important positions or recently been featured as rising stars of the campaign world by its magazine, *Campaigns & Elections*. I asked everyone I met with if they could connect me with others to talk with, and most did. I conducted most interviews in person, in 2009–10 and 2017, and talked to some people twice; I also did phone and Zoom interviews, including some in 2021. In all, I did eighty-four interviews with people ranging in age from twenty-four to over seventy when I interviewed them. My interviewees, like politicos in general, were disproportionately White and men, but I made an effort to talk to as many women and people of color as I could, and to supplement and compare my interviews with published accounts and the patterns in my database.[14]

I talked with campaign managers, political directors, polling consultants, spokespeople, state-level field directors, media producers, and so many more. I interviewed field staffers who had coordinated ground-game efforts like door-knocking and phone-banking on the first Obama campaign, as well as people who'd worked presidential campaigns as far back as George McGovern's in 1972 and Ronald Reagan's first run in 1976. Each has had an influence on the tone, content, and practice of American politics. The politicos featured in this book developed campaign themes like the Hillary Clinton campaign's "I'm With Her" and "Stronger Together" taglines. They crafted attack ads against Barack Obama, like the one for John McCain casting Obama as a shallow celebrity, or the one for Hillary Clinton that said Obama was not quite ready to answer a 3 a.m. phone call at the White House. They wrote Mitt Romney's speeches in the 2012 campaign, ran primary campaigns that failed to beat Trump in 2016, and organized voter contact for Bernie Sanders and Joe Biden in 2020. These are some of the politicos behind the scenes orchestrating nearly everything that happens in competitive, high-level US elections.

Researching this book meant being invited into some of the fanciest, most expensive houses and offices I've ever seen, just as it brought me into fairly humble, jumbled working campaign offices. Most political professionals I met had extremely good social skills. I almost always had good conversations with people from both parties, despite personally being on the opposite side of nearly every political issue from the Republicans I interviewed, and to the left of most of the Democrats as well. Whatever I felt about the views of the people I interviewed, I focused on my research goal: understanding the campaign industry and how such professionals view their jobs, the candidates, and the electorate. Maybe they assumed I shared their views, since I did request the interviews, and although I am trans, they probably just saw me as a fellow straight White guy. Or maybe they simply didn't mind explaining their work to a geeky grad student (when I started this project) or assistant professor (when I finished). Either way, almost all of them agreed to have their interviews recorded so I could refer back to them when writing, and I promised not to reveal their names or identifying details. Many of them told me things they did not want publicly associated with them.

I met people like Roger,* a lobbyist, high-level Democratic fundraiser, and key player in Democratic presidential campaigns from Eugene McCarthy's in 1968 onward. Other than in a museum, I'd never seen more paintings—or bigger ones—than those lining Roger's walls. He let me interview him at his kitchen counter, barely granting me his attention as he juggled calls, managed renovation work, chatted with family members, and watched a football game. Roger has been a prominent figure in Democratic Party politics for over forty years. He has raised money for every Democratic presidential nominee since before I was born. His ability to raise and direct money through his networks of wealthy friends and powerful Democratic leaders grants him the ability to insert his input into everything from the themes candidates put at the center of their campaigns to the laws they enact if they reach office. Except for an occasional mention on the sorts of deep-dive political news most of us ignore, Roger and his views are virtually invisible, yet they are immensely consequential for most American voters.

---

* I have given all of my interviewees first-name pseudonyms. I use the same first name consistently for the same person, but I leave out even a pseudonym or a description when necessary to maintain anonymity, especially when people have told me stories that might make them identifiable, or if they have told me things that are especially sensitive. If I use a first and last name to talk about a politico, that is a real person's real name. When I use only a first name, that is a pseudonym for someone I interviewed. See note 13 for further details on interviewees.

Francis, about thirty years younger than Roger, is also straight, White, and influential, but in other ways he is quite different. This Republican consultant gave me his full attention in his humble Alexandria office, just outside DC, where he told me that his entire professional life has been focused on politics. He isn't a lobbyist, doesn't bundle money for candidates, and hasn't advised a single president. Francis is a communications consultant who coordinates campaigns' public-facing efforts, designing advertisements, conducting "opposition research" to find potential attack angles against opposing candidates, and forwarding party views on hot-button issues. His work has benefited a California Republican gubernatorial campaign, the party's efforts to repeal the Affordable Care Act (Obamacare), and officials seeking to defund reproductive health initiatives. When we spoke in 2010, he had notched another victory as part of the successful Proposition 8 effort that overturned California's law legalizing gay marriage. Because of this, Francis was my least enjoyable interview; I had a hard time putting myself or Francis at ease knowing his role in challenging the legal status of my friends' relationships, and we had a stilted conversation; even so, it added to my understanding of the world of politicos.

At the other end of the political spectrum, I enjoyed my conversations with people like Angela, who works on the left side of Democratic politics, and in the part of campaigns that most overlaps with my work in academia. A pollster, Angela works behind the scenes. She meticulously designs survey questions about policies and politics, figures out whom to survey, and interprets the results for political clients. Her work provides campaign teams with data to inform their sense of key demographics and ideal messaging. That is, pollsters like her lay the groundwork for every campaign ad and political speech you've seen in the last half century. The pollsters don't tell campaigns what to do, but their results can indicate which aspects of a candidate's biography, philosophy, or platform have the best chance to resonate with and motivate voters to turn out and support the candidate on Election Day.

Many books on political campaigns focus on one party or the other, but this book is about both parties. The dynamics I describe are important for anyone who wants democracy to be more representative, in any party. A lot of people who share my political values only study Democrats. And although I have to confess that I want the Democrats to be more effective and the Republicans less, I think it is important to understand *all* campaigns. What I found is that although the two parties have very different policy goals and political ideologies, Democratic and Republican politicos' views about how to run campaigns are remarkably similar. I did not find many differences in what they told me about the technologies and techniques, or the norms and culture of campaigning. In fact, while regular Americans are becoming more polarized, less likely to know or talk regularly to people who don't share their political beliefs, and more likely to see members of the opposing party as bad people, many campaign professionals told me they have good friends across the partisan aisle.[15] Famously, two politicos from different parties, Mary Matalin and James Carville, even went so far as to get married. Political professionals share experiences, a work environment, and a level of access to power that most of the rest of us cannot begin to wrap our heads around.

That said, this book is not an indictment of campaign professionals. I met a lot of committed people in both parties whose work was anchored in sincere values and beliefs. They want to run good campaigns and elect people they believe will be good for the country and possibly beyond. But the expectations and norms set by their industry—the rules of the game, as it were—mean they can end up doing more harm than good. Those rules determine who can become a political professional in the first place, and then constrain how politicos think about and do the work of politics.

The approach to voters—to regular people—that politicos learn in campaigns permeates many other parts of the American power structure. Campaign professionals often move into other elite roles, dispersing outward as consultants for advocacy and lobbying groups, representatives of corporate interests, advisors and staffers for elected officials, and even into government office themselves.

Almost all potential voters, on the other hand, live lives far from all the work that leads up to an election or happens afterward. In hard-fought elections the cyclical tides of our system bring a deluge of campaign communications to voters' doorknobs, phones, mailboxes, television and radio channels, and, these days, to their inboxes and social media feeds. These messages, often focused on fear-mongering and attacks on opposing candidates, can be off-putting to people who aren't obsessively following the polls. For many Americans, these communications from campaigns are the only connection they have to candidates, electoral politics, and elected officials. A substantial portion of Americans rarely or never vote, and an even bigger portion of adults usually vote but are otherwise not interested in electoral politics. Few seek out political news, follow politicians and pundits on social media, or even discuss politics with extended family. The 40 percent or more of eligible voters who rarely show up in voting booths are by and large ignored by campaigns.[16] And when campaign materials that hold no meaning for them do show up on their doorsteps, they're put out with the recycling.

A campaign could be a conversation between political elites and regular people. But only a very small portion of contemporary campaign budgets are dedicated to talking with potential voters. Instead, contemporary campaigns tend to be performances more than conversations: one-way communications in which consultants, staff, and candidates send the messages they think will be most effective to the people they believe are most likely to be determinative for election results. Each campaign is conceived and executed as an isolated event rather than part of an ongoing party project. In the process, campaigns ignore countless potential voters, even in competitive states, and may turn as many people away from politics as they mobilize. Observers of US politics have long suspected that much of what campaigns do is bad for our democracy, but they've had fairly limited insight as to exactly what (or whom) to blame.

Campaign professionals mediate and manage the relationship between people and political power. Their work defines the practice of democratic politics in the United States. This is why we need to gain insight into their world: their beliefs about the effects of their work, the ways they get jobs, the organization of their work world, their goals and how they evaluate each other, their understanding of voters, and the power they wield beyond campaigns.

PRODUCING
POLITICS

★ ★ ★ ★ ★

CHAPTER 1

DO CAMPAIGNS REALLY MATTER?

In the last months of his 2006 reelection campaign, a fairly conventional Republican candidate for the US Senate from Virginia, former governor George Allen, pointed out the only person of color in the room, an Indian American staffer from his opponent's campaign, and referred to him as "Macaca."[1] The word wasn't familiar to most people, but its racist implications were obvious, and the story peppered the political news cycle for weeks.[2] When Allen lost the election by just a fraction of a percentage point, observers largely agreed with Todd, a Republican pollster I met with in 2010, who told me the "Macaca moment" was to blame: as Todd put it, Allen was "supposed to win" and then he "did something stupid."[3]

Less than a decade later, Donald Trump undertook a presidential campaign by gliding down a golden escalator and calling Mexican immigrants criminals, drug-runners, and rapists. He went on to mock a disabled reporter, was accused of sexual assault by dozens of women, and was exposed as having bragged about grabbing women "by the pussy" and getting away with it because he was "a star." Despite all of that, as we know, he won the presidency.

Observers of American politics have been surprised a number of times since Allen's loss. In the wake of 9/11, few of us would have guessed that a Black man with the middle name Hussein could be elected US president, but Barack Hussein Obama won decisively, twice. Before 2015, you'd be hard-pressed to find scholars or pundits who would predict that a Jewish socialist from Vermont could come anywhere close to winning a major-party presidential nomination, but Bernie Sanders gave Hillary Clinton a run for her money in 2016 and mounted a strong challenge in 2020 as well. Most pundits were calling Trump's primary and general election wins very unlikely right until they happened. Did something fundamental change about our politics between Allen's loss and Trump's win? Did saying "Macaca" hurt Allen while "Grab 'em by the pussy" failed to stop Trump? Public conversations about American electoral politics often focus on such high-profile moments in campaigns, but that attention is largely misplaced.

Much scholarly research, far from focusing on the particularities of candidates or campaigns, sees campaigns as pretty predictable. In this view, election results are mostly a function of macro-level forces that make for a more or less favorable environment for one party or another. Incumbents tend to get reelected unless the partisan makeup of their districts has changed substantially, presidential candidates running after their party has already held power for two terms often lose, and the party of the president tends to lose seats in midterm elections. If the economy is good or the country is at war, incumbents and the party currently holding power do better than their opponents.[4]

On top of these "fundamentals," campaigns work as marketing efforts, in which candidates do their best to sell themselves to potential voters. In the primaries, campaigns try to capture a party's nomination—that imprimatur will secure the largest swath of votes. Then, in the general election, they focus on motivating the party-affiliated and eking out some votes among the much rarer truly independent voters.[5] To this end, campaign staff work to figure out which of the candidate's beliefs, attributes, or positions are most likely to gain enough interest and votes to get them to 50 percent + 1—that is, to clear the threshold for winning office. They craft a coherent message highlighting their candidate's strengths and their opponents' weaknesses, and deliver it through television and other media, the internet, and person-to-person communications. The side with the most money to spend on disseminating their message, the most favorable environment, and the most polished and likable candidate should win the election.

That's what mostly happens, but there are exceptions. In 2006, Democrat Jon Tester narrowly beat incumbent Republican Conrad Burns in a US Senate race in deep-red Montana. In 2010, Scott Brown (R) defeated Martha Coakley (D) in a special election for what was considered an entirely safe US Senate seat in heavily Democratic Massachusetts. Hillary Clinton's campaign spent nearly twice as much as Donald Trump's in

2016, and Clinton won the popular vote but lost the electoral college; four years later, Trump and Democratic challenger Joe Biden both ratcheted up the campaign spending enormously, the Democrats again doubling Trump's spending.[6] Scholarship on campaigns would predict that such a huge spending disadvantage would hurt Trump, and that already being the president should help. But this time Trump lost even more substantially in the popular vote and also narrowly lost the electoral college, making Biden the first challenger to beat an incumbent president in twenty-eight years.

Attempting to explain these outcomes in election postmortems is a reliable ritual of our national politics. Pundits, parties, and politicos argue about why the winners won, and why the losers lost. They eventually settle, more or less, on an explanatory story about the country, the electorate, or the particular campaign or candidate: the national mood, what voters wanted, what voters were ready for. Obama won because of his "ground game," getting out the vote and opening previously untapped sectors of the electorate. Martha Coakley lost because of a lackluster campaign. Hillary Clinton lost because she wasn't "likable," because of Americans' sexism, or because the media hyped the story of her private server emails. Trump won because America refuses to grapple with White supremacy, past and present; or because his "authenticity" and willingness to say offensive things without apology was so appealing to so many people. True as far as they go, none of these is a complete explanation of an election's outcome. In the 2016 case, had roughly seventy thousand people, spread across the states of Pennsylvania, Michigan, and Wisconsin, done something different on Election Day, we would have had an entirely different postmortem conversation about the country's mood and its "readiness" for a woman leader, about media coverage, the economy, and the Clinton campaign's effectiveness.

To put things differently, in late November 2016, the story of Trump's win depended on whom you asked. In the immediate aftermath, you could hear anything from his election's being a one-off "fluke" to its necessitating a total rethinking of everything we know about campaigns and American politics. Some commentators argued that his presidency was the predictable culmination of a long-simmering stew of anti-elitism, racism, misogyny, and disaffection among substantial swaths of the American electorate; others emphasized how effective Trump's campaign was at mobilizing and engaging White people who lacked college degrees. Or maybe Trump won because Attorney General James Comey released that "October Surprise" memo, which made Clinton's emails salient again, or because Cambridge Analytica and Russian troll-farm operations manipulated people through fear and misinformation.

Now, as I write in 2021, I'm looking at the results of the 2020 election. The outcome was certainly different from 2016, since it ushered in a "traditional" president by historical standards: an older White man with plenty of political experience, family ties to the military, and a compelling personal story. But the election result was strikingly similar to 2016's: the vast majority of the 63 million people who voted for Trump in 2016 did so again in 2020, along with over 11 million more, while the vast majority of the 65.8 million who voted for Clinton in 2020, plus about 15.5 million others, voted for Biden in 2020.[7] Those extra votes Biden got made the difference, but even so the outcome was still very close. If 43,000 people, less than .05 percent (one twentieth of a percent) of the electorate, in three states—Arizona, Georgia, and Wisconsin—had voted for Trump, there would have been a tie in the Electoral College and the election would have been decided in the House of Representatives.

Candidates who aren't "supposed" to win, do, and those who seem like shoo-ins sometimes lose. But despite all the attention given to campaigns, most voters don't change their party choice from one election to the next.[8] Eighty-nine percent of people who reported voting in both 2008 and 2012 voted for the same party both times.[9] Over and over we hear that Americans are exposed almost wholly to information that confirms their preexisting beliefs as a result of political polarization and echo chambers and social media bubbles. Most voters side with one or the other major party no matter what. Trump boasted in the run-up to the 2016 election that he "could shoot someone in the middle of Fifth Avenue" without losing Republican supporters. Truly, there wasn't much Trump could have done to shake the commitment of the vast majority of his 2016 voters. And even though Democrats tend to say it with less bluster, many of their party faithful are in fact equally unmovable.

Given all this, how do the people who run campaigns make sense of how and whether campaigns' or candidates' actions move voters? And how should we?

· · ·

I met Todd on a hot afternoon in June 2010. Todd was, according to the industry publication *Campaigns & Elections* magazine, a "rising star" among Republican politicos: vice president of a polling firm and an increasingly frequent guest commentator for TV news outlets. His office was the former living room of a charming blue-painted townhouse a few blocks from the Capitol in Washington, DC, now kitted out with a full-sized refrigerated cold case stocked with water, soda, energy drinks, and beer, all visible through its clear glass door. Todd, White and about thirty-five, wore khaki shorts, leather sandals, and a short-sleeved shirt embroidered with palm trees. Well-made and comfortable, everything from Todd's clothes to the décor exuded casual excess.

When we spoke, Todd was working as a pollster and general strategic advisor on a long-shot Republican senatorial campaign. We talked about how he got into political consulting, what makes for good polling and campaign messaging, and his understanding of how campaigns are won or lost. His conflicting explanations exemplified a tension in how both campaign professionals and political scientists think about campaigns.

First, he told me that his and his team's effort would determine the outcome, stating: "If we win, it will definitely be because we had the superior strategy and we were able to fully take advantage of the environment." This is a common and common-sense way of interpreting election outcomes—whoever wins must have run the better campaign! But Todd almost immediately contradicted himself. He would like to tell me, he said, that "consultants can make the race" but "at the end of the day," it comes down to uncontrollable or even unmeasurable factors like "momentum" and "the way the race closes" and "which candidate naturally resonates—something you can't fake." Nonetheless, he told me, "consultants are always wanting to take credit for it." Todd was not consistently convinced that his expertise made much of a difference—and this was even before the rise of Trump and the growing understanding in many quarters that most people are going to vote for the party they always vote for, regardless of what any campaign does. Most other politicos I spoke to were just as ambivalent about whether and how campaigns matter for election outcomes.

The first part of Todd's pronouncement—that the winner is determined by which side has the superior strategy—is the way many commentators and observers view campaigns. Most of us who pay attention to campaigns care a great deal about the outcome: whether the candidate or party we support emerges on election evening with a victory that gives them a position of power in our government. In the aftermath of the 2016 election, you could find countless tweets, op-eds, articles, and, not long after, even books, explaining how Clinton's loss to Trump was due to poor campaign decisions, or how sophisticated data analysis and online manipulation techniques brought Trump over the finish line. In other words, almost all the punditry and public-facing analysis of campaign outcomes implies that we can know with certainty what campaign actions will have what effects and that campaign professionals do too.

Since at least the 1970s, some observers have seen campaign professionals as almost puppet masters, sounding the alarm about the erosion of true democratic deliberation and its replacement by manipulated mass participation. The basic task of an electoral campaign hasn't changed—to convince a sufficient portion of voters to turn out and vote for your candidate, party, or referendum. But the way this goal is pursued has shifted substantially since the first half of the twentieth century. Up to that point, political parties were the primary mobilizing forces during campaigns, from choosing candidates to providing staff, from crafting messages or themes to making strategic decisions throughout a campaign. With the increasing size of the electorate, transformations in the technology of mass communication, and reforms to election laws, the "candidate-centered" campaign and the candidate-centered politics we are used to replaced the party-run campaign.[10]

This shift brought with it the expansion of the politics industry, a rapid rise in the number of people whose full-time jobs involve working for or advising campaigns. Many of them are political consultants who have their own firms and sell their services to campaigns; many others are campaign and party staff, who work as employees of different short-lived political organizations. Adam Sheingate, in his book on the consulting industry, identifies 1,765 political consulting firms that received $25,000 or more in the 2012 election, and I have counted over four thousand people who have held at least one significant role on a presidential campaign in the twenty-first century.[11] Some people I counted worked at firms on Sheingate's list, but many didn't.

The rise of political consultants especially triggered a wave of concern and a slew of books. One of the earliest of these was the one penned by

David Lee Rosenbloom, a political science professor and veteran campaign staffer. In 1972, he published *The Election Men: Professional Campaign Managers and American Democracy*. In it he warned that new technologies were making it ever easier for mercenary political consultants to manipulate the electorate into voting for the consultants' preferred candidate. Describing the transformation of Hubert Humphrey between his 1968 and 1972 campaigns, he wrote, "The heart of the new Humphrey was a computer."[12] Larry Sabato, a well-known pundit and political scientist, made similar points in *The Rise of Political Consultants*, in which he worried, as many political scientists did at the time, about the shift in responsibility for electioneering from parties to independent consulting firms, who would (and could) do anything at all to get their candidate across the finish line.[13]

This kind of concern has waxed and waned, but in the aftermath of the 2016 election there was once again a widespread belief among Democrats that Trump had won through masterful and probably unethical manipulation of gullible voters. We heard a lot about Cambridge Analytica's unauthorized use of Facebook data to target campaign ads. A former Trump staffer, Christopher Wylie, even published a tell-all book, *Mindf*ck: Cambridge Analytica and the Plot to Break America*, taking responsibility for what he saw as his role in helping elect Trump.[14] There were also allegations of Russian state–sponsored actors placing targeted ads and running misleading social accounts, which spurred a special investigation in Congress; Hillary Clinton is reported to have blamed her loss, at least in part, on "the KGB."[15]

In all of these accounts, the implicit—sometimes explicit—view is that people who work in (or in the case of Russian agents, on behalf of) campaigns are brilliant master manipulators, selling their analytic prowess to the highest bidder and then playing voters like marionettes. This tracks with most popular representations, especially of political consultants. Television shows and movies depict them as strategic geniuses, like Bruno Gianelli on *The West Wing*, or Olivia Pope on *Scandal*. They're ruthless and expensive, and they just know how to manipulate the people into doing what they want. But they're fictional.

Much of popular and journalistic discourse approaches campaigns' outcomes the way my interviewee Todd did at first: as directly traceable to the efforts and decisions of campaign decision-makers. This is an appealing, intuitive approach to campaigns: elections almost always have unambiguous results, campaign staff and political consultants made decisions along the way, and so we must be able to trace their success or failure, a win or a loss, back to something those politicos did.

But when we think about campaigns and campaign professionals that way, we tend to make assumptions that get in the way of a genuine understanding of what campaigns do and how they work. If we assume that campaigns' effects are always calculable and knowable and that campaign professionals are essentially strategic masterminds who compete to manipulate voters into making the choices they want them to make, we are getting campaigns, and by extension, American democracy, wrong.

In fact, most political and social scientists are much less willing than Hillary Clinton and many other Democrats to blame Trump's 2016 victory on Russian interference or Cambridge Analytica. A team of political scientists who wrote an extensive account of the 2016 election stated: "Although Russian interference was and is deeply concerning" on an ethical and political level, "there are many reasons to doubt it changed the outcome of the election." More specifically, "Russian-sponsored content on social media likely did not change the outcome of the election."[16]

Christopher Wylie, the guilt-ridden former Cambridge Analytica staffer who published a book-length confession about his role in Trump's election, should be happy about what social science has to say about his company's efforts (although if people read social science as avidly as they read campaign tell-alls, he might not have sold so many books). Political scientist Kris-Stella Trump (no relation to Donald Trump) published an article in the *Washington Post* summarizing the "four and a half reasons" to doubt that Cambridge Analytica could be credited with or blamed for Trump's victory. Her "four and a half reasons" to be skeptical are worth quoting directly:

1. Personality is not a good predictor of political views. . . .
2. Predicting personality is hard. . . .
3. Changing individuals' choices based on their personality profiles is harder than it sounds. . . .
4. They had stiff competition from other campaigns. . . .
(4.5) And it's not clear that Cambridge Analytica could do any of this. . . .[17]

You can start to see a pattern emerging here: campaigners, candidates, and pundits make sweeping pronouncements about how campaigns are won or lost; social scientists do careful analyses and show that a lot of what campaigns do might not matter at all.

Political scientists have devoted a lot of time and energy to answering the question of whether and how much campaigns matter, and much of the research on campaigns supports Todd's second assertion about his role much more than his first: it's not often clear that campaigns' activities can determine the outcome of the race.[18] There are at least three ways that campaigns' effects are often unclear: one, it's hard to change how or whether someone will vote; two, it's hard to know how to change someone's mind even when it is possible; and three, it's hard to assess—even in hindsight—whether campaigns' actions were responsible for what the electorate did. There is reasonably good evidence that contacting people directly and asking them to vote increases the chances they will indeed turn out; there is very little evidence that most of the rest of what campaigns do makes a measurable difference in election outcomes.[19]

One reason campaigns have limited effects is that a lot of the forces that shift votes from one election to the next are well outside campaigns' control, as Todd pointed out. Many of these are identifiable even before the actual candidates are nominated, before the general-election campaigns even start. This is brought home by election-prediction exercises, where political scientists model the future on the basis of factors that have tended to predict outcomes of elections in the past. Every August or September, in even-numbered years, at the annual American Political Science Association meetings, professors present their forecasts for the upcoming elections. These forecasts are then published in October of national election years in the academic journal *PS: Political Science and Politics*.[20]

These scholars make their predictions about the outcome well before the election, based on little to no information about the campaigns' strategy, tactics, or even the resources at their disposal. In other words, neither the quality of the campaign nor the candidate is factored into these models. Instead, the forecasts are usually based on just a few big-picture factors, like the overall approval rating of the current president, the state of the economy, how long the current president's party has been in power, and whether or not the United States is currently at war. Incumbent presidents usually win; when one party has had two terms in the White House, there is a good chance that the other party's candidate will be voted in. A strong economy, or the widespread perception of a strong economy, generally favors the party currently in office. Using such general information, the political scientists' predictions usually are right.

For example, in the October 2016 election-prediction issue of *Political Science and Politics*, although only two of the nine forecasts predicted Trump's victory, seven predicted a small popular-vote majority for Hillary Clinton, which was indeed the result. All nine predicted a fairly close election, which was also the case. Only one of these predictions was based on polling data asking people directly about their voting intentions or candidate preferences, but that, too, can be predictive long before an election (2016's result notwithstanding). Nine of the twelve articles forecasting the 2020 election correctly predicted a Biden win.[21]

How can this be? With so much breathless coverage of every move that campaigns and their candidates make; with so much effort invested in putting together the public events, speeches, photo opportunities, and online ads; with so much data science behind campaign decisions, why aren't campaigns successfully manipulating us into doing whatever they want? There are many reasons, of course, but in some sense they all start with the people who are supposed to be on the receiving end of this relentless campaigning.

We often think about campaigns as simple mechanisms for getting relevant information to voters so they can assess which candidate best fits with their political values or preferences, and vote accordingly. But that assumes that people's political beliefs exist outside or before politics, and that they make political choices rationally, so they only need to select the candidate who comes closest to their ideal. In this scenario, every voter would sit down before every election to examine the extent to which each candidate—regardless of party—espoused positions and values they could support, and would vote accordingly.

In reality, most people do not have well-thought-out or even internally consistent political philosophies.[22] Whether and how people vote has something to do with the information they receive and gather, but just as important, it's about the groups they identify with and the relationships they have. Our connections to unions, churches, and neighborhoods, to personal contacts with strong political views, to government agencies, and sometimes to individual campaigns and candidates are powerful drivers of our political orientations and engagement.[23]

Most people's political orientation, to the extent we can be said to have one, then, is not based on stable preferences or beliefs, but is about our sense of identity and belonging and our understanding of what politics and parties are, and who they are for. Instead of starting from an internally consistent set of values and beliefs to choose candidates to support and a party to affiliate with, most of us work the opposite way. We come from communities whose values we learn and share, and where those values are often entangled with partisan identities.[24] Those partisan-inflected identities then shape how we see the world and evaluate social and political issues. For example, Democrats were much more likely than Republicans to report a strong economy under Obama and a weak economy under George W. Bush (vice versa for Republicans), regardless of actual economic indicators.[25] And in the wake of the 2016 election and Trump's apparent warmth toward Russia, the partisan divide in public opinion on foreign relations entirely reversed from its usual: Republican voters became more in favor of "friendly cooperation" with Russia while the percentage of Democrats who supported "actively working to limit Russia's power" doubled.[26]

Group identity and partisan identity are becoming more and more closely linked. White Evangelical Christians, who were credited with bringing Jimmy Carter, a Democrat, into office in 1976, are now nearly all Republicans.[27] They reliably vote for the person with the *R* next to their name, whether that candidate is claiming to be on the side of "family values" (George W. Bush, Bob Dole) or has children from three different relationships (Donald Trump). A majority of Black Americans, of any religious or economic position, have voted for Democrats since 1936; since the civil rights era, that majority has been consistently 80 percent or higher.[28] Race and partisanship especially have been becoming more and more tightly entwined over time, in fact, but other aspects of identity are entangled with our voting patterns as well.[29]

Whatever community or social groups we belong to, Americans who identify with a party (about 63 percent of registered voters) increasingly believe "our" party has better values, is more responsible, and is better than the opposition, for our interests and the country's.[30] We believe that the "other" party is full of "other" kinds of people who don't share our values: 75 percent of Democrats and 64 percent of Republicans say that those in the other party are more closed-minded than other Americans; 47 percent of Democrats and 55 percent of Republicans say those in the other party are more immoral than other Americans.[31]

Most of us are essentially always going to vote for "our" party's candidate. If nearly everyone you know is unquestioningly loyal to one party, there is going to be very little that campaigns can do to change your vote. It is hard to break that sort of attachment. This is true for the relatively few people who actually pay close attention to politics, who are especially likely to also have strong partisan identities and ideological beliefs, as well as being higher-income and more educated than the rest of the country.[32] It's also true for many less-engaged voters, who are frequently just as deeply attached to one party and as deeply averse to the other.

Even though about 30 percent of the American electorate identify as independent when asked about their party affiliation on surveys, the number of true swing voters is much lower—these self-described independents vote for one party or the other about as consistently as those identifying as Democrats or Republicans, and they are nearly as unpersuadable.[33] Estimates vary quite a bit, but it may be that about 5 percent of 2016 voters had switched from voting for Obama to voting for Trump, and about 2 percent had made the opposite switch, from Romney in 2012 to Clinton in 2016.[34] In all, about 7 percent of the electorate "swung" in 2016, but some of them canceled each other out.

Campaigns do whatever they can to get their side's base—the loyal partisans who make up most of the electorate—to turn out in full force on Election Day, and they also spend a lot of time and money on the swing vote. This small portion of the electorate is what campaign professionals are often fighting over, attempting to persuade them with every tool in their arsenal that the opposing side's candidate is bad, and their candidate is better. Yet there is also another kind of swing voter who might matter more: the inconsistent voter. The percentage of those eligible who show up every four years has ranged from a recent low of 52 percent in 1996 to 2020's high of nearly 68 percent; in midterm elections the turnout is even lower, reaching a high of 50 percent in 2018.[35] For some voters, the swing is between voting or staying home, participating or choosing not to choose. This is a larger and less visible portion of the potential electorate.

Both kinds of potential swing voters, though, generally pay precious little attention to the campaigns courting their votes, the analysts parsing their behavior, or the nitty-gritty political details—Biden promises X! Trump's campaign broke rule Y!—that capture the attention of the highly politically engaged.

It turns out that a lot of those "big" moments that pundits talk about when they cover politics never affect the outcome at all. A team of political scientists published studies chronicling the effects of events in the 2012 and 2016 elections. They reported that most big stories and ads, even the ones you hear about for years afterward, don't sway enough voters for long enough to make a difference.[36] For example, those of us who follow the news closely heard all about Mitt Romney's secretly taped comment in May 2012 that 47 percent of Americans would vote for Barack Obama no matter what and "are dependent upon government, who believe that they are victims. . . . These are people who pay no income tax."[37] But that comment had no lasting impact on Romney's standing in the polls. And there's no evidence that the much-discussed "Macaca moment," credited by Todd and many pundits for George Allen's defeat by Jim Webb, is what sank Allen.[38]

In *The Timeline of Presidential Elections*, political scientists Robert Erikson and Christopher Wlezien collected the results of hundreds of opinion polls and surveys taken during fifteen presidential campaign cycles.[39] They matched campaigns' time lines to people's reports about whom they intended to vote for, and they found very few events that shifted voter intentions enough to matter for the election results. Generally, a big portion of voters' intentions are set by January of election years, and another portion crystallizes after the nominating conventions. After the summer, and until the election—the autumn months when campaigns are in full swing—voter intent shifts only incrementally, though last-minute shocks can occasionally sway a tight race.

Again, this seems counterintuitive, doesn't it? There may not be very many swing voters, but in tight elections, 5 percent or even as little as half of 1 percent of the electorate in a few key places is enough to decide the outcome. So campaigns flood the airwaves with advertisements in the last few months of an election, doing everything they can to persuade those precious swing voters to swing in their direction.

But it turns out that such persuasion mostly doesn't work. Political scientists Joshua Kalla and David Broockman show that communications in general elections rarely change many voters' minds or determine election outcomes; instead, they say, the "best estimate for the persuasive effects of campaign contact and advertising—such as mail, phone calls, and canvassing—on Americans' candidate choices in general elections is zero. Our best guess for online and television advertising is also zero, but there is less evidence on these modes."[40]

Because of these kinds of findings, some political scientists have even argued that campaigns hardly matter at all for election results. Their predictions seem solid even without campaign-specific information and voter data.

There is also some evidence for a somewhat more optimistic view of campaigns' effectiveness. In her book *The Message Matters*, the political scientist Lynn Vavreck argues that campaigns may affect outcomes through helping voters connect macro-level concerns such as the state of the economy to particular vote choices. She writes, "The economy matters because the candidate who benefits from it talks about it a lot during the campaign and this makes voters more aware of the condition and this candidate's relationship to it."[41] A review of the research up through 2014 similarly concluded that campaigns mostly work by connecting people's evaluation of candidates and issues to the economic and political fundamentals. Campaign messaging and media coverage help give persuadable voters a reason to come to the conclusion they might have anyway—about whether it's time for a change or better to stay the course. In other words, campaigns' effects may be mostly about framing big issues effectively. Despite the fact that most people's votes are either reliably for the same party every time or shift based on the state of the economy or their own sense of their personal economic well-being, campaigns' messages can do a better, or worse, job of reminding people to blame a bad economy on an incumbent, or to give credit for a good economy to the party currently holding the presidency.

Taken together, untangling these campaign effects is profoundly challenging. In *Identity Crisis: The 2016 Election and the Battle for the Meaning of America*, political scientists John Sides, Michael Tesler, and Lynn Vavreck examine claims about what did or did not decide the 2016 election and in the process explain what political science has learned about how campaigns do and do not matter to election outcomes. In the acknowledgments section of their book, published in 2018, they remark that the process of understanding what happened "took longer than we wanted"—even though two of the authors had written a book on the same topic, with the same format and approach, on the 2012 presidential race.[42]

Sides and his coauthors work through a variety of what-ifs about 2016. What if Clinton had run more ads? Well, although many political scientists are convinced persuasion doesn't work, Sides, Tesler, and Vavreck conclude that ads did probably help Clinton get the votes she got. However, given the very small measured effects of advertising on vote share, it would have taken more ads than it was possible to run to put her over the edge in the battleground states that she lost. They find no evidence at all that Facebook ads could have won the election for Trump or would have made a difference for Clinton.[43]

What about "field"—the ground game, efforts to get out the vote? Unlike persuasion efforts, there is reliable evidence that voter contact aimed at getting out the vote (called GOTV in political circles) can substantially increase turnout for a candidate and that Obama's proliferation of field offices probably helped him win in 2008.[44] In 2016, Clinton did have fewer field offices than Obama, more concentrated in heavily Democratic areas, but the percentage of Democrats who reported being contacted by a campaign was the same in 2016 as in 2012 (among Republicans, it was substantially lower). So it's not clear that Clinton underperformed Obama in reaching voters to mobilize, especially when compared with their respective opponents. Based on estimates of how much vote share an additional field office can help capture, Sides and his coauthors conclude that increasing Clinton's number of field offices to Obama levels wouldn't have been enough to flip even Wisconsin, where Trump's winning margin was the narrowest.[45]

Sides, Tesler, and Vavreck spend pages systematically assessing even more counterfactual scenarios and concluding that no single change in the Clinton campaign's approach could have made up the difference. But, they note, "of course, this analysis and earlier academic studies cannot conclusively determine what would have happened if the Clinton campaign had made different decisions. If the hypothetical involves a wholesale remaking of the campaign's strategy—message, field operation, coalition, and so on—then *no analysis can credibly speak to that hypothetical*" (emphasis added).

The Clinton campaign's advantages in spending on field and ads did lead to more votes than she otherwise would have gotten, "at levels typical of recent presidential elections." But "as is often the case in presidential general elections," deploying campaign resources differently "would likely not have overcome the other forces at work."[46]

Put another way, even after an election is over, even with two years of data-crunching by some of the political scientists most knowledgeable about elections and campaign effects, it remains impossible to establish that some action of either campaign would have definitively changed the outcome—or, conversely, that it would not have changed it.

Amid this uncertainty, why is the campaign postmortem such a stalwart tradition? Occasionally, but rarely, claims about the causes of campaign outcomes are based on, or at least align with, good research that can identify key factors. Many observers credited Obama's victory in 2008 to his field program, and later research confirmed that.[47] But attributions of Trump's 2016 victory to Cambridge Analytica or Russian interference are not supported by evidence. As with most outcomes in the social world, a definitive conclusion—if only X had happened, Y would have happened instead!—is usually out of reach.

Without going into a deeper dive, it's probably worth knowing that this issue of understanding and identifying "causality" turns out to be deeply complicated, not just for campaigns but for the social world more broadly—I once spent three days at a Harvard conference of philosophers and social scientists convened to discuss just this question. Presentations included my work (with Sam Friedman) on how class origins matter for career trajectories, one by a sociologist who compared Hurricane Katrina's effects on those who moved out of New Orleans and those who stayed, and one that featured a thought experiment in which philosophers puzzled over the assignation of blame for two kids throwing balls at the same window at the same time.

At the start of the conference, I was confident that I could say that if I use a saw to cut a two-by-four in half, I am the "cause" of the wood's bifurcation. But over twenty hours of conference discussions, we considered whether the grain of the wood might also be a cause (if it were harder wood, I might not be able to saw it with my handsaw), whether my breakfast might be a cause (if I were too hungry to focus, I might not have been able to cut the wood), or whether maybe the air around me was a cause (if

I can't breathe, I can't saw). All these educated, inquisitive people couldn't come to a conclusion on causality beyond "It's complicated!"

Campaigns are a lot more complicated than splitting wood, and so they are particularly challenging places to try to untangle the threads of causality. In national elections you have not only a few hundred million people whom campaigns are trying to influence but also more than one campaign trying to influence them, and all kinds of things matter to how or whether they will be influenced at all—from their choice of news media to their friends' opinions to their perception of their economic circumstances. In other words, campaigns attempt to act on sentient human beings with unpredictable lives and personalities and beliefs, and causality is tricky even when we're describing the simple act of a saw cutting wood.

Given all that, how do campaign professionals make sense of their work? They don't generally disagree with political scientists about how difficult it is to capture campaigns' effects, to know what is going to determine the outcome of an election, or how much their work will matter. Most politicos I spoke with in 2017 had some ideas about what the Clinton campaign could have done differently, but Lindsey, a senior Republican pollster, put it most clearly when he told me what he thought about Clinton's campaign slogan: "'Stronger together' for what was never very clear. Would that have made the difference? Who the hell knows? Nobody knows. And those folks who are out there telling you they know this factor would have changed the outcome are blowing smoke, they're carnival barkers, because they don't know either." This is the kind of comment most professional politicos won't make on the record, because they need to be seen as experts in predicting and interpreting political currents. But Lindsey is entirely right when he continues: "You can make a compelling argument for a number of things. And when it's this close you can make a compelling argument for almost anything." That was true for 2016, and it continues to be true for 2020, although that outcome was less close in the popular vote.

Ken, a an experienced Democratic media consultant, had a similarly limited take on what his work can really accomplish. "In a presidential campaign, we may do some agenda-setting, we may help to set up the narrative that people are talking about, but so much more—or maybe put it a different way—there are so many other factors that are impacting how people perceive the race and the candidates that go beyond what's taking place in online advertising or paid or even necessarily somebody out door-knocking."

And Tom agreed, even after experiences in strategic decision-making in the general election campaigns of George W. Bush, Mitt Romney, and John McCain. He recounted talking after a meeting on a Saturday morning with a friend who was also "a longtime presidential campaign operative." They discussed how nobody "in the rest of America has any idea what it is like on the inside" of a presidential campaign. Tom told his friend that, from the outside, everyone thinks that campaign strategists have good reasons for everything they do. But, Tom remembered, his friend said, "There is so little you have control over. It just careens from day to day; it's like a roller coaster that you're on. And you're hangin' on, more trying to make sure that you don't go off the tracks than driving." So, Tom told me, "I think what people see on the outside is less carefully planned than most people think it is." He recalled one of many narrowly averted mistakes, where "a million [mail] pieces might have gone out with a message that wasn't exactly on point. And then people would have looked at it and said, 'Well, there must be some reason they said that.' [But] in reality there wasn't a secret brilliant strategy. And that's not just us; that's every campaign I've been in."

Political professionals by and large know that factors outside their control matter as much as or more than their own efforts. This was not just excuse making by people who had recently lost; Alexis, who worked in field on Obama's 2008 campaign, described reading David Plouffe's account of the campaign: "Oh, gosh, right, that happened, that was bad and like that happened and that was bad. . . . How did we win? Just kept on messing up." When I asked Tom directly how much his work matters, he said, "No, the candidate's much more important than we are. The candidate, the issues, the environment." I started to ask, "Does it matter though—?" He interrupted, saying, "I'm belittling my own profession, but I mean—[my mentor] always says, and I think he's right, that there's like a five to eight percent margin, you know, that we're dealing with."[48] In other words, roughly the same percentage of actual swing voters estimated for 2016.

Only three of the politicos I spoke with insisted that sufficiently brilliant campaign strategies, given enough resources, could win any reasonably close race. A few others seemed to have almost no faith in their profession. Everyone else, especially those with the most experience in the highest-level roles, sounded like Todd, sometimes focusing on the aspects of campaigns they can control, sometimes emphasizing the importance of factors they can't. They generally came to a conclusion that roughly matches scholars' assessment: sometimes, especially in close races, campaigns can make a bit of a difference, but exactly how and whether they do so is always hard to nail down.

Although politicos' beliefs about campaigns' effectiveness overall roughly matched the research, their beliefs and choices about tactics—how much emphasis to put on ads versus direct voter contact—were much less in line with scholarship on campaign effects.

Study after study has shown that ads, whether online or on television or the radio, have very small effects on how many people ultimately vote for a candidate. This finding has held however and whenever political scientists have tried to test it, except possibly in the last few days before an election.[49] So if political professionals and political scientists agree that campaigns have limited effects and that those effects are hard to measure; and if political scientists are fairly convinced that ads are among the least effective ways for campaigns to make any difference at all, why do we keep seeing so many political ads?

Jason, a Republican who worked in polling and microtargeting, was very familiar with the research on the minimal effects of campaigns. He said, "I read all that literature, I totally understand it, and I think that what they offer is important in that ultimately you need to be aware of these things, you need to understand the climate you're working in and know what your strengths are and know what your weaknesses are at a macro level and be able to adjust yourself accordingly." But his take was that "campaigns don't matter until they matter." He acknowledged that that "sounds like a Yogi Berra quote" but pointed out, "What if somebody threw a campaign and nobody showed up?" He scoffed at the prospect: "I would like to see a candidate run and say that—'I know that campaigns don't matter, so I'm not gonna run a campaign.'" Jason saw campaign competition as an "arms race" akin to the cold war philosophy of "mutually assured destruction." What happens on both sides is that "you've got to build up your arsenal and they're gonna build it up to match and you're gonna be right [back] where you started." Part of the reason most campaign actions have few or no measurable effects on outcomes, in other words, may be that their efforts are counterbalanced by opposing campaigns.[50]

Political scientists and other observers of campaigns have often noticed that their staff do not make the decisions research implies they ought to.[51] Part of the reason for this is that the research is often contradictory or hard to apply; another is what Jason says about "mutually assured destruction." Many commentators, though, have speculated that politicos, especially political consultants, prioritize advertising over other campaign activities because it is the most lucrative for them. An example of this logic is found in Adam Sheingate's *Building a Business of Politics: The Rise of Political Consulting and the Transformation of American Democracy*.[52] When he shows that consultants don't always do what political scientists have found to be most effective, he surmises that this must be because of financial incentives. Markos Moulitsas, the founder of the progressive political blog *Daily Kos*, coauthored a book that made the same point, if more polemically, in 2008: financial incentives kept Democratic operatives from running effective campaigns, causing Democrats to lose in 2000 and 2004.[53]

If political operatives are not simply doing what will work best, might they instead be motivated by financial gain? That's not really right, either. Of course, campaign professionals, like many of us, would generally like to earn as much as they can where they can. But this is a poor way of understanding the reasons we get the campaigns we do: it misses what really motivates campaign professionals, as well as how many of them are in a position to profit from any given campaign decision.

A survey of political consultants found that only a minority reported entering or staying in political work because of the money they could make, and these tended to be the least influential consultants, those earning the least and working in the smallest numbers of big races.[54] Very few of the campaign workers and political consultants I talked to seemed to be motivated primarily by financial gain. In fact, many of the people I spoke with told me they could make more money if they left campaign work. For example, at the end of my interview with Lindsey, the senior Republican pollster, I asked if there was anything else he wanted to tell me. He immediately responded: "There's so many shibboleths about campaign consultants. You know, that they tell candidates what to think, they're all just these greedy, money-grubbing people. I'm sorry, if the goal were simply to make money, I'd be in commercial market research—a *lot* more money in commercial market research." He told me, "One of the main reasons that people like me do what we do is because we believe that the people we helped elect will make a difference for the country. And that's the big distinction between Republican and Democratic pollsters. It's not the methodology, it's not the role they play, it's where they want to take the country." He compared his work to what he might be doing if he moved into market research, exclaiming, "I do not give a damn whether the toothpaste box is green or red! I just don't. But I care a whole lot about who gets on the Supreme Court. I care a whole lot about who gets to be president. I think it makes a whale of a difference for the country who gets to be president."

I heard comments like this over and over, from both Republicans and Democrats. Almost all of them are deeply passionate about politics and believe in the party and candidates they work for.[55] A Republican ad producer, whom someone else I interviewed described as one of the best and most creative in the business, told me about his shift from working in advertising to working in campaigns. He said that, before he worked in politics, "every day I would go to work and what I did for my clients really wasn't very important. If you drive a Ford or a Chevy, who cares? If you bank at Bank of Oklahoma or Bank of America or Wells Fargo, who cares? That doesn't affect much. I was always just the slightest bit embarrassed, because of what I did." Now, he said, whether "David Perdue or Michelle Nunn gets elected in Georgia has an enormous degree of influence on how somebody in Fremont, Nebraska, or in LA, or in Portland, Oregon—how they live their lives. You know, whether Obamacare gets fixed right or wrong, that's really important to people." Kirk, a Republican general consultant, told me that he "wanted to work with people who I agreed with" and that he tries to "be a little bit picky" about the candidates he works for, because "the worst feeling in the world is to help somebody get elected and then six months later, say, my goodness, maybe they should have lost. You know, that's a bad feeling." And Jay, a Democratic political director, said, "I should say what goes without saying: you should have an interest in electing someone who you think is going to advance the things that you believe in." When these people make decisions that seem irrational from the perspective of effective campaigning, it is generally not because they are trying to line their pocketbooks at the expense of their clients' chances of winning.

A number of studies and commentators nonetheless blame questionable campaign decisions—especially the large numbers of ads relative to their proven effectiveness—on financial incentives. This argument focuses on the one group whose members *can* increase their earnings through campaign decisions: consultants in media firms who deal with ad buys. People in these roles usually get a percentage of the cost of each chunk of airtime a campaign buys, but they are not the only decision-makers on campaigns.[56]

A few people I interviewed did agree with the scholarly research showing that the number of ads is excessive; many told me that absolutely part of what happens in campaigns is that every consultant is trying to get a bigger slice of the campaign-budget pie for their services, whether they provide direct mail, phone-banking, polling, or online or television advertising. Rufus, a Democratic consultant, explained that many firms' advice to a campaign will be to use more of that firm's services. Michael, a Republican who ran the field department for a major presidential candidate, told me, "I don't think most people I work with are bad people, like, overly greedy, but at the end of the day, all things equal, you're going to advocate for what you think works, and what you think works is what you do, and what you do is what makes you money."

Decisions about the allocation of resources on a campaign are ultimately in the hands of the campaign manager, with advice from their staff, advisors, and consultants. If representatives of the main consulting firms are in a room with the campaign manager and their key staff discussing strategy, only a few people in that room are going to be richer if the campaign places additional advertisements. Outside observers and researchers may think a larger portion of a campaign's budget goes to TV ads than is reasonable, but very few campaign decisions are made solely by people in a position to make extra money directly from those decisions.

The rest of the players may sometimes go along with spending moves they're not sure about in order to keep in everyone else's good graces. I heard about a few instances where people were concerned about a campaign's decisions, including the amount of advertising airtime being purchased, and didn't say anything for fear of being considered hard to work with and losing out on future consulting opportunities. One Democrat had recently worked on a campaign funded in large part by Michael Bloomberg's resources. He got a call from another consultant involved with the race who said, "I really want to say this isn't right what you're doing, but I want to be hired by the Bloomberg people again." But he and his friend weren't going to say anything that time, because "if you tell the Bloomberg people they're wrong, they won't hire you again. Even if they are wrong." Similarly, Barry, who worked in field and political departments, told me that he thought his side, the Republicans, were locked into spending far too much of their campaign budgets on television advertising, but he would never say so. "I'm as establishment and inside as they come," he told me, and "a lot of my friends are in the TV business," so if "I ever said this out loud—it's heresy." Nonetheless, he did not think his TV friends were charlatans in the least. "They're very good people that believe in the cause."

A few people weren't in politics primarily for a cause, of course. Todd told me, laughing, "I never really was ideological, but I have become less ideological as time goes on—if that was even possible." A Republican, he'd even worked with a few pro-choice candidates recently. He was motivated mostly by the thrill of competition and the money he earned.

Generally, however, politicos are committed to their party, and believe that the decisions they're making are the best ones they can make. Most think spending a lot of money on advertising makes sense. Ethan, a Democratic pollster, had no particular love for the media firms where so much campaign cash flows. He resented what he described as the "change-your-life, buy-a-yacht, live-on-an-island money" that media consultants, who produce and place advertising, can earn in a single campaign. He thought that kind of money might influence the advice media professionals give, but he disagreed that ads are bad strategy. He was very skeptical of the research showing that campaign advertisements don't matter; he believed that more advertisements do, in fact, generally help a campaign. He explained that his "political science friends are utterly, utterly convinced that television is a giant waste and no one should run any ads." But, he had read the same studies and come to a different conclusion. First, he explained, "So much of the research is taken from presidential general elections," when there is so much else going on. Talking about some studies described in Sasha Issenberg's two books that were conducted when Rick Perry was running for governor of Texas, Ethan said that although the results were fascinating, "The guy had been governor three times. He was about as well known as a governor could be.

There was not much you were going to say about him, positive or negative, that was going to be new to most people. So it seems logical to me that whatever effect would dissipate almost immediately."[57] Despite his resentment of media firms' earnings, Ethan believed that ads work, and that's why campaigns use them.

There are very reasonable critiques of the role of money in campaigns, but it is not the money itself that causes what look like bad campaign decisions to researchers.

I've spent a fair number of pages and words here explaining all the reasons that campaign effects are hard to predict, hard to measure, and are often quite small. You might be wondering why I think this is so important to understand. A lot of people who think deeply about American democracy, its flaws and its promise both, have ignored campaigns and the people who run them. So I want to explain why what happens inside campaigns, or in the heads and hearts of campaign professionals, is relevant to understanding American politics. Many political scientists assume that everyone in politics is acting in a fairly straightforward manner to maximize some obvious interest or utility for themselves—that is, they believe in the rational choice theory of human behavior.[58]

I'm not at all convinced by this theory—indeed, most sociologists aren't. Sure, people sometimes act rationally, but in many situations we do what we do based on a complex mix of factors—our habits, our social conditioning, our desire to adhere to norms and be what we think of as a "good person," our interest in the respect of our peers, our fears and emotions, and so on. In other words, it's part of who I am as a sociologist to focus on the fact that people are social beings, not isolated individual calculators of their maximum chance of increasing their utility functions.

If campaign professionals' actions are geared to one of two obvious external interests, winning or earning, we don't need to know who they are, or what they think. And if we assume those external interests are what explain campaigns, we miss what's really happening in American politics, as well as some of the ways it could be different.

Since the people running campaigns are not simply implementing the best possible path to victory, and they're also not primarily cynically wringing as much money from the process for themselves as they can, what does account for the choices they make? The answer to that question drives the rest of this book, which focuses on four key aspects of the work world of campaign professionals that are essential to understanding how American politics are produced.

First, although campaign professionals absolutely want to win campaigns, most of them are even more concerned with becoming one of the people "in the room where it happens." To them, this means contributing to decisions about campaign strategy and tactics at as high a level as possible in the campaign structure, on as big a campaign as possible. This is where they can have the most influence, where they're the closest to the candidate and the power center of the campaign, and where they'll be given the most credit (or blame) for a win or loss. Reaching this level is the clearest sign that they have "made it" in the political world. In order to gain entry to this inner circle, they need other people in the political world to view them as being good at what they do.

However, because it is so difficult to know which campaign decisions, if any, resulted in a win or a loss, campaign professionals must evaluate each other based on criteria other than the actual effectiveness of their tactics. Data alone cannot tell them how they are doing, but their colleagues and opponents (along with the media) do provide immediate feedback about campaign strategies. It is largely the judgments of other people in politics that matter for politicos' careers.

Thus, the second key aspect of campaign work is that campaign professionals tend to use two main proxies for good campaigning: the extent to which their colleagues are willing and able to work ridiculously long hours, and their adherence to conventional campaign wisdom passed down among campaign professionals. The consensus about what's effective in campaigning rarely changes. When it does change, it's usually because one party has suffered an unexpected loss, and even then the change is so gradual that although new tactics or approaches (such as online advertising) may gain prominence, older ones—even those shown to be entirely ineffective (such as glossy mailers)—remain.[59] "Best practices" in campaigns are largely learned on the job: a few universities offer certificate or MA programs dedicated to teaching campaign skills, but most politicos I spoke with thought these were "nearly worthless." When I asked campaigners what made something a good move in a campaign, they rarely mentioned research or evidence, and instead were much more likely to talk about having a "gut sense" for politics or to say, "You just know it when you see it."

Third, in part because of the use of these proxies, the world of campaign professionals is very insular. It is hard to get even an entry-level position on most campaigns if you do not already know someone involved in politics, and it is difficult to advance if you do not have both the time and financial security to volunteer or work for very little pay for a campaign that may or may not lead to a next job. This is part of why campaign professionals are overwhelmingly men, generally from middle- to upper-middle-class backgrounds, and disproportionately White. This last is true even when you compare within parties. Democratic campaign professionals are more racially diverse than Republicans, but they are less likely to be Black, Latinx, Asian American, Pacific Islander, or Native American than Democratic voters are.[60] The same holds for Republicans. This might not matter if campaigns were simply implementing straightforwardly knowable best practices. But given that those aren't available, this insularity limits the variety of strategies and tactics campaigns might take on, as well as their ability to understand and relate to Americans who are socially distant from the political elite in Washington, DC.

Which brings us to the fourth important consequence of the uncertainty of campaign strategies: a reductive view of voters and their behavior. Tellingly, campaign professionals I interviewed rarely brought up potential voters when I asked about campaign quality. When they did talk about voters, they usually described them as an audience, as passive (if not resistant) recipients of campaign messaging. Campaign professionals even discussed the need to "hit people over their heads" or "pound into them" the campaign's message.

This is because, aside from low-level field operatives and event managers, senior politicos rarely interact with the potential voters they are trying to influence. Instead, their understanding of voters is filtered through polls and the modeling done with voter data, combined with their prior beliefs about the right way to campaign. As if to illustrate this point, one key player in the Clinton 2016 campaign told me that they'd made all the right decisions, but simply based them on the wrong data. I heard from a number of people that the campaign headquarters ignored reports from local campaign staff whose interactions with voters indicated that the reality on the ground was different from what the models predicted. This data- and modeling-driven approach to understanding voters leads campaign professionals to think of them as abstract conglomerations of attributes and data points, rather than as members of families or communities, or actual complex people with whom they could connect.

These four key truths about modern-day campaign workers—their focus on being "in the room," their adherence to conventional wisdom, the exclusiveness of their world, and their approach to voters as variables—mean that in our current system, campaigns are spending huge sums of money to do things that may not be entirely effective at achieving their goal. Politicos tend to see campaigning as a battle between teams as much as or more than an effort to really connect their candidate with potential voters. Consequently, they are missing an opportunity to include people in democracy in a meaningful way.

Campaign professionals are doing work that they believe is deeply important and, simultaneously, might not matter at all. To resolve this tension, they focus on their colleagues, their opponents, and the media. In the end, the all-consuming nature of campaigns serves to exclude people who cannot or will not give up everything else in their lives for the sake of the campaign. All this dedication and devotion isolates campaign professionals—and campaign operations—making it even harder for outsiders to make sense of their work and its implications for American democracy.

★ ★ ★ ★ ★

CHAPTER 2

A FOOT IN THE DOOR

Chris is a pretty typical political professional: straight, White, and wealthy. About fifty years old and a lifelong Republican, he worked on his first campaign when he was "eleven or twelve." Well-dressed, self-possessed, and charismatic, he never intends to run for office, but he looks a lot like someone Hollywood might cast to play the president in a summer blockbuster.

Close to forty years ago, one of Chris's paper route customers was running for a county-level office and gave Chris his first taste of politics. He was fascinated by the man whose name dotted the neighborhood lawns, and he eagerly accepted when the candidate asked for help distributing campaign literature. When Chris's candidate won, he took all the neighborhood kids to a fancy skating rink to celebrate. Chris was hooked. Throughout high school and college he worked on campaigns whenever he could, then got his first full-time job in politics right after graduating. He parlayed his job as spokesperson for a family friend running for local office into a job working for that friend when he won, then applied for a job with a Republican member of Congress in Washington, DC. By the time Chris got hired on the Hill, five different people claimed to have gotten him the job—that's just how many contacts he "worked" to try to secure his position.

His résumé since then is impressive: Chris has worked in communications for three serious Republican presidential contenders, has served as a campaign spokesman at public events and on every major news network, and has commented on current politics as a pundit on cable news programs and in the country's best-known newspapers. Although Chris decided he was done with campaign work in 2012, he continued to wield outsize influence in American politics as a consultant at a high-end Washington public affairs firm, helping big corporations influence law and policy, then as a spokesperson for a well-funded foundation, where his job was to try to convince elected officials to adopt policies that fit with the organization's values.

Chris stands out for his charisma and the high-level positions he's held, but he is not at all unusual among political operatives. The people who work on campaigns are members of a strange and exclusive club, and they know it. Susan, a White Democratic consultant who worked on fundraising and canvassing efforts, explained that "people that work in politics are not normal people," and Rufus, a White Democrat who runs mass phone-call operations, told me, "A lot of the people in this field are odd—very odd people." As a group, they are different from most Americans, but similar to each other: disproportionately White men from well-to-do backgrounds, nearly all have been passionately interested in politics since they were young. They now have substantial influence on what happens in Washington, DC, around the country, and beyond.

Politicos are as passionate about campaigns and politics as some "regular" people are about their hometown football teams or favorite artists. Derek, a White Democratic consultant who has worked on campaigns since high school in 1968, nearly got a PhD but dropped out because he "got the bug again" and joined yet another campaign. Arthur, a White Republican media consultant, told me, "A lot of people in politics are the ones who ran for student council president in high school or class secretary [and] they just got it in their blood." These politicos know that most people don't feel the way they do about politics, so they make it their job to get everyone else to at least vote the "right" way. Rufus, summing up his colleagues, mused, "One of the ways they're odd is they really can see and feel how regular people—even though they are not regular people—are going to react to something." Whether or not they really understand the people they aim to influence is up for debate, but most politicos see themselves as both unusually interested in, and unusually good at, politics.

All this matters because politicos like Chris and his colleagues wield enormous power. In consultation with candidates, they decide how campaigns are run, and this shapes how regular people feel about and envision their places within politics. They advise office holders, contribute to media coverage of elections and governments, and lobby government on behalf of major corporations and interest groups. In other words, they are key to the operation of political power in the United States.

How did they get to be part of this club of "odd" political professionals whose decisions affect so much about our politics? Despite their own generally quite privileged backgrounds, politicos describe the world of campaign work as uniquely open and meritocratic. Todd, the Republican pollster, called his profession "one of the last American Dream careers: the harder you work, the further you get." He claimed that his colleagues all started out on the ground floor, whether they were rich or poor, highly educated or possessed nothing more than a GED certificate. Leon, a Black Republican consultant, echoed Todd, noting that not only does your alma mater not matter, but a college degree is not even necessary: "I've seen examples of folks that haven't gotten a college education and have done tremendously well in campaign politics. You know, just because they were willing to put in the time, they were smart and they got involved at a local level and followed people on the way up." And Todd insisted, when it comes to hiring for a campaign, "All anyone wants to know is 'Who did you work for?' . . . 'How successful were you?'" Stanley, a White senior advisor and Democratic consulting firm owner, agreed: "I've never asked anybody where they went to school. I always want to know what campaigns they've been in."

Most people I interviewed returned to meritocracy talk over and over again: Do well in entry-level positions, they told me, and you'll be rewarded with more work. Family background and educational level or prestige do not determine campaign career success. Judgments about coworkers come down to straightforward assessments of their campaign abilities (or whether they are rumored to be campaign liabilities). This isn't exactly wrong: Hard work is rewarded in this field, as is the ability to produce acceptable work on tight time lines, work punishing hours, and stay calm under pressure. Everyone I spoke with agreed that, no matter their connections' or pedigree, a politico who couldn't do all those things wouldn't be a politico for long.

But campaigns are not really meritocracies in any meaningful sense. When you ask most professionally successful people in the United States how they achieved career success—no matter what job they do—they will likely tell you they got there through hard work and individual merit.[1] And yet a disproportionate share of people in highly paid, highly respected, and highly influential positions in the US are White and from families where at least one parent held a similarly high-powered job.[2] Meanwhile, countless Black, Brown, and working-class people work incredibly hard at jobs that bring little pay, respect, or career mobility.

A work world that was truly meritocratic would be accessible to anyone with the necessary motivation and talent, and it would be equally likely to reward anybody who demonstrates their merit.[3] That is, both "getting in" and "getting ahead" would be based on what someone can do, not who they are or whom they know. But that is not the case in campaigns, which are nearly as exclusive as the halls of Congress or the hallways of academia.[4] Indeed, hardly any work world is truly meritocratic. Consequently, the more interesting questions about campaigns are how people in campaigns define and recognize merit, and who is in a position to have their "merit" recognized in the first place.

My database of political professionals and their career trajectories has the names and attributes of most people who have worked in national-level campaigns in the last few decades.[5] With these data I can make inferences about the race, gender, education, and to some extent the class background of politicos. There are of course other important types of exclusion in the US that undoubtedly apply here as well; no prominent politicos that I know of have identified themselves as disabled, for example, nor have I heard of any who are out as transgender or non-binary. Some are certainly lesbian, gay, bisexual, or otherwise queer, but I could not collect systematic information on disability status, gender identity, or sexual orientation.

Still, the evidence is clear that campaign work is not at all accessible to everybody. Taken as a whole, 83 percent of politicos who have worked on major national races in the twenty-first century are White, 65 percent are men, and 80 percent attended college.[6] These are stark differences from the adult US population, which is about 60 percent White, 49 percent men, and 32 percent college-educated.[7]

Race, gender, and education are all areas where the two parties' constituencies and policies are quite different from each other. Republican voters and campaign staff are both far more White than the country as a whole. While 60 percent of adults in the US and 69 percent of registered voters

are non-Hispanic White, about 81 percent of Republican-identifying voters are White.[8] But for Republican campaign staff and consultants who
worked on national campaigns from 2004 to 2020, I estimate that number
is 93 percent; only about 2 percent of Republican politicos in my database are Black, 3 percent are Hispanic/Latinx, and less than 2 percent
are Asian American.[9] Despite fielding a candidate in 2016 and 2020 who
was much more willing than his recent predecessors to be explicitly and
openly racist, Republicans have diversified their campaigns somewhat
since the beginning of the twenty-first century. In 2004 and 2008 only 5
percent of Republicans working on national-level campaigns were people
of color; by 2020 that number was 11 percent, still substantially less than
the 19 percent portion of Republican voters.[10] People of color are deeply
underrepresented among Republican politicos when compared with the
electorate as a whole, and even when compared with their representation
among Republican voters.

Although the Democratic Party is far more racially diverse in both its
voters and staff than Republicans, Democratic operatives are also disproportionately White compared to the country as a whole and to their own
registered voters. About 73 percent of Democratic campaign operatives in
my database are White; about 15 percent are Black, compared with 19 percent of registered Democratic voters. About 7 percent are Hispanic/Latinx
(versus 13 percent among Democrats overall), and less than 5 percent are
Asian American or Pacific Islander (versus 8 percent of Democrats).[11]

There has been some improvement in the racial representativeness
of Democratic campaign politics over the last two decades. In 2004 and
2008, 78 percent of Democratic operatives in national-level campaigns
were White and only 12 percent were Black (about 65 percent of registered Democratic voters were White in 2004). In 2012, a picture of the
nearly all-White staff at Barack Obama's Chicago headquarters caused
controversy, and Obama's campaign subsequently worked to diversify his
campaign staff.[12] In 2020, the Democratic presidential primary campaigns
included the most racially diverse group of viable candidates in history,
and they reported collectively that 42 percent of their top staff were people of color.[13] Maya Rupert, a Black woman, served as campaign manager
for Julián Castro and then held a key role on Elizabeth Warren's campaign; she was only the third Black woman in history to manage a presidential campaign. The Pew Research Center estimates that, as of 2019,

59 percent of Democratic registered voters were White, at the top levels of these campaigns were broadly representative of the racial composition of their party's voters.[14] When I count the broader set of Democratic campaign staff in my database working in key roles in any national-level campaign in 2020, however, the campaign teams are still disproportionately White—about 68 percent—but closer to the racial composition of their voters than they had been.

It is not clear whether the increased racial diversity highlighted in the primary candidates and their top staff in 2020 will persist in the ranks of Democratic operatives beyond that one primary season. Diana, a Democratic Latina field staffer, said that Democratic campaigns are "intentional about hiring when the campaign season starts. But what about building a talent pipeline of non-White people? That's missing." Doug Thornell, a Black Democrat who worked at all the big national Democratic Party organizations before becoming a consultant with the strategic communications firm SKDK, pointed out to *Campaigns & Elections* magazine that Democratic consulting firms' senior levels are still very White: "There are virtually no African American political ad makers on the Democratic side. I think we, as Democrats, need to change that and make the consulting world look more like the Democratic Party."[15]

National-level Democratic campaigns are even less racially representative when I look at the roles people worked in. White people filled 69 percent of campaign manager, deputy campaign manager, and state director roles in 2020, similar to Democratic campaigns as a whole in that year. But Democratic communications departments in 2020 were 81 percent White, and campaign staff in field departments and in roles outside management, communications, and political departments were about 74 percent White. People of color were concentrated in political departments, where only 40 percent of staff were White. They often had titles like "director of African American outreach." As Diana explained, "There's definitely this thinking that if you're Latino, then you know maybe they'll only put you in states that have a sizable Latino population" or in positions doing outreach to Latinos. She went on to talk about the effects on her career: "So what does that mean? It means that through the years it's made it a little bit harder to expand. And so that means less opportunities."

The few non-White Republicans are also concentrated—one might say pigeonholed—in political departments. A Black Republican I spoke with said he didn't feel that race had hindered his "professional success in campaign politics." But he had definitely "been put in weird positions, where it's like, 'Well, okay, you know, in this instance we're speaking to an audience of Black businessmen in this area—all right, come along politically.'"

The gender gap in campaign involvement is at least as stark as the racial one. Women make up only about 26 percent of the Republicans who have worked on general presidential elections, and only about 42 percent of the Democrats. Both parties have become somewhat less dominated by men over time, while neither party is yet representative of their voters. There were many high-profile women campaign managers in 2020 races, and just over half of Democrats working in national-level campaigns were women. This is still not quite representative of registered Democrats, about 57 percent of whom are women.[16] Still, it's much better than the gender ratios in 2004, when women made up only 38 percent of people working in Democratic campaigns. Democratic campaign staff are far more representative of their constituents along gender lines than Republicans. Republican campaign staff in any kind of national race were about 27 percent women in 2004, and about 33 percent by 2020, whereas Republican voters were about 48 percent women.[17]

Despite what many campaign professionals told me they believed, their ranks are even less representative in terms of education than in terms of race or gender. Only 32 percent of people over twenty-five years of age in the United States have a college degree or higher level of education, but 75 percent of Republican campaign professionals and 85 percent of Democrats included a college or university alma mater in the biographical material I could find.[18]

Moreover, campaign professionals attended exclusive, often elite, colleges and universities—Democrats even more than Republicans. Economist Raj Chetty and researchers at the Opportunity Project, drawing on an analysis by *Barron's*, categorized colleges and universities into a set of tiers, from "Ivy Plus" at the top down through "elite," "highly selective," "selective," and "other," which includes two-year colleges as well as a few four-year institutions.[19] Chetty et al. report that less than 1 percent of Americans who attended college went to institutions they designate as Ivy Plus, such as Harvard, Princeton, Yale, Duke, and Stanford. But close to 5 percent of Republican campaign operatives and over 15 percent of

Democratic campaign professionals attended these schools. Another 22 percent of Democrats in my database and 20 percent of Republicans went to "elite" schools such as Amherst, Georgetown, Rice, or Swarthmore. These schools have enrolled only 3 percent of college-going adults in general. Similar percentages (23 percent of Democrats and 21 percent of Republicans) went to "highly selective" schools such as Rutgers, the University of California at Berkeley, Colorado College, or Boston University, which enroll only 9 percent of college students. Finally, almost all the remaining politicos in both parties went to "selective" colleges and universities; 2 percent or less went to the kinds of "other" colleges that enroll the largest portion (44 percent) of Americans. Taken together, 61 percent of Democratic operatives and 46 percent of Republicans attended schools designated as "highly selective" or above, as opposed to just 13 percent of college-educated voters.

So far I have discussed race, gender, and education but have said nothing directly about class origin. Inferring someone's race based simply on their web presence may be difficult, but it is nearly impossible to systematically ascertain their class origin.[20] Most people don't include their parents' occupations, educations, or income in their online biographies. Those who do generally want to make a point about coming from "humble origins" and so are not representative.

Nonetheless, tomes of sociological research make it exceedingly clear that class origin has a profound impact on access to education, high-status occupations, and high incomes.[21] The fact that almost all politicos went to college is good reason to guess that most of them had parents who went to college. The schools people attended are another clue about their class origins. The Chetty project collected data on the earnings of the parents of people who attended different sorts of schools; the median parental income for the "Ivy Plus" schools was $171,000, more than twice the median for college-educated adults' parents overall and more than three times the median for all US households. All the tiers of colleges politicos attended in any numbers have much higher median parental earnings than the US as a whole.

Interviews also painted a picture of the class exclusivity of campaign work. Only seven of the seventy-two people I spoke with told me they came from what sociologists would call working-class families. Two of my older interviewees had fathers who worked in factories; one grew up with a firefighter dad and church secretary mom; another had a father in telephone repair and a stay-at-home mom. These families may very well have thought of themselves as middle class, and probably had steady incomes and job security. Only one person told me he grew up "poor." Almost everyone else told me about growing up at least comfortably middle class. Many had parents who were teachers or owned small businesses, and a substantial portion were children of the upper middle class or even elites. One told me his parents "developed and managed coal mines throughout the world"; another's father was a prominent member of Congress; others' parents were lawyers, engineers, professors, doctors, and business executives.

The gender, race, educational, and class-origin differences between politicos and the rest of the country are not simply about who happens to occupy these roles at any given moment; they are also about the constitution of the political sphere itself. Historically, parties and campaigns in the US were run entirely by White men, most often well-off ones; voting was restricted to these groups too. Incisive observers of US history from W. E. B. Du Bois through Nikole Hannah-Jones have pointed out that American political conflicts are almost always, on some fundamental level, about race and racism. But most of those battles in electoral politics have been fought by White people.[22]

As sociologist Victor Ray put it, organizations are "racial structures—that is, cultural schemas connected to social resources."[23] Spheres that historically have been predominantly White tend to continue to advantage White people in ways both obvious and subtle, both inside the organization—pushing some people to excel and stymieing the careers of others—and beyond it. The same applies for gender and for class.[24] When organizational and professional cultures are structured around the norms and culture of the privileged, inequality gets reproduced unless conscious, well-supported efforts are made to counteract that tendency.

· · ·

It is clear that campaign professionals are far more likely to come from privilege than from poverty, but there are exceptions. The stories of two people, Don and Robby, from relatively disadvantaged backgrounds who nonetheless entered campaign work illustrate both the barriers to access and ways to overcome them. Now very successful Republican politicos, each had an atypical path into his career: one happened into the work unplanned, whereas the other spent a full year trying before gaining his opening.

Don figures that when most people meet him, they see a "White man who is southern, and wears a bow tie, has a great family, and a wife and kids and house." He reckons they assume he comes "from money and got connected to politics that way," but "it was just the opposite." He grew up in extreme poverty, "living on welfare, food stamps, Section 8 housing." But when his school district proposed putting the kids from the poorer side of town in a different high school, Don was livid. He was going to be sent away and separated from his friends. Don took his anger and testified at the school board meeting, then "kind of accidentally became the face of these poor kids." A local politician, impressed with the kid's chutzpah, asked Don to volunteer for his campaign, and even though Don "didn't know shit about politics!" he was soon being paid to put up signs.

When Don got to college at the flagship state university, that same politician gave him a job as a page in the state senate. "Frankly," Don remembered, "I didn't even know that politics was a career. I didn't know that was something you could do. . . . I didn't know lobbyists, I didn't know campaign consultants, I didn't know this was a thing." But he "fell in love" with the State House, joined the College Republicans, and "just met all these different politicians" who asked him to work for them. From his perspective, he'd gotten his career in campaign work without really trying. It was as if his interest in it came after his entry into the profession.

Even though Don's entry into politics was not at all standard, his trajectory thereafter was typical: he worked on a number of campaigns until some people he met on one of them started a consulting firm and invited him to become its first full-time employee. Six years later, Don left to start his own firm and has been based there since. Over the years he's worked for state and national GOP organizations and on state-level and presidential campaigns.

Robby, like Don, lacked the early passion for politics that characterized most of my respondents. The youngest of four, Robby grew up in a working-class immigrant family in Washington, DC, just a few miles from the White House. "I can't really remember outside of, like, government class, really giving any serious kind of consideration to government and politics," Robby told me. But then came the 2000 election, in which Bush was the Republican and Gore, the Democratic candidate. Gore won the popular vote, and the count in the Electoral College came down to Florida, where court battles over the counting of votes stretched into December before being resolved by the Supreme Court in Bush's favor. Robby had just finished college, not having "really considered" what his political views were, but he "got very interested in politics because of the recount."

In contrast to Don, who essentially just happened into politics and built his political connections organically through jobs and campus groups, Robby realized he wanted to go into politics but had no idea where to begin. "Even though I was from DC and grew up in DC, I really didn't know anyone in politics."[25] He knew this was an unusual origin for a politico, and told me that "a lot of people in politics have relationships or someone that they know, or someone that they're close to has a relationship that kind of provides them an [opportunity] as an intern, or a staff assistant, or something along those lines. You know, I was a little different in that I didn't [know anyone]." Getting his first political job was tremendously difficult, in part because he had no idea how the system worked. He remembers, "I went about trying to get a job in politics the only way I knew how, which was to update the résumé, kind of walk the halls of Congress, hand it out. . . . I ended up hitting probably about a hundred House offices and Senate offices and committees and whatnot." With plenty of interest but very little opportunity, Robby spent close to a year in this effort before someone on Capitol Hill took his résumé seriously and offered him an interview.

Don and Robby's stories illustrate that it is possible for poor and working-class people to enter careers in politics. There are no formal barriers to entry into political work: You don't need a particular degree or certificate or anything except the interest and someone to give you that first job. But the very informality of the process of starting out into political work can make it harder for people from backgrounds like Don's and Robby's.

The lack of requirements for specific credentials or formal training make it harder to spot the inequalities in access to participating in decisions about national campaign strategy—to being in the room where it happens. The difficulty is not in gaining admission to competitive programs or passing a challenging exam, as with law and medicine. Instead, there are what might be called filtering effects at every step on a potential path toward a career in politics.

These filtering effects are especially likely to exclude people who are poor or working-class, women, Black, Latinx, Indigenous, or Asian American. There *is* a fairly clear path into the higher echelons of campaign work, but it's only clearly visible from the top. Unlike tech companies, management consultancies, and investment banks, campaign organizations are not known to hold career-recruitment events on college campuses.[26] Nonetheless, stories of how people got into and advanced in campaign work were remarkably consistent across my interviews, starting with first getting a foothold in the field. Getting an initial job in campaigns or an entry-level position in national politics involves knowing that such jobs exist, finding a connection or an internship to get in the door, and being incredibly persistent—all of which are far easier when you look like the people in charge of hiring. Those hurdles alone keep many people from ever getting a first political job. The characteristics of these entry-level jobs are also likely to "weed out people who are either not that into it or not that good at it," as Michael, a White Republican operative, put it, as well as to weed out anyone without the resources to withstand regular interstate moves, low or no pay, and near-constant uncertainty about their next job or source of income.

WHO WANTS TO WORK IN POLITICS ANYWAY?

Even before anyone has started looking for jobs or internships, the pool of people who might want to work on campaigns is severely limited by interest. Most people who work in campaigns have been passionate about politics since they were kids. When other kids were getting excited about football or fashion or film, future politicos were following election returns or running campaigns for student council.

Even Claire, a White Democratic campaign manager who was in her early thirties when I spoke with her in 2010, felt she had gotten a late start because she only became interested in politics midway through college. She said she wasn't like "these kids, I mean, they live, breathe and eat it. You know, all through high school, some of them back into middle school, definitely through college," adding that "a lot of people in this business" had a parent who ran for office or was regularly volunteering for campaigns. Most people I spoke with said something similar; one recounted a story of handing out campaign flyers with his mom before he even got to kindergarten.

If you're not in a setting where this is common or reasonable, chances are you won't develop this kind of taste for politics. People who did not grow up thinking of politics as interesting, important, and relevant to them are unlikely to pursue it as a career.

To some extent, kids' interests are simply a function of their personalities or what they happen to be exposed to at a critical juncture. But who happens to be exposed to what, and how they react, is in large part about their family's social position. As sociologists and political scientists have confirmed, your parents' socioeconomic class has a big influence on what kinds of hobbies and tastes you develop, especially with regard to politics. People who grow up in families where no one pays much attention to politics are probably not going to wax poetic about the thrill of watching their candidate win in a close race. And on average, poor and working-class families are less likely than their middle- and upper-middle-class peers to be regular voters or to follow politics closely.[27]

Which brings us to another problem with how people are recruited into politics and also how campaigns work. For most people who do think of themselves as politically engaged, politics is a lot like a spectator sport, as Eitan Hersh points out in *Politics Is for Power*.[28] These types of political citizens get excited about knowing what's happening, following the news, and discussing possibilities with their friends: How will the Senate vote on this bill? Who's going to win the primary? Will the Republican eke out a narrow victory? They might get involved here and there, on an issue-by-issue or candidate-by-candidate basis, but they're not, as Hersh puts it, actually working for *power*. Building political power requires joining groups, trying to recruit others, building networks, and staying invested in politics beyond the campaign cycle. But that's not how a lot of politically engaged upper-middle-class White people approach it.

People who come into political work from this kind of background already see politics differently from how most Americans do, and also differently from the vision put forth by democratic theorists. They see political work not primarily as about winning representation for communities that need it but as beating, outmaneuvering, the other team, as a sport that they're playing—one with real stakes, real outcomes for power.

Politicos care about these outcomes, but they aren't always central to how they think about what they're doing, once they get to be the athletes instead of just the spectators.

National-level politicians, another source of potential role models for kids who might be interested in politics, are also distinct from most of the rest of us. As political scientist Nick Carnes points out, no matter how often they speak of their working-class roots (or some semblance of them), people who run for and win office are very, very disproportionately likely to hold professional positions before starting their first campaign. Carnes found that just 2 percent of members of Congress worked doing manual or routine labor before being elected, although 52 percent of US citizens work in such jobs.[29] Only about one-third of Americans over twenty-five have college degrees, but all but ten members of the 117th Congress do.[30] No wonder so many people feel that politicians don't understand them.

Young people are most likely to get excited about careers in which they have role models who resemble them—but poor and working-class people in all racial groups and people of color in all classes have few chances to see reflections of themselves in national politics. This lack of identification becomes a self-reinforcing cycle.

Obviously, there are deeply politically engaged poor and working-class people in this country. There are plenty of people in these communities who are passionate about improving their neighborhoods and the lives of people around them, though they don't always do this political work through the electoral system. Many of our most important and transformative social movements have been led by people of color and by poor and working-class people of all races, from the labor movement, which "brought you the weekend," to Black Lives Matter, from the civil rights movement to movements of poor people, regular people have taken steps to change society for the better.[31] Working-class community organizations and movements are often also focused more directly on community needs and propelled by personal introductions—that is, your neighbor or aunt invites you into the work, which tends to be grassroots, unpaid, and local.[32]

Generally, however, the electoral political arena has been reserved for people with most forms of privilege—White, upper-middle-class, nondisabled, straight, and cisgender men—as both the key players and the most involved spectators. You might think that the more ways in which a person is distant from that description, the less likely they are to participate in politics. But the social world is more complicated than that, so to consider how race shapes individuals' connections to politics, we have to look at a set of identities and characteristics beyond race alone. One fundamental insight of Black feminist scholars like law professor Kimberlé Crenshaw and sociologist Patricia Hill Collins is that identities are not simply additive but, to use the term Crenshaw coined, intersectional.[33] Being a Black woman can't be understood as just being two degrees distant from being a White man.

In fact, Black women constitute one of the most politically engaged groups in the United States.[34] In a paper I wrote with Hana Brown and Ankit Rastogi, for example, we show that poor Black women vote at higher rates than poor White men, poor Black men, and poor White women, and by a substantial amount.[35] Their voting rates in presidential elections rival those of middle-class Whites. Moreover, though socio-economic status strongly predicts voting among White people—many books have been written on the overall class inequality in voting—the class-voting line is essentially flat for Black American citizens.[36] White Americans earning over $100,000 annually are about 1.5 times as likely to vote as White Americans earning under $30,000 per year, yet Black people at all income levels vote at roughly the same rate. That means that rich Black people vote somewhat less than rich White people, but poor Black people vote more than poor White people. The race-class intersection works differently for other minority groups in the United States. Asian Americans as a group are the least likely to vote across all class positions, and Latinx people vote at higher rates than Asian Americans but at somewhat lower rates than White people.[37] There is some evidence of a class gradient in voting and political participation for Latinx people, and less evidence for Asian Americans. Most research on race and voting tends to ignore Indigenous/Native American people, who are among the least likely to vote in US elections.[38]

All of which is to say that nothing inherent in racial group membership or class necessarily makes people more or less likely to vote or pay attention to politics. Black South Africans, who were mostly very poor, voted in their country's first all-races democratic election in 1994 at far higher rates than even well-off people in the US.[39] In the United Kingdom, people at all income levels had similar voting rates until around 1987.[40] So what explains patterned differences in balloting? In part, it has to do with people's level of connection with the actual institutions of politics.[41]

In response to concerted efforts to exclude Black people from democratic participation, from the end of Reconstruction onward, American Black organizers from the civil rights movement to the present have invested their time and energy in securing and protecting voting rights and amplifying voter turnout.[42] This has generated direct connections to politics for many in Black communities. Many cities have Black political dynasties, and Democratic politicians and operatives court certain Black leaders to win primaries and general elections.[43] One example was Joe Biden's come-from-behind-win in the 2020 South Carolina primary, driven in large part by the late endorsement of Congressman James E. Clyburn, who had served in Congress for twenty-seven years.[44]

The book *For Colored Girls Who Have Considered Politics*, written by a quartet of Black women political operatives, also demonstrates the close connection of many Black Americans with politics.[45] None of the four came from a wealthy family, yet each was in a position at a pivotal point in her youth to be in the room with a politician or community leader and to get involved in a political organization or campaign. Networking is how most White politicos enter politics, but the authors of this book exemplify the difference in Black politicos' motivations for and interpretations of their political work. Unlike nearly every White power player I interviewed, the authors of *For Colored Girls* say they saw the work of political engagement as a way to give back to their communities. This kind of direct link to political power is less common in other communities of color, and for poor and working-class White people, especially for the vast numbers of White workers who don't belong to a union.[46]

Scholars who have looked at these dynamics have concluded that a substantial reason for lower rates of voting among non-Black racialized groups is that political parties and campaigns have not historically made efforts to connect with them and get them to turn out; this is shifting somewhat for Latinx in the last few elections but hasn't yet changed much for Asian Americans.[47] Members of minoritized racial groups in the US, of course, also have very good reasons to be suspicious of government and elites in general, and some members of these groups (though not a majority) eschew voting on purpose, out of an unwillingness to participate in a system they know does not have their best interests at heart.

And none of that touches on issues of voter suppression, felon disenfranchisement, and other ways Whites in power have tried, since Reconstruction, to limit democratic participation from Black people and, to a lesser extent, other people of color, and poor and working-class White people.[48]

In many, many ways the pool of people who vote regularly, let alone are actively interested in politics as an occupation, is not at all reflective of the population as a whole, and that is the first part of the story of why the political profession looks the way it does.

CLIMBING THE CAREER MOUNTAIN

Interest is one thing. Actionable knowledge is quite another. Thus, a big challenge for potential politicos is understanding the types of jobs available in campaigns and then figuring out the first steps toward a career in politics.

Politics lacks a clearly visible career path with identifiable stages and criteria for advancement. Think about a career as a path up a mountain toward its peak. Every career's path is more or less well marked and more or less difficult to traverse. For instance, the career path to becoming a medical doctor is difficult to navigate but extremely clearly mapped: complete pre-med requirements and get a good GPA as an undergraduate, take the MCAT, get accepted into a medical school, complete the coursework, choose a specialty, get matched to and complete a residency, pass some more tests, and you will be qualified as a doctor and can almost certainly reach the mountain peak: a stable and high-paying job in your chosen field. Each of these parts of the path is hard. Many people will drop off the path at almost every stage. Nevertheless, the way from point A to point B is perfectly visible; smart, motivated, and hard-working aspirants frequently navigate it successfully.[49]

When the criteria for advancement in a given field are murky—when the path lacks signposts and checkpoints—it is far easier for discrimination to creep into the journey. For example, in organizations where "fit" is highly valued, the biases of those in charge of hiring and promotions are much more likely to smooth the way for people who already look like the people in key decision-making roles. That means a hefty disadvantage for Black and Brown applicants, as well as other people of color, women, people from poor and working-class backgrounds, and anyone else who isn't sufficiently similar to the people with power.[50] Someone like Alexis, the daughter of a well-known Democratic politician who worked on get-out-the-vote efforts in the Obama campaign, will tell you that "there's a fairly clear path to sort of leadership within campaigns" (cautioning that "it's not looked upon all that fondly if you try and skip three levels"), but that path is most visible from the top, to those who have already ascended it. Anyone outside the world of campaigns and the social networks of campaign professionals would be hard-pressed to know how or where to begin.

Even politicos who were passionate about politics from a young age often struggled to connect with political work. Over half of those for whom I could find this information majored in political science. Some had parents who helped them make the move to Washington, DC, even before they landed a job. Still, most had to put in a good deal of time and effort to break into the field in a meaningful way. They had to work their networks and prove their dedication before getting to do the kind of work that had me asking for interviews.

Say you're twenty-two years old, with a fresh bachelor's degree and a desire to go into campaign politics. Where would you start? Most people find that getting an introductory job is about using your connections—it's "who you know" rather than what you know or what you can do.

This is especially true in campaign work, where hiring is often fast and informal. These are not the kinds of positions for which hiring managers post ads for positions, sift through résumés, and conduct round after round of interviews. To even know there is an opening, you need connections of the sort cultivated through privileged childhoods, membership in politically connected communities, or shared college experiences. Whether on the Hill or in campaigns, the key is often to show up in person and be willing to do whatever you're asked to do.

Chris, the lifelong Republican politico in communications, described finding a job in a campaign as "not one of these things where you send out blind résumés." His strategy relied on a sort of connections-based strategic knowledge gathering: "If you get a lead, you've gotta basically run a campaign to get that job, and you've gotta call people to serve as third-party advocates, you have to find out all the information you can about the status and what it is that you need to do, if anybody's out there beating you, what is it that you need to do better." Such a campaign to get a position requires having already built connections, then using them to access other networks: "A lot of [getting my job] had to do with cross-pollination. . . . I knew a guy who knew a guy who knew a guy who knew a guy, and they all—next thing you know, I found out I had five different avenues of access to this job and that was how I have it."

Clayton, a White Democratic operative who has done research for multiple campaigns, told me that people running campaigns "just never put out an open call for résumés. They just don't operate that way. If they have an opening, they'll ask a few friends, and their friends will ask a few friends and they'll get a couple people on the side." That's how the first decade of his own political career went: he got an internship, then followed his internship mentor when he started a think tank and again when the mentor joined a major presidential campaign. Clayton actually bucked the trend when he was put in charge of hiring: he believed he was "able to put together a better staff" by advertising for jobs in his department rather than hiring "the way people traditionally do" in politics. Still, he wasn't about to rely only on open hiring: "I mean, obviously, there's people that you're bringing in because they're getting good recommendations and things like that from people you know, but I try to expand it out." It was "a lot of work" to go through piles of résumés from applicants he didn't know, but Clayton was proud that he'd identified "good people that way" and they were "now doing very well for themselves." These individuals might not have gotten into campaign work otherwise, he added: "I'm sure there's a lot of people who are pretty talented who just never break in and then end up doing something else."

A small number of my interviewees—six out of seventy-two—got into politics without deploying already-forged connections. Three of the seven people of color I interviewed were in this group (and, just to be really clear, only three of the sixty-five White people I interviewed). One of them was Robby, the determined working-class kid who canvassed the halls of Congress until someone eventually gave him a job. Another saw a posting for an organizing institute run by the Obama campaign and made her way onto the Obama campaign from there. The third applied for an advertised job with Bernie Sanders's 2016 primary campaign.

The other three responded to advertisements for entry-level jobs in political consulting firms and, once hired, used those positions as springboards to more influential jobs in politics. Unlike campaigns, which almost always rely on a combination of networking and head-hunting for hiring for important positions, consulting firms often do post ads for their open positions and even hire people they don't already know. Instead of—or ideally, in addition to—connections and campaign experience, this particular path requires some credentials—at least a college degree.

Debby is one of those six exceptions. She was always interested in politics, though she was sure she didn't want to be a politician herself. A White Democrat who graduated college in 1998, she was planning to get a PhD in political science when a professor suggested she work for a year or two before applying to graduate school. She sent out résumés during the spring of her senior year, successfully finding a path straight from college to a job at a major polling and political consulting firm in DC. Instead of applying to PhD programs, she found she loved the work and rose up the ranks. Twenty years later, she started her own consulting firm.

Jason is another one of those six; a White Republican who now runs his own highly sought-after political data and polling firm, he had been working as a teacher when he decided he wanted to work in politics. To make the transition, he, like a few other people I interviewed, decided to go to Georgetown University's Graduate School of Political Management and get a master's degree. Unlike a number of the other people I spoke with, however, Jason told me what he learned and the credential he earned were genuinely useful to him; he was hired into a consulting firm on the basis of the schools on his résumé and the data analysis skills he had acquired.

For almost all politicos, though, first jobs came through networks. Family friends made introductions to people in politics, college buddies passed along phone numbers, or professors passed along information about internships. Although three people I interviewed were hired as junior associates by political consulting firms (following the more-credentialed, less-networked way into campaign politics), most consultants I spoke with also started out working in campaigns through connections.

Campaign ad guru Jeff, a White Republican, insisted that connections were not necessary for success in politics: "I think that obviously helps, but, no, that's a very defeatist way of looking at things." Instead, he advised "going into a situation and knocking on doors or showing that you have a talent or abilities that people need, and then they will—and, you know, things will work out. Worked out for me." Later, however, Jeff recounted how he got his first job in politics, as the luggage boy on a presidential primary campaign, through a friend from college who had gone on to become a political consultant. That experience brought Jeff into the orbit of other political staffers and consultants, helping him secure jobs on the 2004 Bush-Cheney presidential campaign and the 2008 McCain-Palin campaign. Today, Jeff is a highly respected and sought-after consultant who owns his own firm and creates cutting-edge ads. Though he's obviously talented, it's not clear that he would have found his way into this world without that old college buddy.

Likewise, Democrat Brian's first job in politics, in 2003, came through his mother—she served with the candidate on a local nonprofit's board of directors—yet he doesn't see himself as having entered politics through family connections.[51] The candidate "knew who I was because we are from the same community," he began, before conceding, "I mean, he actually knew my mother, so there was a little bit of a personal connection." It seems that however they tell their own stories, politicos also grasp that, as Alexis explained, "relationships and knowing people is huge" for gaining a foothold in the field. Alexis, the White daughter of a politician, worked in the Obama campaign, then in an administration job on climate and energy issues, and now works for a powerful environmental nonprofit. She got her first formal campaign job "through a friend of mine who was working on a campaign, and then the relationships that I built there are the ones that sort of got me onto Obama, and those relationships, obviously, are what got me into the administration."

When I asked Brian about the unrepresentativeness of campaign politics, he responded, "Well, look at the makeup of most candidates. They're mostly White male. Right? And because it's such a small community, there's only like a couple hundred, maybe a couple thousand people in the whole space if you include pollsters and you know television people and direct-mail people—it's such a small circle that there's a lot of inbreeding in that sense. They all know each other."

Even a preexisting connection frequently needs to be backed up with a good deal of persistence. Kerri worked on the buildup to a presidential primary campaign through a college-semester-in-DC program. As she ended her stint as a data entry intern at the candidate's DC leadership PAC, Kerri was approached by a staffer who asked whether she might want to come and work on the campaign. In retrospect, Kerri conceded, it might not have been a very serious job offer. But "I'm like nineteen, being asked on the steps of the Capitol if I want to work on the presidential campaign. And I about, you know, peed myself, and—of course! And I guess I had a lot of . . . maybe not misplaced faith in my boss at the internship, but a certain naïveté." After finishing that spring semester on her home campus, Kerri quit school in order to take the campaign job she believed she'd been offered. It was a rude surprise when she called the campaign office to firm up her plans—no one would take her calls.

So, Kerri said she drove to DC and sat in the office until they talked to her again. She remembered telling the staff in the campaign office, "Look, I quit school. I need to know, either I have a job or I don't. I need you to make a phone call and get me a job." Looking back, Kerri believes it was her persistence that paid off, not some off-handed hint of a job offer. What ultimately got her situated with a campaign job, in her assessment, is that the campaign "thought well, you know, I mean, 'She's kind of crazy, but that's kind of what we need—is somebody who's willing to do whatever it takes and stick with it.'"

When Kerri finally got her campaign job that summer, she was told to get to New Hampshire, ASAP. She went home and packed, then drove three days, all the way up the East Coast from Florida. She spent her first couple weeks as an official campaign staffer sleeping on the floor in the attic of her boss's house. No one sugarcoated the details: "They told me, 'You're going to work from 8:30 a.m. to 8:30 p.m. six days a week for a couple months, and then we'll work seven days a week and you'll be done whenever we end." No vacation, no days off. In return for all the effort she put into getting the job and then getting herself there, she remembers the first days with a laugh: she made photocopies and "got sandwiches for people for most of the first year . . . and laundry and dry-cleaning and took out the trash." Soon, "quitting time" had "quickly progressed to nine o'clock, to ten o'clock to eleven, to midnight and got longer, which they don't tell you at the very beginning, probably with good reason. I don't tell people that either."

This sounds like an extreme way to break into a career, but Kerri's story is not unusual. Entry-level campaign jobs are almost always entirely unglamorous and unpaid or poorly paid and require incredible hours and dedication. No one disputes this—even Kerri now asks junior people to get her lunch. But she hastens to say, "I'm not asking them to go get a sandwich because I'm too lazy to go get a sandwich. It's because, no offense, but for whatever reason, I'm a more important cog in what's going on right now than you are, and one day you will be more important than the kid you asked to go get you your sandwich, who hopefully will one day be more important than the person they asked to do that." You've just got to start at the bottom, because someone needs to be doing those jobs.

Alexis explains: "From a field perspective, they're pretty clear: everyone starts as an organizer. You move up to a regional field director or field director and then from there you can transition into something that's more of a leadership role." To her, starting at the very bottom and moving up is reasonable: "I think you really do need to put your time in and learn what it's like." It's about gaining the necessary institutional knowledge without forcing anyone on the campaign staff to step away from their jobs and explain yours. You do the work, you move up, and you do it over and over again.

Mick, a White Republican who trained other conservatives in political work, described his consternation upon being assigned as an intern when he was hired by a member of Congress in DC, despite having gone to college and graduate school at "two prestigious universities" and his past work on a presidential campaign. "A lot of people come out to DC and they think their [previous] success is going to translate into success in this city," he told me, but for him it turned out that there is "a ladder you just gotta work your way up on," and to do that "it's hard work, dedication, willingness to do anything and who you know."

All this starting-at-the-bottom seems reasonable to politicos, but it has consequences. Privilege limits the potential pool of politicos, not only through connections, or a lack of them, to people already in power, but also by determining who has the sorts of resources and networks that can sustain them through the lean years of working their way up in campaign politics. Kerri, for instance, had the freedom to move for work on a moment's notice, a car to drive up the East Coast, and the capacity to take a job in a primary campaign that could end at any time, without any guarantee or expectation of another job to follow. Kerri's candidate dropped out in January, just after the Iowa caucuses. After six months, her first campaign job was over, and Kerri was unsure what to do next. Luckily, her aunt helped her land on her feet.

For our book *The Class Ceiling: Why It Pays to Be Privileged*, Sam Friedman and I interviewed people in high-powered, highly sought-after jobs. Some had working-class origins and others came from privileged backgrounds.[52] The interviews revealed a wide variety of ways that these kinds of careers are harder for poor and working-class-origin people to navigate successfully. Many stories paralleled what I learned about work in campaigns. For example, a working-class actor described his career, in comparison with that of his privileged peers, as trying to "skydive without a parachute." Because an acting career, like campaign work, involves landing a series of jobs with different organizations, of varying and sometimes uncertain durations, people from families with money could rely on the "Bank of Mum and Dad" to keep them afloat between gigs, which can be few and far between, but just one might provide the crucial big break. Many of the working-class people we interviewed had moved out of the most creative but also the most unstable roles in their industries in favor of less exciting but steadier positions. Thus, aspiring actors who want to be in television entertainment may opt to take an HR job at a television production company—it's a steady salary and a chance to stay in the TV field.

Elections run on set schedules, so lulls in campaign workers' work schedules are somewhat more predictable, and their fallow periods tend to be shorter than those of actors. But many of the other dynamics are very similar. Introductory positions in US politics are frequently unpaid or carry only a token salary. Often they require moving. The hours rival the grueling schedules of medical interns, but without any guarantee of work after the campaign ends. Without family or savings to cushion your landing should a campaign job end abruptly, politically passionate people may reason that it just doesn't make sense to accept low-paid, eighty-hours-a-week work of an uncertain duration just to be part of a campaign. One reason why there are so few people in politics from poor and working-class families may be that they lack the resources to weather the uncertainty of campaign work and leave the field.[53]

One example of someone who almost was excluded from politics is Maya Rupert, Julián Castro's campaign manager in his 2020 presidential bid. She told the *Wall Street Journal* that when she wanted to get into politics, she was deterred by how many entry-level positions were unpaid internships. She told an interviewer, "I was not in a position to be working for free."[54] Instead of going right into electoral politics, she found a job at an advocacy organization after law school, and then got work in the Department of Housing and Urban Development. That resulted in a connection to Julián Castro, which led into her work on his campaign. Still, she noted that her relative lack of experience in electoral politics might be seen as a problem by many of her peers, who generally believe only experience in campaigns can lead to good campaign decisions.

There's no way to know exactly how many people are kept out of political work, as Maya Rupert almost was. The low numbers of people of color and people from poor and working-class families suggest that the number may be considerable. Diana, the Latina Democratic organizer, summed up the barriers people like her face: "A lot of folks got their foot in the door being interns in some way," which allows them to "prove themselves" and get "known and get the check mark that they're okay. And so then they get recommended for campaign jobs." But, she asked, "who are those people, people who can afford to work for free and live for free or live, you know, without income for a few months? And so that's already like a certain segment of the population."

Susan, the White Democratic consultant, put it clearly: "Being involved in this type of work is almost like a luxury." The way the campaign industry is organized works to exclude people from poor and working-class families, people of color, people without college degrees (even though, as Susan said, "the fact that I happened to major in political science does jack shit for me in this business"), and anyone else who is not able, for whatever reason, to take a temporary job with little or no pay, often no benefits, and little job security.

Even though almost all of the people who currently work in politics extol it as a meritocracy, when you look more closely at how people get into this kind of work it becomes clear that it is anything but. There are certainly some ways that campaigns reward those who are able to work hard, but the systems and the culture filter out most people before they get a chance to show how hard they can work. All along the path to becoming a politico, from developing a passion for politics to getting a first job and being able to keep it, a person encounters numerous barriers to entry and advancement in the campaign profession. They combine to keep many people out of campaign work—or, put another way, to let only specific kinds of people in.

All of these challenges, combined with the racial and class segregation that mean most White middle- or upper-middle-class people grew up around people in similar social positions, mean that even before they get involved with political work, campaign professionals often have little direct experience with the lives and concerns of the majority of Americans. Campaign workers, especially consultants and those at the highest levels of campaign hierarchies, have more in common with members of Congress and workers in other elite professions than with citizens in general, voters specifically, or even the voters of their own parties. They are producing politics for people from whom they are not only geographically but also socially quite distant.

CHAPTER 3

THE HIDDEN WORLD OF CAMPAIGNS

Working on an election campaign is all-consuming, intense, time-hungry work. In this way, it's aptly named: like a military campaign, a political campaign requires pulling together a group of professionals and new recruits who will give their all to a single goal and who are willing to upend their lives in pursuit of a win. The camaraderie and pace, however temporary, are intoxicating, and many campaign workers, once the votes are tallied and the balloons are dropped and the offices are packed up, will find another campaign to join and do it all over again. It's a work world of committed insiders, and it can make you never want to leave.

Tom put it this way: "When you do a presidential, you feel like you are in the middle of the most important thing going on in the world." Tom grew up in New York, the son of a White conservative Republican banker father and his White apolitical homemaker wife. Until the end of high school, in 1969 or '70, Tom doesn't remember caring much about politics. A "knock-down, drag-out" study hall argument with the anti-war captain of his school's debate team changed that. Tom's opponent was "totally against" US involvement in Vietnam, but Tom disagreed: "I thought any war is terrible, but I thought that a war in which we were standing with (a) the democratic side and (b) an ally was a justifiable war." According to his friends, Tom "kicked ass" in the argument. As the debate captain walked away, he commented, "Well, I have to do a debate on this tomorrow, so thanks for helping warm me up." That moment of condescension was galvanizing, and Tom resolved to care a lot more about politics.

In college Tom joined a campus conservative group, then got a job in the organization's national office upon graduation. In 1976, at age twenty-four, he worked on his first presidential campaign, and he went on to build a whole career in Republican and conservative politics.

Now Tom is a partner in one consulting firm and president of his own. He intersperses his work with his corporate clients with work on congressional and Senate campaigns. And for the last eleven or so presidential election cycles, every four years he works in some capacity for a conservative Republican candidate's campaign. Tom's specialty is helping candidates connect with their party's base—White, conservative, religious constituencies—and making sure that campaign strategy teams tailor their outreach efforts to match these communities' language and approach to political and social issues. He prides himself on knowing a fair amount about the communities he's charged with managing, as well as his willingness to ask and learn from those who know better than he does. This is important because while Tom specializes in Evangelical Christians, he is not an Evangelical himself.

Tom really enjoys campaign work. He keeps a picture on the wall in his office purely because it hung in the office of his most recent campaign. It's signed by the candidate, but Tom says the image "has no significance other than the fact that it was on the wall. I love having it there because it reminds me of how much I enjoyed the experience—despite the fact that we lost." For Tom, "there is a pace and a feel to a presidential campaign that is like nothing else. It is like being in the World Series. And I love it. I really do."

Political campaigns, like battles, also foster intimacy among the combatants. Staffers travel together, miss sleep together, and invest deeply in the work they do together. Their commitment is rooted in their partisan and ideological alignments as well as their competitiveness, tenacity, and team spirit. The sociologist Matthew Mahler has written about what he calls the "sensuality" of campaigns, which threaded through my interviewees' accounts of all-encompassing closeness and intensity.[1] Jerry, a White Democratic communications consultant, made the military comparison explicit, telling me, "You work very closely with someone, right? And it's like going to war: like you're in the bunker, you're in the foxhole together, and you have that bond because you've gone through this horrific experience with a person."

For many politicos, the all-encompassing nature of campaigns is part of their appeal. For everyone from the lowest-tier field organizer to the top-level campaign manager, the work is both intense and intensive, nearly round-the-clock as election dates near. This intensity is a defining feature of political work, starting with the love of politics for itself which brings people to the work, and continuing into the long, grinding hours and the requirement to prioritize the campaign over all other endeavors. It also sums up the emotional bonds forged in the campaign crucible.

The people who work in politics by and large love what they do. They are convinced that their side, their party, whichever it is, is on the side of what is good and right. They are willing, even happy, to sacrifice their relationships with family and friends, their free time, their health, in order to give everything they can to the campaign. The most successful campaign professionals command incomes that put them comfortably within the top 1 percent of American earners, but very few of them got into or stayed within the politics business for the money.[2] They genuinely believe in what they are doing, and they equally embrace the thrill of being part of a competitive team giving a world-class performance in a high-stakes race.

Larry is a White Democrat, roughly the same age as Tom, and his first campaign, like Tom's, was shortly after he graduated from college. He knew quickly this was the career he wanted. He "felt that this was something I was really good at." But it wasn't just his capacity to do well in this work that motivated him; it was the intensity of the work, the camaraderie. On that first campaign he spent five months with his Senate candidate, and they "traveled together for 153 days with 3 days off . . . 93,000 miles without leaving the state." To him, it was wonderful: "That's an experience like going through a war with somebody." Win or lose, politicos have strong feelings about the campaigns they've worked on, even decades later. Larry still recalls hearing that first election called in their favor, describing it as "one of the greatest nights of my life."

Terry McAuliffe, a former chair of the Democratic National Committee, governor of Virginia, and advisor to and fundraiser for the Clintons, describes his life in politics in his book *What a Party!* In one passage, he recalls heading home from the hospital with his wife and their newborn baby. He wanted to pick up a check from a campaign contributor, but knowing his wife would object, he didn't ask her but directed their driver to stop by the person's house. He collected the check while his tearful wife waited in the car. Don't worry though, he assures the reader; by the time they arrived home, his wife was "all smiles." As McAuliffe affirms, "No one ever said life with me was easy!"[3]

David Plouffe, a political strategist who with his partner David Axelrod ran Barack Obama's 2008 campaign, tells a similar story of prioritizing politics above all else.[4] In the midst of the 2008 primaries, he received a tearful call from his wife. Their beloved elderly dog was going to be put down, and his family was devastated. He wished he could be there for them, but the campaign was simply too important; he said goodbye to his dog over the phone.

Anecdotes like these and the stories I heard in interviews make us wonder what kind of inconsiderate, self-centered people would recount this callous behavior with apparent pride. But prioritizing political commitments over everything else is absolutely a badge of honor for campaign professionals—it signals their insider status and hints that they are uniquely valuable, indispensable to candidates who want to win. It affirms the strength of their work identity. That's why Plouffe and McAuliffe and many other politicos put such anecdotes in their memoirs for wide audiences to read.

Sam is a White Democrat in his forties. He is unusual in that he has tried to avoid letting his life be consumed by his work. In fact, it's why he worked in an organization that provides data and analysis for Democrats running for Congress, rather than accepting any of the offers he'd had to work on presidential campaigns. He considers himself lucky that this position is among the few political jobs that allows for some semblance of work-life balance, telling me he's home every evening because he refuses to work during dinner and his kids' bedtime. Of course, he's flexible: "If you want to do a call at ten at night, whatever, I'll do it." He shared a well-known anecdote about Obama's 2008 national field director, Jon Carson, whose first child arrived just three months before Election Day. Sam couldn't decide which was worse: having to miss out on your child's first few months, or not being fully available to a presidential campaign. "I felt so terribly for him," Sam said, "because it's this amazing time and you're exhausted anyhow, and to not be able to just completely experience that—either one of them. To not be able to either completely immerse yourself in the presidential campaign and that experience, or having your first-born child, it's just terrible." Ethan, another White Democrat, graduated from high school in 1981 and works in polling. He explained that "there's a culture of campaigns, because it's so driven by fundraising, so candidate time is all structured around fundraising." Calling major donors to ask for money needs to happen during business hours, so campaigns have to "cram all meetings in at night or on weekends. And so you inevitably end up doing these conference calls on Friday night, on Saturday morning."

Most campaign workers echo Anna, a White Republican who runs a conservative firm that places ads online. She explained of her commitment to the job, "You have to be willing to do whatever it takes. If it takes until three in the morning to get it done, then you've got to be willing to do that. And if you miss somebody's wedding because there's something going on, then that's what happens. You have to basically be willing to devote your life to this."

And in fact, for most politicos, missing weddings, angering spouses, or absentee parenting are acceptable trade-offs. Debby, the Democratic polling consultant, told me, "There's not a lot of, let's see, demarcation between business and personal life." People who "are interested in the nine to five or whatever today's equivalent is, you know, do not succeed in this field. [You have to] really live, work, and play in the space." It may not be "your job to follow that individual race, but it's part of who you are and what you care about and what you talk about at cocktail parties and so on," so that "you still know what's going on around the country. You know what's competitive, you know what's not, and you're able to identify, you know, down-ballot candidates and sound smart in conversations about them." If you are a true politico, says Debby, you have politics "pulsing through your blood." Or as Candice, a Republican who worked in direct-mail fundraising, put it: "You have to sleep and breathe it. During the election, I'm here from seven in the morning 'til midnight, seven days a week. Everything I do is to get these guys elected. So this isn't a part-time thing. You have to love it."

To be seen as a "good" politico you have to love politics so much that you'll give up most of the rest of your life for it. Those who cannot or will not make that kind of sacrifice are not likely to succeed in a career in political work—making those who are willing to do so and remain in the campaign world even more distinct from most people.

War and sports metaphors proliferate among people in the politics industry, not only because they are great for explaining the intensity of the campaign experience but also because campaign professionals see their work as focused on a struggle between themselves and their opposition. If campaigners see elections as wars, you might expect them to see potential voters as foot soldiers or recruits. But I think the better metaphor positions voters as the "terrain" on which the war is fought—the prize campaign professionals hope to win through their efforts.

Tom's mentor, a major figure in conservative politics, sums up this worldview: In a campaign, he says, "The only question you ever have to answer is: How do you get to fifty percent plus one?" Getting the votes needed to win a contest for political power ultimately requires voters, of course, but the world of campaign professionals is not centered on voters themselves.

The campaigns fighting for political victories are workplaces for campaign staff, clients for political consultants, and production sites churning out enormous quantities of political messaging. Thousands of people earn their living working on national-level campaigns. What campaigns do is governed as much by the culture and passions of those professional politicos as by the science, such as it is, of vote gathering. So to make sense of American politics, we need to understand the way campaign battles work.

In the US, national campaigns for federal offices start early in odd-numbered years, nearly two years (sometimes more) before the general election will be held. This is when candidates are deciding whether to run, forming exploratory committees, and hiring consultants and party-affiliated staff. Jimmy, a campaign manager and consultant with twenty years of experience in Republican politics, is a White man who has been working in politics since shortly after his college graduation. His talents have been invaluable to senatorial, gubernatorial, and even presidential primary campaigns. Excitedly, he told me, "Running a presidential campaign is really the ultimate startup. You start on day one by ordering office supplies, and within twelve to eighteen months, in a primary, [the campaign becomes a] $100 million a year corporation with 150 employees nationwide. So that is a quicker scalability than even an Uber or a Facebook or any of the tech startups that everyone now thinks of as examples of rapid growth."

Today's national-level campaigns are conducted primarily by relatively short-lived organizations, many of which last only as long as the duration of the campaign.[5] These include campaign-specific entities such as Biden for President, and other political organizations, such as allied PACs (political action committees) and super PACs formed to support a particular candidate or issue. Other political institutions, such as party organizations like the Democratic National Committee or the National Republican Congressional Committee, are more permanent, though they also organize short-term campaign efforts. Campaign finance laws govern the extent to which these different organizations can coordinate with one another, and how.

All these types of organizations, across both parties, share common elements and approaches. There is a great deal of consistency in how campaigns are conducted. If they're lucky, campaign startups will last less than two years—just through the November election and a short wrap-up period. If they're less lucky or less skilled, the campaign organization may dissolve even faster as the candidate drops out before primaries or caucuses or loses their party's nomination.

Either way, when the campaign ends, the organization scatters. Some young staffers will have had their taste of politics and decided it's not for them—they'll head back to law school or into other kinds of work. When a candidate loses or drops out, consultants continue to work for their firms and for other candidates, and campaign staff hustle to find out what's next. They take to Twitter to hunt down job opportunities, go on unemployment for a bit, work for a party organization or an affiliated think tank or PAC, go back to nonprofits, or seek out another candidate who'll be staffing up their own campaign shortly. When a candidate wins, some staff and consultants will get offers for jobs in the now-elected official's office or administration, while the rest are on the hunt for a new position.

A few months after one election ends—sometimes even sooner—the cycle repeats. The players shuffle, coalescing into new campaigns, new all-encompassing political contests. But political professionals are journeymen: they know their niche within a campaign, and even when they move into unfamiliar territory, their understanding of their own roles and those of others allows politics to keep churning. What roles do they play?[6]

Political consultants are the campaign warriors whose names we are most likely to know, and the ones who tend to get the most attention from both academic researchers and the press. People like Karl Rove and David Axelrod have national name recognition; they own their own firms and earn six- and seven-digit figures working on major campaigns. They are regularly asked to comment on political news and talk shows. They're the ones most people think of, if they think about campaign professionals at all.

But, similar to the entertainment industry, the really successful people you've heard of are just the tip of the iceberg. The people who don't get press, or haven't yet, include less exorbitantly successful consultants, along with campaign staff without their own firms who are hired directly by the campaign organization. Many consultants work on more than one race in each cycle, unless they have a central role in a presidential campaign, whereas campaign staff work full-time on a single campaign. But other than the number of races they're working on at once and whether they're paid a salary or as contractors, there aren't a lot of important differences between campaign staff and most consultants.

Campaign staff don't command the lucrative salaries of top consultants, but they are no less crucial to elections. Staff members write speeches, run door-to-door canvassing operations, recruit and manage volunteers for phone banks, conduct opposition research, craft fundraising emails, seek endorsements, set up campaign events, and do so much more to ensure their candidates come out on top. Some roles, such as field organizers, are nearly always held by staff, and others, such as ad creation and placement, by consultants, but there is more overlap than difference. Both types of workers can be involved in making key decisions, inside or outside a campaign's inner circle.

Most prominent political consultants started out as campaign staff, and many current campaign staff report it's their goal to one day "hang out a shingle" of their own as a consultant. But this is not a universal goal. Many politicos spend good portions of their careers moving from one campaign to another, into and out of party jobs and as elected officials' staff, without ever establishing their own consultancies. I asked Sarah, a Democratic consultant and field organizer, whether there are differences between "people that end up in consulting versus being party staffers or working directly for candidates." She told me, "That debate makes no sense." There might be a difference between *policy* people and the rest, but "the consultants, the party staffers, the campaign operatives are pretty much the same."

If we pay attention only to big-name consultants, we miss a key part of the story of how campaigning, and thus American politics, works.[7] Political operatives, whether they are consultants or staff, are part of what political scientists call the "extended party network" of party organizations like the Democratic National Committee or the Republican National Committee, the political action committees and partisan and related organizations aligned with one party or another, political consulting firms, and the staff who move among them.[8]

The bigger differences among politicos may be in the size and importance of races they get to work on. Smaller local races generally have a lot fewer resources, hence they often have less experienced and in-demand staff and consultants. Jimmy, a Republican, put it this way: "On one end of the spectrum you've got state house races and things like that, legislative races. That's more like dirt-track racing. And then you've got on the other end the presidential race, which is more like NASCAR. And where you're talking about one-hundredth of a mile per hour is the difference between winning and being blown out of the back of the pack. Whereas in dirt-track, you can flip over a car in the middle of the race, get it right back up and still win the race." Ken, a Democrat, also contrasted the bigger versus smaller races. In presidential campaigns, everyone is at the top of their game, but "perhaps further down-ballot, perhaps with people who aren't maybe as actively involved all the time" in a "congressional race or a state house race, maybe you fall into more of a rhythm" and do less creative work. Many politicos drew similar distinctions between smaller races where they might not need to bring their "A-game" and larger, more competitive races where they absolutely did. Most of this book is focused on politicos' work in national races, but much of what I discuss applies to races at all levels.

On nearly every race, there are clearly differentiated roles and responsibilities; politicos may move between them, but generally they specialize, especially as they move upward in their careers. To get a sense of what campaign staff and consultants actually do, let me take you through the key parts of every political campaign.

CAMPAIGN DEPARTMENTS

The foot soldiers of political campaigns are the field staff, the lowest rung of the campaign hierarchy. Their work is often referred to simply as "field." Field staff actually talk to potential voters, on the phone, through canvassing, and increasingly via text messaging. They also organize volunteers and sometimes paid canvassers or phone-bankers to do the same tasks; these temporary and part-time workers, while working for the campaign, are not generally considered part of the campaign. A typical day in an often-dingy field office starts with field staff receiving or pulling lists of the day's voter contacts, then apportioning the lists to the people who will be doing the door-knocking or making the phone calls, and readying the office to receive the day's in-person volunteers.

The volunteers and canvassers arrive, hopefully in numbers sufficient to accomplish the day's contacts. Field staff train volunteers, often making calls and canvassing alongside them. They also set up volunteers with the scripts the campaign has written and the forms to record voter responses, either on paper, or using apps such as MiniVAN, which accesses the Voter Activation Network, to assign to tech-savvy volunteers the names of voters they will call, text, or visit. Then field staff turn to recruiting, scheduling, and confirming the next round of volunteers, then ensure that all the data from the day's work is carefully fed back into the databases, by app or by hand.

Early in the campaign, a field operation's main goal is to identify whether and to what extent potential voters support the candidate, and update voter files to allow for more efficient resource distribution in later months. Campaigns are reluctant to use their scarce resources on calling or knocking on the doors of people who are staunch opponents, rarely vote, or seem to be otherwise poor investments, not to mention people who are no longer at their listed address or phone number at all. So the data gathered in early contacts and recorded by field staff can be thought of as reconnaissance, aimed at improving the accuracy of the campaign's voter data. In addition to information-gathering, field workers are given "persuasion" scripts, with talking points to use to try to bring undecided voters on board.

Nearer Election Day, the campaign begins shifting into GOTV—get out the vote—mode. Field operations ramp up as the campaign focuses on contacting known supporters who may need a nudge to actually go and vote. In places with early voting, this period involves accessing lists of people who have already voted, then calling or knocking on the doors of anyone who hasn't.

Nothing about fieldwork is glamorous or high status. The field staff are usually among the most junior in any campaign in terms of age, placement within the hierarchy, and political experience. Frequently, they work in places they don't even know. Kerri drove from Florida to New Hampshire to do her job, and the Clinton campaign office I visited in West Philly in 2016 was staffed entirely with people from out of state.

Roger, the influential Democratic insider we met in the introduction, spoke about "field" the way many regarded "essential work" throughout the Covid-19 pandemic: the work is necessary, and I'm so glad I don't have to do it. Or, in Roger's words, this work is "important and I believe in it," yet "it's easier to do" than other campaign work, "more mechanical and less theatrical," and "you won't learn anything other than—yeah, you'll learn a little bit on how voters think." Fieldwork isn't, to his mind, "a bad thing to do," but it's no sure path to a political future. Candidates aren't particularly interested in giving postelection staff jobs to their best canvassers. "I mean," Roger said, if the candidate "sent ten people to North Dakota for six months," well, "I wouldn't want to be one of them." Jason actually did fieldwork on one campaign in South Dakota, but even though he was he "pretty much the lowest-level paid staffer you could be," he "didn't do a lot of door-to-door. Fortunately, we can give that to other people." David Plouffe recounts being called field scum when he first worked on a political campaign.[9]

Field, when it's aimed at turnout, as opposed to persuasion, is also one of the most heavily researched and clearly effective aspects of campaign work. Political scientists Donald Green and Alan Gerber have published countless articles and a book (now in its third edition) testing the effectiveness of different methods of voter outreach. They consistently find that calls and, especially, in-person visits increase actual voting turnout.[10] Campaigns, knowing they can't contact every potential voter, analyze voter databases to prioritize who gets contacted, how often, and how; field operations represent the campaign as they carry out those contacts and refine voter databases.

Volunteers and staffers work with scripts tailored for reaching out to different universes of voters from the data file. Matt, a Republican communications specialist who worked on the campaigns of both President Bushes and many others, explains that as technology changes, the particulars of targeting and matching voters to scripts changes. As recently as 2012, campaigns still used mostly printed lists for field operations, which limited the diversity of scripts field staff could use.[11] By 2016, though, the landscape had "completely changed." Matt described volunteers "knocking on a door with an iPad and there's a custom script for everybody on the block. . . . Say you're going to twenty houses in a block, there could be fifteen unique scripts, based on somebody is a Second Amendment person or if they're pro-choice." As campaigns gather data, "You know who the hardcore Republicans are, and their issues, and you have their scripts, you have who votes that you believe are undecided, and you know, based on the issue matrix, based on their type, what you should be saying." So by the time field staff knock on the door, "You have somebody who looks a lot like [the voter], saying exactly what that person at the door probably wants to hear."

That's the theory, at least. But when political communication scholar Rasmus Kleis Nielsen spent a fall volunteering for two campaigns, he saw a somewhat different reality. Although this was in 2010, before the advent of the technology advances Matt extols, the relationship between canvassers and their scripts is unlikely to have changed much. In Nielsen's research neither volunteers nor paid canvassers stuck to the scripts they were given for canvassing. Canvassing is hard, tiring, and often unrewarding even for the deeply motivated. Walking and driving unfamiliar neighborhoods to find the addresses on your list is tedious, and few people will actually be home, answer the door, and be willing to talk. Those who do engage with a canvasser on their doorstep may just want to tell you how much they hate politics or your political party or your candidate specifically. Every interaction is a chance for the field worker to experience rejection and rudeness.[12] It's always nice when a few enthusiastic supporters come to the door, though it's hard for canvassers to see what effect these visits have in terms of reaching campaign goals.

So those doing voter contact often drop the script—and that may not be a bad thing. Lisa García Bedolla and Melissa Michelson conducted experiments in getting out the vote in California elections in the 2000s and found that who was talking to whom mattered a lot more than the content of their message.[13] Despite all the effort that goes into customizing scripts, it appears that the contact is the key. But campaign volunteers are not necessarily that similar to the people they're most often trying to mobilize. Volunteers for campaigns earn a good deal more on average in their regular daytime jobs than the population of eligible voters.[14] Compared with the electorate as a whole, undecided voters, or registered Democrats, Obama campaign volunteers had far higher incomes, were more likely to be White, and were far more college-educated than the voter they canvassed. In other words, they were more similar to professional politicos than to potential voters. They also had much more liberal political views than regular voters overall and even Democrats in general, but when asked, they guessed—incorrectly—that regular voters more or less shared their priorities.[15]

Despite all the challenges and pitfalls and messiness of organizing regular people to go and talk to each other, field operations work. It may take hours of work for a canvasser to find a single person who intends to vote but needs a nudge to turn in their ballot, or a potential voter in need of information on how and where to vote. But thousands of canvassers working every reasonable hour adds up.[16] If canvassers' work in an area adds a few extra thousand votes, it absolutely makes a difference.

Running a field operation is primarily a numbers game, a volunteer management task measured by numbers of doors knocked and calls completed. But field operations usually only want their volunteers to talk to the specific potential voters on their lists—not just anyone who answers the door or phone. That risks the outside possibility that campaign contact with someone whose positions aren't known ends up activating a voter for the opposition.

Recently some campaigns and firms have begun shifting their approaches to voter contact. In experiments with "relational" organizing, people are asked to get others within their personal networks to vote; in "deep canvassing," volunteers with in-depth training are encouraged to engage in longer, less-scripted and more reciprocal conversations with potential voters about issues of common concern.[17] But by and large, fieldwork—at least when run by mainstream campaigns, rather than the partisan groups more committed to organizing—is wide rather than deep; field staffers are dropped into communities that are strategically important for the campaign, spend weeks or months managing voter contacts, and then go back to wherever they came from or on to their next campaign when they're done. In two or four years a new field office will be set up in that neighborhood, and the process will start all over. The data gleaned along the way will be saved, but the chance that the same two people talk to each other again is vanishingly low. Thus, fieldwork isn't about building institutional knowledge or relationships for the future; it's about simply trying to tip the balance for the contest at hand.

Ground-game workers are distant from the actual candidate, especially in the larger races. In a presidential campaign, in addition to the on-the-ground staff, there will be local, regional, state, and national field directors setting targets and managing strategy and encouraging their subordinates to meet their numbers goals—unglamorous and unheralded work. Some people really love doing field, making connections with strangers at their doors, but however they feel about the work, it is usually happening far from the campaign's centers of power.[18]

Unless a campaign decides to publicize its ground strategy, or things go wrong and problems are leaked to the press, that work is also largely unnoticed by those outside the campaign. Exceptionally impressive ground games, like Obama's, make news, but in most races, whether field staff knock on ten doors or a hundred, whether their volunteers stay on script or go rogue, and whether they actually increase the chance that some number of people will vote for the candidate—none of this is visible except to those doing the work and tracking the results.

For fledgling campaign professionals who want to move up the ranks of the campaign hierarchy, Roger's advice was not only to avoid fieldwork but to seek out positions in "more theatrical" campaign roles such as "scheduling and advance."

Advance teams travel where the candidate does, so in a presidential election, they are on the road almost constantly. Any time you see media footage of a candidate shaking hands with voters in a diner or addressing a huge campaign crowd, you're witnessing the advance team's work. They figure out where the candidate will walk in, which people should be visible on camera, and a thousand other details that serve to create the best possible representation of the candidate and their supporters. Josh King, in his book about his time working as an advance man, says that working advance means being "entrusted with protecting the image of a politician."[19]

Infamous campaign gaffes often can be traced back to advance staff. According to King, the widely ridiculed image of Michael Dukakis wearing a helmet with his name on it and looking out of place in a tank has "haunted" him, "as it has most advance men or women." In what King calls the "Age of Optics" in campaigns, there is always the possibility that an unfortunate moment on the campaign trail will be turned into memes or attack ads by the opposition, and advance teams try to minimize the chances that that will happen. We still don't know the full story of

Rudy Giuliani's press conference for the Trump campaign during the prolonged counting of the votes in November of 2020, but we can surmise that harried, overtired campaign staffers made the mistake—or very strange deliberate choice—that led to a comical scene at Four Seasons Total Landscaping in Northeast Philadelphia that day.[20]

Advance teams are in charge of making the events happen, but campaign managers and their closest advisors decide when and where events should be, largely on the basis of polling results.

Polls conducted by campaigns aim to uncover voters' perceptions of the candidates and the race, the issues voters care about, and the links between the two. Which issues and which approaches might be most effective at persuading voters to check the box for their candidate? That's the sort of question pollsters try to answer. They will typically conduct multiple polls over the course of the campaign, and their position of having more or less direct access to voters' perceptions of the candidate and the issues gives them a key role in most campaigns, often in the inner circle near the top of the campaign hierarchy. Lindsey, a senior White Republican pollster, says of his job, "What I do is look at data to help strategy and message and strategic decision-making. And people who do well in this business tend to be people like you and me. There's a reason why there are more PhDs in the polling niche than in any other field" in campaigns. Aaron, a Democrat who worked in communications and new media, explained the role of polls: "So much of these arguments, these messages that we've been talking about, this branding, comes from polling at the beginning. And I just think that it's really interesting that people probably don't really get that."

Pollsters almost always work as consultants and have their own firms, and they often have a master's degree or a PhD in political science or a related field. In addition to designing the questions that will elicit the information campaigns need, polling firms build representative samples within the pool of potential voters they want to understand, conduct the polling, and analyze the results.

Polling has gotten a lot of attention since 2016, when sites that collected poll results predicted a Hillary Clinton win that did not ultimately materialize. In early 2017, I spoke with a top advisor from Clinton's 2016 campaign. He was still clearly shaken by Trump's victory, telling me, "I thought we were going to win, and I'm a 'glass half empty' guy—and I never say those words. And I was absolutely convinced we were going to win, by every indicator, every piece of data. Not just our own data—everybody else's data." He placed a lot of the blame for Clinton's loss on that polling data. "I don't think we made bad decisions, based on the data that we were looking at," because "if your data says you are up nine in Wisconsin and you're up two in Florida," of course "the logical answer is we're going to [campaign in] Florida. And that's a correct campaign decision to make. [But] if you're data's off," if you're wrong about "who's actually going to turn out, or not turn out, and all of a sudden Wisconsin's a two-point race or a three-point race, it's a very different calculation that we make."

In theory, polls and surveys work because they collect information from a randomized sample of the population of interest; if the sample is truly random, you can get very good estimates of the true contours of public opinion. In practice, especially with the short turnaround needed in campaigns and the declining numbers of people willing to talk with pollsters at all, this is a challenge. A poll is only as good as the representativeness of the people responding to it, and Ken, along with substantial portions of the political polling and survey research worlds, is concerned. He told me there are a lot of "people who think [polling] is really, really broken. And I'm not quite sure how we're going to fix it."

Pollsters had some of the same issues in 2020, even after trying to correct for the errors of 2016.[21] It's worth noting that the national polls actually came very close to the final national popular vote tally in 2016. But individual states' results decide our national elections, and polling in key battleground states was off, largely because a big share of voters who told pollsters they were undecided ultimately voted for Trump.[22] Polls and surveys can still be important sources of information, but they are not the crystal ball that many wish they were or make them out to be.

Getting a representative sample in your poll and using weights to make up for variability in who responds certainly is tricky, but many pollsters pointed out that polling isn't rocket science. Sophia, who worked in Democratic polling, said, "To be a pollster, . . . it's not sophisticated. The analysis that all pollsters do is very simple. Just crosstabs. I mean, we do some regression analysis but that's like—it's not accessible for the campaign, so we don't really rely on it that much." In other words, while social scientists and the parts of the campaign world that specialize in data analytics may put together models involving multiple variables, pollsters for campaigns mostly just look at tables that show them, for example, the percentage of White Democrats who say health care is their top issue.

Reading the results of a poll may not be rocket science, but designing good polls is another endeavor. Response rates for phone and in-person surveys are way down, skewing the extent to which actual respondents are chosen sufficiently randomly from a larger pool to be representative and making it harder to infer knowledge about that larger population from the small group's answers. Moreover, even subtle or apparently meaningless differences in the way a question is asked, the order in which questions are asked, and the response options provided can yield radically different distributions of answers. For example, if you ask people whether they are Republicans, Democrats, or independent, around 35 percent of people will say they are independents. If you leave it at that, you might think most Americans aren't aligned with either party. But if you ask those "independent" voters which party they "lean" more toward, about 75 percent of them will pick one of the two major parties, leaving only about 7 to 10 percent of people who are genuine independents. The leaners turn out to have voting behavior and beliefs on issues nearly indistinguishable from those of people who align with a party when first asked.[23] The people who say they're independent aren't lying; that is indeed how they think of themselves. But if you assume that means they are really different from partisans, you'll misunderstand them.

This issue can be compounded by the distance between pollsters and the people whose opinions they are trying to understand. Any poll question will be understood differently by different people; whether people understand the question as pollsters intend is linked to race, class, and other aspects of social position. Take, for example, a very commonly used question on political polls and surveys: the seven-point ideology question that asks you to place yourself on a spectrum from extremely conservative to moderate to extremely liberal. Many Black people say they are conservative but nonetheless reliably vote for Democrats, which has puzzled political scientists. The political scientist Hakeem Jefferson has shown that Black people frequently have a different understanding of this question than the one that White survey researchers expect; when Black people say they are conservative, they are reporting on something other than their political views. Poor and working-class people of all races are also far more likely to simply say they "don't know" the answer to this and other questions about politics.[24]

Nearly every pollster will tell you that designing and interpreting a poll is, as Angela, a Democratic pollster, put it, "a little bit of art and a little bit of science." Derek, a Democratic campaign manager and strategist, told me, "Reading a poll is like reading a novel. There's the protagonist; that would be your candidate, [and] there are issues, which are part of the background and the scenery. There are certain characters that will play an important role in the storyline, and you have to look at a poll in those terms. What's the overall narrative, and who are the players, and what's influencing them?" Bad pollsters, according to Derek, even if they have the needed numerical literacy, "really don't read the numbers, or understand the numbers"; they interpret the poll results as "very cut and dried." But "it isn't quite that way." Angela pointed out that being a good pollster not only "requires being trained in a methodology" but also requires being a good listener. "Not everybody has it, but I think to be a really good pollster, you have to have respect for the voters and really be curious about what they're thinking and why they're thinking it." When mostly White and well-off pollsters are trying to interpret the stories told by people very different from themselves, there is a serious possibility of misunderstanding that is larger the further removed pollsters are from the people whose views they are trying to analyze.[25]

Ethan, a Democratic pollster, pointed out that, as with other campaign positions, it can be hard after the election to know whether the pollster did a good or a bad job. "I think it's really tough to put yourself in the perspective of a client. What do they want to know? Are you accurate? There's no good way for a consumer in this marketplace to measure that. What they can measure is reputation. And reputation is a combination of, well, who seems to have the most clients—so, who's the pollster for some—and essentially, who's recommended by people they trust? So that may be the high-profile governor or senator in their state. That's certainly going to be the person their other consultants recommend or have worked with, or some candidate they know." Performance matters for pollsters' future employability, but it's mediated by their professional connections.

The other kinds of data campaigns rely on to understand the electorate include information on past elections' results and voter databases.

Nearly every politico thinks of voters as positioned along two axes: their likelihood of voting and their likelihood of voting for the "right" party or candidate. Thus, as conservative Matt explained of this initial data, "Let's say that you basically know which hundred thousand people are going to vote. You basically know that forty percent of these people wouldn't vote for you if you were the Second Coming"—that is, they are unmovable supporters of the opposition. For Matt, these are ardent Democrats, and he can ignore them. He also knows "who the hardcore Republicans are" and knows that they don't need a lot of his candidate's attention either. If the reliable Republicans are another 40 percent of the electorate, by his reckoning, he's trying to figure out whether a given campaign can lock up at least 10,001 votes (50 percent + 1) from the 20,000 remaining, especially the much smaller portion who might switch their preferred party from one election to the next. This makes Matt's estimate of the persuadable universe about 20 percent, which is higher than most recent studies estimate.

Most states make their voter rolls public, so anyone can find information on registered voters, their addresses, and the number of times they've voted in local, state, and national elections. Most states also share voters' age and gender, and many states also collect and share party registration and racial identity. Campaigns have long used these data to decide which voters they will focus on in an election; the general wisdom is that you don't pay much attention to members of your party who always vote, or to staunch supporters of the other party, or to people who have never voted despite being registered for many election cycles. As Republican strategist Matt put it, "The key to this business is to know what votes you can't possibly win, and not spending a dime on them. And then identifying everybody who would vote for you and your party, even if Jack the Ripper ran. And you don't need to spend a lot of money on them. You just need to make sure they get out to vote."

Vendors of political lists have made a business of building and maintaining their own databases, which combine public voter roll data with other kinds of information. When field workers or phone bankers contact potential voters, the voters are targeted on the basis of these lists, and their responses—support or oppose a candidate, plan to vote or plan to stay home, etc.—ideally are added to the database.

Recently, voter-list vendors have also started adding information from consumer databases to allow for microtargeting of potential voters. This kind of data has received a lot of attention: campaigns and consultants and cautious observers all claim that political actors can target and manipulate voters using information derived from their social media use, their consumption habits, and very detailed demographic information. If a campaign knows, say, that Doris is a White stay-at-home mom who lives in a fairly wealthy suburb, is married to a banker, has two elementary-school-age kids, and buys a lot of soccer supplies, they might tag her as a soccer mom and figure she's persuadable to their side. Of course they don't go through millions of voters one by one and look at their individual characteristics. Instead, these data analysis firms build models based on the available data: if the campaign has called a number of people similar to Doris and they all said they were firm supporters of the opposing candidate, they might assign Doris a score as a low-likelihood voter for their party. Campaigns have increasing amounts of information about voters at their disposal, but at the end of the day they still have to make their best guesses about whom they can persuade, who is already on their side, and who will need a lot of reminders to actually show up at the polls. Data analysis firms provide scores, usually a set of numbers ranging from 1 to 100, indicating the estimated probability that Doris will vote, or will vote for the candidate. Campaigns use these scores to decide who goes on field canvassers' lists of people to contact.

Where the field campaign is sometimes referred to as the ground war and the workers and volunteers as foot soldiers, communications can be seen as the air war. It's not a stretch to say the guys (again, it's mostly men) in charge of campaign communications see themselves as something like fighter pilots. For many political professionals, communications, the province of media professionals, is where the war for voters is fought. It is certainly where the bulk of campaign finances go—to producing ads and buying airtime or online placement, and to the firms that do that. Spending on ads across all local, state, and federal campaigns in the 2020 election reached $8.5 billion; the presidential campaigns accounted for about $1.5 billion of that.[26]

Media professionals are the consultants who get really rich in campaign work. They're usually at the heart of a campaign, brought on early and part of the inner circle. Sarah, a Democratic field strategist, complained about "the media consultant being the big guy. Everyone's going to listen to him or her. So the media consultants are often hired first.

They're often the ones that dictate the entire message strategy." Pollsters come next, she said, and "while I really respect polling and I really—of course you want to have that information" and "I love all my pollster and media friends," but "I think they often are too listened to, rather than having this sort of collective of different input" from people with other expertise.

A communications department's campaign staff members handle speechwriting, function as spokespeople, and interact with the press, while their media consultants handle ad creation and placement. Both may work on developing and fine-tuning the slogans and overall messages of a campaign. In the 2016 campaign, slogans and talking points included "I'm with her" and "Clinton is reasonable and competent and responsible, unlike that maniac" and "Make America Great Again" and "Trump is authentically himself, says what he's thinking, and isn't cowed by those awful PC people who are always telling you what to do and looking down on you." Aaron told me these messages come in large part from reading the polls "at the very beginning" of the campaign, and "figuring out what is going to work for us, and conversely what's not going to work for the other side. And you're going to hit them for that negative message and you're going to push forward your positive one. But it's not just like . . . this sort of organic thing, it's not like, here's what I believe, a lot of the time, unfortunately."

Ken, the senior Democratic media professional, told me that his job is to figure out how to connect the campaign to voters' lives and priorities, saying, "I'd like to think that you need to be honest. I'm not sure that's true." Instead, "Those of us who are responsible for communicating" need to look for "the stories, what is the narrative, what is the emotional connection that will actually get someone's attention and [that person will] say, yes, this is relevant to me, and I want to pay attention, or I want to get involved, or I want to vote."

Communications professionals try to craft messages that will move the swing voters they believe are the "fulcrum demographic"—think soccer moms starting in 1996, or hockey moms in 2008—while not alienating too many existing supporters, and hopefully will also rally the faithful to come out and vote on Election Day. That is a hard needle to thread.

Ken explained that with the advent of "addressable advertising" it is possible to narrow-cast campaign messages to some potential voters.

There are about fifty-five million households with the kinds of smart TVs and similar technologies that allow advertisers to create profiles of viewers, therefore allowing advertisements to be targeted to particular sets of people.[27] In theory, "you now know, from your data analytics, what people that you are targeting look like." Then you get anonymized data on the characteristics of households, so you don't actually know the identities of the people you send ads to, but you know a lot about them—whatever consumer data is available, what they watch, ages and racial groups, and so on. That information is used to score voters on how likely they are to vote for the Democratic candidate, and then, in the example Ken gave, different households watching TV will receive different ads. He told me to imagine three households: "Daniel is a Trump voter, Ken is a Hillary voter, and Sue is an undecided or swing vote or target persuasion vote. In Daniel's house, *60 Minutes* is on. At 7:12, an ad comes up." Because (in this example) I'm not someone the campaign is trying to win over, I won't see an ad purchased by the Clinton campaign. But "next door, same break, Ken gets a turnout spot. And same break in the next house over, Sue gets a persuasion ad."

Again, this is the theory, an example of the kind of sophisticated analysis-based targeting that gets a lot of attention in the media. As with many issues in campaign communications, it is not actually clear from research that this kind of targeted communication is more effective than broad-based appeals. It may actually be counterproductive, as Eitan Hersh and Brian Schaffner showed in a 2013 article.[28] Despite the hype, this kind of targeted ad was still only a small percentage of total advertising spending in 2020.[29]

There are big questions about how much political ads affect either whether people turn out to vote or how they vote when they do. It is more clear that campaigns' broad themes and party nominating conventions can matter for the election's outcome. But regardless of how much they affect outcomes, campaign communications are one of the main ways regular people hear about politics. In competitive elections, up to 90 percent of people surveyed can recall seeing some form of campaign communication.[30]

And these ads do more than promote one candidate over another. In looking for emotional connections, they frequently deploy dog whistles or outright racism to get their points across. This was the essence of the Republicans' "Southern strategy." In the wake of the successes of the civil rights movement and the increasing political participation of Black people, Republicans solidified their hold on southern states' electoral college votes by appealing to racist White people who had formerly been staunch Democrats. Lee Atwater, a political consultant who worked for both Ronald Reagan and George H. W. Bush, notoriously described how Republicans moved from using the language of overt racism to expressing opposition to forced busing and to calling for more indirect policies, such as cutting taxes and other economic policies with the byproduct that Blacks get hurt worse than Whites."[31]

There are countless examples of ads using this strategy, such as the infamous ad—part of Atwater's campaign for George H. W. Bush against Michael Dukakis in the 1988 presidential race—featuring a Black convicted felon, Willie Horton, who had committed further crimes while on a furlough from a Massachusetts prison. The ad deployed and reinforced racist beliefs about Black criminality to smear Dukakis as "soft on crime." Or the entirely fictional "welfare queen" featured in Reagan's presidential ads and speeches, or Trump's 2016 ad featuring footage of a Central American migrant caravan, focused on a man (who had previously been deported, then reentered) convicted of murdering two policemen, with overlaid text claiming that Democrats let him into the country and let him stay.[32] Republicans are much more likely to deploy dog whistles and overt racism in their campaign communications, as they've solidified rather than reduced their party's reliance on White voters over the forty years since Atwater's interview—80 percent to 90 percent of the party's voters are White.[33]

But Democrats' campaign communications are not always paragons of antiracism and solidarity. Al Gore was the first to bring up Massachusetts' furlough program in a primary debate with Michael Dukakis, though he didn't mention Willie Horton directly. In 1992, Bill Clinton held a press conference announcing his "tough on crime" stance at a Georgia prison while standing in front of a group of mostly Black prisoners. Most recently, Biden's 2020 ad blaming Trump for not being tougher on China at the start of the coronavirus pandemic played on xenophobia.[34] The Democrats' coalition relies on people of color, though, and especially Black voters, so they are far less likely to use the same overtly racist tactics as Republicans. Nonetheless, they have frequently minimized or delegitimized

Black grievances and resisted coming out too strongly in favor of racial justice for fear of alienating White voters.[35]

Both parties regularly depict their opposition, whether in intraparty primaries or interparty general elections, as selfish, unconcerned with regular people's needs, power-hungry, or otherwise corrupt. Many of the political professionals I spoke with loved this kind of down-and-dirty political fighting, but regular people get the message that all politics—not just one candidate or party—is corrupt and uncaring. This kind of messaging contributes to increased cynicism and distrust of politics and politicians.[36]

There are a lot of other important components to campaign work, and people move around to various degrees within and between these different departments. I've focused here on the parts of campaigns that are most directly concerned with interacting with or understanding voters, but it is worth having an overview of the other kinds of staff and consultants in political campaigns.

One standard campaign department I haven't mentioned yet is the political department. Having a political department inside a political campaign may seem redundant. But political departments are all about finding and mobilizing allies for the campaign. Political directors and people who work for them seek to make connections with other campaigns and community groups. These other political actors—politicians, group leaders, or other influential people—may give the campaign their endorsement, send volunteers for field efforts or participants for rallies and events, and ultimately help persuade potential voters to vote for the candidate.

Jay, a White man who has been a political director on a number of national campaigns, explained that for Democrats, that means you make a list of stakeholders that includes "elected officials, unions, depending on where you are, it could be environmental organizations and then minority leaders." And then "you try to identify an honest broker that's perhaps been in your role before" and get that person to "sort of explain the lay of the land." Then, even though you may be working in a place you don't know at all, you "begin to be able to get a picture of the state, of the terrain, who's going to be willing to cooperate with whom. And then it's your job to put your guy or your cause or your ballot initiative or what you're working on in the mix." He points out that "all that's happening, you know, while the ads are actually communicating with the regular voters." His job is working with other political figures and leaders, "making sure that we have a presence in African American churches, you know, making sure that we were represented. If there was a Latino street fair or an Asian—you know, I mean you gotta do the outreach and you gotta try to not get anybody saying, 'Hey, you're ignoring us.'"

Under the political director there are usually a number of positions linked to particular key constituencies: Democratic campaigns usually have positions such as director of LGBT outreach or labor union coordinator; Republican campaigns frequently have people in charge of connecting with Evangelical communities and gun owners, among other groups. Both parties usually also have directors of outreach for particular (non-White) racial groups; political departments are where staff who are people of color are concentrated in campaigns.

Another key, if small, part of campaigns is the opposition research team. Clayton described his role as the research director in a presidential primary as having "a comprehensive knowledge of all of the opponents and their positions and their strengths and weaknesses." Opposition research involves digging up information on the opponent to be used in contrast or negative ads, or to leak to the press. That kind of work is how we found out in the 2008 cycle about John Edwards's "$400 haircut" and his affair.[37] Trackers, like the young Indian American whom George Allen called Macaca while he was filming, are another part of these operations. Part of this work is essentially scandal-mongering, but it also includes finding records of the candidate's positions on issues, and trying to ensure that everything in the other side's opposition research—everything they might dig up on your candidate—is already known.

A candidate's policies are central to how they'll govern, and they often get a good deal of discussion in primaries, but no one I spoke with in campaigns told me that the particulars of a candidate's policies were key to their electoral chances. For most people I spoke with, policy and politics were two different worlds. Leon said, "If you're more policy oriented, you should go work for an [elected] official." Sarah explained that if there's a division among types of politicos, it's not between the consultants and the party staff but between all of that set and the "policy people." She talked about the distance between "the policy and the campaign world," and told me that "because of my personality, I was more attracted to sort of the outgoing engaging people" in campaigns "versus the policy wonk side of things."

When politicos brought up policy as a part of campaigns at all, it was usually to say that too much focus on policy in a campaign is counterproductive. Jerry said, "A big problem with Democrats is they constantly barrage people with ten-point plans before they communicate a vision and connect with people in an emotional and visceral way." When I thought I heard Chris, the Republican communications consultant, say that policy knowledge was important, he corrected me emphatically, laughing as he said, "Policy knowledge—whoa! Who said anything about policy knowledge? Policy guys wreck campaigns!" He then explained he was being "halfway facetious" because of course policies are important, but "campaigns are often driven less by policy specifics and more by attributes of candidates and their policies." If a candidate "introduces a tax plan, that tax plan reinforces the fact that he understands the working man. Or understands the economy. Or is going to totally reform the way Washington works. So, it's the reform and the connection with the common man and the connection with the accomplishment on the economy that drives winning campaigns." But the "policy people will ruin it" because "they worry about the specifics and they say, 'Well, you know, it's two-point-five, it's not two-point-one, and actually the fact-check on this shows that that really is only going to cut six hundred million.'"

The policy folks think that's important, but, Chris went on, people outside politics "don't sit around worrying about that stuff. They really don't. And so what I always get frustrated about with the policy folks is that they really, they kind of—they mess up an important argument that we're making to the American public or to the voters on the contrast between two candidates, you know?" On the other side of the aisle, one Clinton 2016 insider told me he thought that campaign lost because John Podesta, the campaign chairman, is "really an issues guy, he's not really a political guy. He's been involved in politics all his life, but that's not really his strength, his strength was in policy."

Nonetheless, major campaigns all have policy directors who craft policy statements. They usually work with policy advisory boards in the relevant domains, which are made up of prominent endorsers from those fields, not campaign staff or paid consultants. The size of the policy staff on even large presidential campaigns is usually small compared with other departments. Even though they mostly thought policy was bad for campaigns, the politicos I spoke with absolutely thought that what people do when they get into office matters. Many told me about the policy issues they cared most about. But by and large they didn't think voters cared about the details, or even the broad outlines, of policy proposals, and so they thought campaigns should focus on other things: the candidate's biography, their vision for the country, their slogans such as "Make America Great Again" or "Change We Can Believe In."

Two other key parts of campaigns are finance departments and operations departments. Finance departments manage campaign fundraising. Most of the actual fundraising is done by the candidate making calls to major donors and by surrogates for the campaign who bundle donations. The finance department coordinates donation drives for smaller donors (often working with a consulting firm specializing in fundraising), and also manages the processing, accounting, and budgeting. Operations departments handle all the administrative and legal tasks associated with being a large organization—paying salaries and bills, filing financial statements with the Federal Election Commission, securing insurance. Both of these functions are essential to the successful operations of a campaign, but they are much less involved in determining what campaigns do and say than the other departments.

And, of course, there are the candidates themselves. The world of campaign professionals is about candidates, and many politicos have deep loyalty to particular candidates as well as to their party as a whole. But candidates are not generally part of the everyday fabric of the work world of most campaigners. Candidates absolutely are part of campaigns, but I'm discussing them last here because they are rarely the principal decision-makers about what campaigns do and how they do it.

That could be a surprise—Hillary Clinton is often blamed for the failures of her campaigns, and Barack Obama is accorded accolades for his successes. That isn't entirely wrong, but it's definitely not the whole story. When campaign professionals talk off the record about candidates (at least, with me), they usually either say that the candidate's characteristics were such that no amount of brilliant or awful campaigning could change an outcome, or they talk about the need to coddle, cajole, manipulate, or manage the candidate. David Plouffe's book about his time on the Obama campaign is full of accounts of Obama's mood and Plouffe's thoughts and feelings about this. It's clear throughout the book that he sees himself, David Axelrod, and Robert Gibbs as managing Obama. He recounts how, early in the campaign, Obama wasn't "locked in on the trail, either in his remarks or in his solicitations of political support," and then compares Obama to a racehorse: "We weren't sure if Obama would turn out to be Secretariat, but we suspected he had some thoroughbred political talent, it just wasn't on daily display." They arranged a dinner with the candidate, "ostensibly to talk about next steps in the campaign," but the "main purpose was to let him know he had to find his inner motivation—or at least better disguise his weariness."[38]

Campaigners generally see this type of relationship of campaign managers to candidates as the proper and natural order of things. Jerry, for instance, complained about "new candidates or candidates who are working with new team members" who don't trust their staff and "so they micromanage like hell." That can create real problems, he said: "Unless there's someone at the top of the operative or consultant food chain who has the trust of the candidate to tell them to butt out," there can be a "bitter internal struggle to get the candidate to stop micromanaging and stop interfering with the operations of the campaign."

Sam, a Democratic data analyst, put it even more strongly, talking specifically about campaign managers: "You have to have a strong personality to be a good manager, because you're dealing with candidates who are almost always going to be very strong personalities." Campaign managers have to stand up to candidates, because "while the candidates generally have very strongly held beliefs about what you need to do to win, they're almost always wrong when it comes to the day-to-day of a campaign." Leon, a Republican, explained that a good candidate "makes their phone calls" to raise money, and "you're a bad candidate if you can't follow your schedule that the staff puts together for you."

Of course, campaign staff want to work for candidates who, in addition to being tractable, make winning more likely. A few features of candidates matter a lot to campaign professionals. Sarah, the Democratic field specialist, said, "They need to know why they're running, first of all. That's the first question to ask them: Why are you running? This is an intense situation. What are you trying to do this for? . . . You want to make sure they know that, and [that] it's a good reason, it's compelling, it's something that voters would listen to." Sam told me that candidates also need to have an "ideological profile" that is a fit with the "geography they're running in. How in line are they with their district, generically from a partisan and an ideological standpoint? And if they tend to be out of line in a lot of areas, how eloquent are they in . . . dealing with those differences?" You also want someone who "has a good background, an impressive résumé, former elected office helps—if they have a proven track record of winning races, that means something. Money is a huge aspect of it. Either can they raise money or do they have money they can spend?"

For politicos, a candidate's role in their own campaign is actually rather limited: they need to raise the money the campaign needs and to perform well in ads, speeches, and meet-and-greets. Sarah put it very directly: In a campaign, "Candidates have a very specific job: they need to be talking to everybody they can be talking to and they need to be raising a butt load of money. And the raising-the-money part is the most important thing." Leon summed up how most politicos think about candidates: the ones who "let their staff do their jobs are great."

It's worth noting that, even though politicos agree that the candidate should not be in charge of the campaign, the campaign manager isn't always in charge either. For smaller and local races—for Congress, city council, mayor, or state representative—the campaign manager may be a relative political neophyte, and despite their title may end up taking advice and possibly direction from consultants and party committees involved in the race. Rufus, the Democratic consultant, recalled how he got his first campaign management role with a call from someone he hadn't heard of who said, "We hear you're good with difficult personalities." And Rufus said, "Who's we? And what is this about?" The guy on the phone said, "I work for the chair of the Democratic Congressional Campaign Committee," then asked, "'Do you want to manage a congressional race in Illinois? We have a chance to pick up a Republican seat.' And I said, 'Oh, that'd be kind of interesting.'" So Rufus "went down to the DCCC, met with them, I said, 'I never managed.' They said, 'We're eight weeks out, there are no managers, we'll tell you what to do, and we'll help you out.'" And so Rufus managed his first congressional race.

Smaller races generally have far fewer paid staff and consultants, and in some races the person called the campaign manager may be more like an administrator or sophisticated office manager, reporting to a general consultant who is actually handling all the coordination and strategy. In larger races, the campaign manager is the true head of the campaign organization, the ultimate decision-maker, who hires and fires consultants, sets overall campaign messaging and strategy, and sets the candidate on their tasks. They are the generals on the battlefields.

.   .   .

Politicos describe their experience of campaigning as very like being the officers and soldiers in a war, or the coaches and players in a football or basketball game. But there are important differences between politics and these other forms of competition. In sports you always know the actual score, and in war the generals can be reasonably sure what territory they hold and whether they won or lost the last battle. In campaigns there are no objective scorekeepers to tell everyone how the teams are doing. In fact, as we saw in 2016, the media trying to act as scorekeepers by posting poll results and forecasts may actually end up influencing the "game's" outcome: at least one study suggests that Trump may have been able to eke out his 2016 victory in part because Clinton supporters saw the projection that Clinton was a safe win and decided to skip actually voting.[39]

In addition to seeing campaigning as a competition, I think it makes sense to see its similarities to theater or filmmaking, as a site of cultural production. This is straightforwardly the case for those politicos who are creating advertisements, writing speeches, and setting up photo-ops for their candidates, but it is true more broadly when we think about what a political campaign does. Focusing on the fact that campaigns are about meaning, culture, emotion, and perception moves our attention to the people receiving campaigns' messages, rather than just the two sides fighting each other. Campaigns attempt to connect emotionally with masses of Americans across vast differences in life experiences and social position and geography. Although the producers of our politics often portray themselves as masterminds, strategists, and tacticians planning a series of battles to plot a course to victory, they are also like writers and directors, using data along with creativity to bring their vision of the world to the public. As in other forms of culture and meaning-making, the effects aren't always direct and measurable, but they contribute to how we understand politics, ourselves, each other, and our country.

CHAPTER 4

THE ROOM WHERE IT HAPPENS

E than was a tweedy, professorial sort who spent fifteen years as a Democratic pollster before shifting to writing and corporate work. Perhaps because he had been outside the world of political production for a while, Ethan, in his late fifties and White, had a very clear view of how the game worked. When he saw *Hamilton* with his kids, the song "The Room Where It Happens" really stood out. To him it was a "wonderfully universal rendering of the ambition of those of us who don't necessarily run for things. You want to be in the room where that decision's made, when the deal is cut on Capitol Hill." Ethan recognized the desire for influence, as did Sophia, a White Democrat about twenty years younger than Ethan who also worked in polling. "Everyone wants" the strategic roles, she said, and "the smaller the campaign, the larger the role" of any individual staff member. Likewise, "the larger the campaign, the more you're fighting to be in that role." For many politicos, being trusted by candidates and others to participate in shaping campaign strategy is deeply important, for their own enjoyment of the work, for their ability to market themselves to future campaigns and clients, and for their sense of worth—getting to be "in the room where it happens" means they have arrived.

Nearly everyone who is well socialized into the campaign world wants to be "in the room" or "at the table" on any campaign they work on. They want to be involved in the decision-making at as high a level as possible. The currency of campaign work, and to some extent of politics more broadly, is inside knowledge, and that's what people tend to seek. Whether or not you are "in the room" indicates your status on the campaign: it matters more than your job title, more than how many people you supervise. This is the organizing principle of work in campaigns.

The campaign decisions politicos make are marked by their understanding of what it takes to get ahead, to get into the "room where it happens." So to understand our politics, we need to figure out how people in campaigns evaluate each other's worth, skill, and insight.

Notably, politics involves a lot of different rooms. Rufus, a White Democrat, definitely valued being in charge, yet he had no desire to work in presidential elections. "No, presidentials suck," he said bluntly. He didn't want to be one of "ten or twenty top people" on a campaign. Plus, he added, "It's such a cauldron of assholes that get to that level that I don't want it." Rufus understood that being in the inner circle was the goal for most people working on campaigns, but he was happy to run things as the principal of his own consulting firm.

Brian, the Democrat whose mother's connection to a candidate landed him his first political job, also pointed out that some people do not share the goal of getting to the inner circle: "For some people, the last thing they would ever want to do is be around the candidate all the time. Maybe they want to develop the new web strategy, that's their dream." Although he acknowledged that "those people are going to be incredibly valuable for a campaign," he immediately pointed to a perceived limitation of that approach to campaign work: "They'll never have direct influence over the candidate or the top decision-maker. . . . There's a lot of value in that— wielding power and influence—in politics, and the people who get those responsibilities are the ones who are excited and eager to put themselves in those positions to show that they can do those things. It's the people who want to be in the game."

Exclusion from the inner circle feels like a huge slight to those who believe they have the right qualifications to make important decisions. Some people even told me they had chosen not to work on campaigns at all rather than be relegated to roles they saw as too far from the center of power. Tom, the Republican who had worked on eleven presidential elections, told me he was personal friends with one major candidate in a presidential primary yet worked on a competitor's campaign. "There was this pretty thick palace guard" around his friend, and Tom struggled to pierce it and "get a meaningful role" in the campaign: "They were perfectly willing to have my help on the outside, but nobody wanted me around the table."

Rather than have an outside role working for his friend, who was the candidate he most believed in, Tom accepted an insider position with an opponent's campaign in the primary—though not one whom his friend considered an important threat. And things worked out for Tom by the end of that cycle: when his second-choice candidate "dropped out after New Hampshire, the next day I was on [my friend's] campaign. As a matter of fact, I brought a whole bunch of people with me."

Similarly, Michael, a forty-something White Republican, turned down a number of requests to work on a major candidate's presidential campaign when he was offered roles without enough stature. He said no to three different jobs within the campaign until he was finally offered a position as the national-level director of the field department. Michael was relieved that he didn't have to seek out a job outside politics, though he'd been prepared to sit out that cycle rather than work on a campaign without the access and power he felt he deserved.

Getting to be "in the room where it happens" requires being understood as a serious, mature campaign professional. Invitations to campaign war rooms and inner circles follow status, which in this field is about having a "gut sense" for good strategy that mostly matches others' gut senses, having good relationships with others in the inner circle, and being able to perform with the kind of argumentative authority and confidence that are respected by other campaign professionals. In other words, in campaigns as (to varying degrees) in other fields, judgments of skill, talent, and even hard work are contingent on the social setting in which they are being made. Time and again, the campaign professional finds that the assessment of their merit depends on who has been asked to judge it.

Those assessments rely on proxies for effectiveness or good campaigning, like the dedication to extreme overworking described earlier, the extent to which people just seem to fit, and personality, measured against the assertiveness seen as the rightful territory of White men. Being hired and advancing hinge on knowing, and impressing, the right people who possess the right influence. This makes the inner circles of campaign decision-making even more distinct from the potential electorate in terms of race, gender, and class. It amplifies the distance between political professionals and the people campaigns target, and it reinforces existing ideas about which kinds of people belong in politics, which issues are politically important, and who and what deserves political attention.

The campaign profession has more men, more White people, and more highly and exclusively educated people than the country as a whole. Moreover, although in both parties staff are not representative of their own voters (discussed in chapter 2), campaigns' top echelons are even less representative. Since 2002, the vast majority—75 percent—of top national or statewide positions in big Democratic campaigns for president, a Senate or House seat, or governor were held by White people. The percentage is even higher—almost 80 percent—if we don't count political departments. Close to 57 percent of those leadership roles were held by men, and 43 percent by White men.[1] Looking at the very top of Democratic campaign hierarchies, White men held at least half of national or state campaign manager or deputy manager roles, White people of any gender held 77 percent, and men held 65 percent. Republicans are far more likely to be White and to be men: over the same period, 70 percent of their top roles were filled by White men; less than 7 percent were held by people of color of any gender; and 26 percent were held by women of any race.

My database records position titles, but title alone does not reveal who was in the inner circle of a given campaign. News reports on major presidential campaigns often mention candidates' closest advisors, the people actually in the room for all the key decisions. According to those reports, thirty-three of the fifty-four people reported to be in these inner circles for presidential general election campaigns from 2012 to 2020 were White men. Neither Mitt Romney's 2012 run nor Trump's two campaigns had a single person of color as most-trusted advisors; Romney had one woman in his inner circle, and Trump had four, two of whom were his wife and daughter. Fourteen of the twenty-six people in Democrats' inner circles across those three cycles were White men; six were women of color (four Black, two Asian American), all but one of whom served in Hillary Clinton's campaign. Biden's 2020 inner circle was entirely White.

Many commentators imagine that campaigners' skills can be judged by the tally of successes and failures in their past, especially their recent past: Did your last campaign get the candidate elected? Welcome aboard! But it turns out that this isn't particularly useful information about whether a potential hire is a good campaign worker. So how do campaign professionals really judge each other? In part they do it the way we all do: by evaluating reputation and relationships.

Humans are social creatures, and our relationships pretty much always matter. That's not only true for campaign careers: "Work your network" is advice familiar to anyone who has ever looked for a job. Social scientists use the term "social capital" to talk about the value of our connections and recognize those relationships as a kind of social currency.[2] Thus, the importance of relationships and networks to campaign work is not unique to that sphere; still, the primacy of one's networks in this arena is a bit unusual. Continued work in national-level electoral politics is only possible for those with the reputation and relationships to keep getting hired.

The extra value of social capital is partially tied to the commonalities between political campaigns and military campaigns. Intrinsically, campaigns are short-lived affairs, with a group of people briefly working toward the singular goal of victory. Unlike a military campaign, though, when a political campaign battle is over, the organization that orchestrated it usually disappears or at least goes dormant. Everyone who works in political campaigns is a sort of temp worker, who will change jobs (if they're staff) or clients (if they're consultants) at least every two years. Campaigns are also characterized by quick staffing-up periods at key moments in the election cycle. Very few campaign positions are ever advertised; instead, people find out about jobs through word of mouth. Positions are commonly filled through informal conversations, when one campaign staffer asks a past colleague or contact whether they would like to "come on board." When the time and staff to post jobs or conduct rounds of interviews are lacking, reputation and relationships offer much-needed shortcuts for campaign staffing.

This means recognizable merit in American political campaigns is less about calculating win-loss records and more about whether other people believe in and talk to others about your worth as a staffer. Every single campaigner I interviewed brought up the importance of connections, although in different ways. Some seemed to think that schmoozing was the key to a campaign career, regardless of skill or talent. I heard this most from younger politicos, or those who were not the most successful in getting invited on to big campaigns. More experienced and successful politicos tended to tell me that referrals were the only reliable way to judge their colleagues' quality. However they characterized networking generally, when politicos traced the pattern of their careers, nearly every move they had made had hinged on knowing someone, or someone who knew someone, on the inside of whatever campaign, party, PAC, think tank, or PR firm they aspired to join.

Sophia had worked in politics for a decade when we met. As a pollster she did the kind of work one might think would be easy to evaluate objectively. But, she explained, to be successful in her field, "It's not being good at the job; it's working your network. Like, that's why your good people leave—because you're not rewarded for being clever or insightful. You're rewarded for really wringing as much as you can out of your network." She could have been talking about Ethan, also a pollster. The premium placed on schmoozing, which wasn't strictly necessary to do his work but was essential to getting jobs, is largely what drove him out of the field. "There's this sort of dance—and I will admit, I was not the best at this—but the pitching and getting of business. And it's a difficult thing when your best clients, essentially, either they lose"—and therefore won't hire you again—"or they go inactive" because they've won, and as incumbents they may not need your help anymore. "So, you have to replenish every two years," which Ethan says requires two things: a good story about how you helped someone win their election last cycle and "the network—which I learned the hard way." If you don't have both, you won't get hired.

At a certain point Ethan took stock of his career's costs, realizing "if I'm going to keep doing campaigns as a thing forever, I need to be relentlessly traveling. I need to go to a lot of state conventions and keep up friendships with the twenty-somethings that are running the campaigns. That takes a personality, sort of constant never-ending networking that—I don't know—other people were better at it than I was."[3]

After double-checking that I would maintain his anonymity, Ethan described the scene at the annual American Association of Political Consultants conference as "not the prettiest picture; these are not people who had work-life balance where it should be. There's a lot of lonely White guys who got divorced a long time ago." He also unintentionally underscored his own privileged position: as a White guy with a fair amount of money and a reputation for doing good work in polling, Ethan was able to land very much on his feet, leaving campaign work for polling and analysis jobs in media and the private sector.

Similarly, Jerry, a Democrat who worked in communications, told me that the lists of recommended consultants parties send to campaigns "are not based on merit. Those decisions are based on personal relationships or . . . the consultant's ability to maneuver and navigate the establishment, to ingratiate themselves. That's not to say all the people who get hired or on the preferred list are bad or incompetent. It's just that they're not necessarily there because they're really good."

The networking required to keep up in campaign work doesn't only put off somewhat introverted guys like Ethan. It also can work to disadvantage and exclude people who don't quite fit for reasons of race, gender, or class.

People tend to socialize with, like, and trust people who are similar to themselves in various ways—sociologists call this homophily, and it means our social networks tend to be fairly homogeneous unless we make a conscious effort to diversify them. When hiring to fill positions hinges on social networks in a field that is already disproportionately men and White people, White men tend to get hired. It's the classic old boys' network effect.[4] Diana, the Latina field staffer, explained that a lot of campaign culture is about "Do I feel comfortable with you? You know, are we going to become buddies? Are we going to laugh at the same things? And so, yeah, to some extent, how you grow up is going to influence some of that." Which is why Democratic operatives, to get past that, have "had to be very vocal and very intentional about their efforts to hire non-White people."

And when they do, those few Black operatives still stand out. Symone Sanders, who was a senior advisor to Biden during his 2020 campaign and then became chief spokesperson for Vice President Kamala Harris, said on a podcast interview, "When I show up, curvy with a low cut, a bold lip . . . and a chilling analysis, people don't know how to take it, because I'm not supposed to be able to give you solid political commentary with a bedazzled nail."[5]

Another woman Democrat who worked in a consulting firm explained that while the campaigns make some effort to be racially diverse, consulting does a worse job. In her firm, as in many elite workplaces, the only Black person was the administrative assistant. She told me, "I don't think we did an adequate job at all in trying to recruit people that were not White. . . . The principals are both Jewish and I think there's this like built-in comfort with—a cultural comfort—I'm Jewish, there's always a lot of Jewish people on staff. And, yeah, I just felt like we were totally inadequate in reaching out like outside of those worlds."

Given the way campaigns staff up, access to important roles requires a connection to the candidate or someone else "in the room" who wants you there. They'll want you there if they know you and trust you and think you're going to bring something valuable. So you need to build your network, and be thought of as good at what you do.

But judging whether someone is good at campaign work is pretty complicated. It doesn't really work to just look at how often someone has been in races that won. Everyone wants to hire people who are good at winning campaigns, so recent wins do sometimes help people get jobs. But at the same time, politicos are also very aware of the randomness of many campaign outcomes, or at least of the fact that the outcome is so often entirely outside their control, especially when they're thinking about judging each other or being judged.

Politicos told me over and over again that ultimately whether the campaign you are on wins or loses is "just circumstances," as Jeff, the Republican ad producer, put it. He gave the example of James Carville, the lead strategist behind Bill Clinton's 1992 presidential victory over the incumbent, George H. W. Bush. Early in his career, Carville was always on these losing campaigns, but was he bad then? No. You know, he was always a very capable guy; he just had bad luck." In fact, he explained, it wasn't just bad luck, but the standard math of reelection runs. Incumbents win in nine out of ten races nationwide, so "you're going to lose most of the time in politics unless you're running incumbent stuff—you're gonna lose," Jeff concluded.[6]

And sometimes you end up on the winning side. Clayton, the White Democratic researcher, told me, "There's also people who, especially in electoral politics, . . . kind of 'luck into' success. Win some campaigns because the things were stacked up favorably and then . . . you're a winner. And then you'll be able to continue to be successful or continue to get hired."

"All you need is one big win," Rufus, the Democratic consultant, confirmed. "You could have fucked up everything! I mean, we could suck, but if our Senate candidate wins, we're gonna look golden. Even if we had nothin' to do with it."

Along with being an incumbent, candidates' success can also come down simply to the letter next to their name on the ballot, R or D. Jesse, a Republican who had just founded his own targeting firm, explained that the "environment" matters—the D or R designation can be an albatross or a boon, depending on the party in power at the time. "If you were a Democrat working on a campaign in 2006, 2008, you could have been subpar and still look like a genius. On the Republican side, you could have been a genius and looked like a fool." Generally, when one party has held federal-level power for a while, the other party tends to do really well with voters. In early 2010, with Obama two years into his first presidential term, Jesse anticipated that it was Republicans' turn to win a lot of congressional seats. He told me that a lot of Democratic operatives looked good in 2008 as their campaigns rode on Obama's coattails. "And this year," he said before the 2010 mid-terms, "I think it's probably flipped where there's probably a lot of subpar Republican operatives that are gonna look great, because the tidal wave is going to carry them across the finish line." That's exactly what happened.

Even politicos who benefit from being seen as good because of a recent surprising win pointed out that election results were bad indicators of their skill. When a campaign wins, everyone involved claims—and largely gets—credit. Kirk understood that his small role in a recent state-level Republican upset was behind the influx of invitations he was receiving to meet with politicians and other consultants. But he cautioned that it was problematic to accord universal credit to anyone associated with a big win. "You get a lot of candidates just desperate for some help," but they don't know how to judge campaigners' skills. "So, there are a lot of folks I meet that . . . I don't know that they really know what the hell they're doing, but there's no way to verify it. Some of these folks who were just on a winning campaign and just happened to be there are considered 'Oh, they must be really good.'" Pointing to his most recent campaign, Kirk noted, "We raised $12 million for the candidate online. That doesn't mean if you hire me, I'm gonna raise $12 million online for you."

Many politicos wish there were an objective system for evaluating one another's skills—a few even suggested that maybe my research could help them out. In a typical statement, Larry, a White Democrat in his early sixties who works providing data to campaigns across the country, said, "It's not like there's someplace you can go easily and see, well, who's won more of the tough races, right?" Maybe, if you needed to quantify a consultant's individual effectiveness, he suggested, wins and losses could be helpful. "But then, like I said, you'd have to control for someone who might win a ton of races, but they're just doing a lot of safe candidates. Or the opposite, because they tend to take a lot of long shots." Overall, Larry conceded that being part of or even in charge of a winning or losing campaign "doesn't mean anything," and "it would be impossible to know" which staff had been really good or really bad behind the scenes. Without a better system in place, and often under time pressure to make quick decisions to bring staff on board, "People fall for more marketing and more of these personal relationships, who they know." When someone Larry knows asks whom to hire, "I'll give them my best recommendation. And now, again, does that mean that I'm going to end up recommending the best possible person? I don't know that. I have to recommend people I feel good about, who I haven't been hearing crap about, who I feel instinctively understand this business and what they're doing and they've done it well." But, he said, at the end of the day, you have to "use your gut. You know, how do I feel about this person?"

Alison, a White Republican thirty years Larry's junior, had worked as a campaign manager for local and statewide races in Virginia, and was now working for a direct-mail firm. She said almost exactly the same thing as Larry, though with a bit more optimism for the prospect of a better system in the future: "I've often thought about, like, it would be really great to do something where there's actually a way that Republicans can keep track of and train good campaign managers. And field workers, field operatives. Because there's no good tracking system of these people." Instead, Alison described an informal and ultimately unreliable system of assessments and recommendations: "They float around from campaign to campaign and you hear names, and 'Oh, I knew that guy, he was working on this guy's campaign like three cycles back.' And you hear things about these people, but you don't know if they're really good—you don't know."

Another common theme among the politicos I interviewed was that, while agreeing that most candidates and other campaigners were poorly equipped to judge job hunters' skills, they were confident about their own abilities to do so. Many spoke with complete certainty about which of their peers were genuinely, objectively skilled.

Campaign professionals reward each other for their good "instincts," appearing "smart" or just seeming to "get it," despite the fact that, in this low-information environment, there's little chance they could make such assessments rationally. Without better ways to assess each other's skills and abilities, they described using track records of campaigns won and lost as well as examples of tactics job seekers used in past campaigns as starting points for these judgments. All scored, of course, on their own sense of what makes for good or effective campaigning.

The acquired, largely implicit sense of what constitutes campaign prowess led my informants to say things like "You just know it when you see it" or to tell me they relied on "political instincts" when evaluating potential coworkers. Sophia remembered looking at a campaign ad with a colleague; Sophia thought "the ad was stale, old but equaling stale, like, out of touch," while her colleague "thought it was establishment, a power broker, whatever." In Sophia's opinion the colleague had "a tin ear for this stuff. . . . We just had totally different reactions." Though she acknowledged "there's no way to evaluate who's right and who's wrong," Sophia concluded that the ad "didn't resonate with where the electorate was at" and her colleague was "off."

A few of my interviewees insisted that anyone can learn campaign work, but the rest doubled down on the need for a politico to have the right political instincts if they were going to make it into the room where it happens. However, it's extremely hard to pin down what those instincts actually entail. Sophia and many others simply feel they can recognize good campaigning. Kerri said, "It's sort of hard to define [but] there are definitely people in this business who just seem to . . . get it. They seem to absorb it, they seem to have the instincts and kind of know, and it's not something you can really teach. Sort of that gut feeling." Francis, a Republican digital strategist, spoke of people who "have a talent—a political gut, so to speak." Echoing fellow politicos who compared the production of politics to other forms of cultural production, he said, "It's like music, you know? You either are born with an ability or not."

Campaign professionals make judgments about one another, and one another's campaign products, based on a tacit, practical sense that is hard to translate into clear criteria. This is not an uncommon feature of expert decision-making, even in contexts with more clearly defined rules and standards. Thus even doctors and psychiatrists, despite their notoriously expansive and detailed diagnostic manuals, nonetheless rely on their own experience and mental shortcuts when it comes to diagnosing and treating patients. Which means it's not necessarily a condemnation of professional political decision-makers to say that they can't and don't use scientific or objective measures to back up their sense of what is and is not effective in campaigns.[7]

Since campaign outcomes can be so arbitrary, this kind of gut sense is essentially the only criterion available for politicos in judging one another. Campaign operatives try to contribute to winning elections, but the best way to do that isn't always obvious or even knowable. If operatives want to continue getting jobs, the most important audience for any given contribution to a campaign might be not the voter, but the peer: the power players in their own and other campaigns, any of whom could be the next person looking to hire staff.

That raises the next question: What determines whether Politico A believes Politico B is skilled? Projecting the right persona is another key to being perceived as a skilled political operative. This includes having the habits and dispositions that people expect, as Adrian, a White Democratic digital media guru, demonstrated when he told me about another political professional, Joe: "He just looks unruffled, totally unflappable. . . . He was one of those people who just exudes an air of being in control. And there is clearly like a premium on that. I actually think his thing that makes him successful and good is almost exactly the same thing that makes David Plouffe successful and good—it's just like a calm in the storm kind of thing." In other words, projecting an air of authority by making decisions quickly and sticking with them is an important part of looking the part—and looking the part, in a field dominated by hiring based on "fit," is half the battle.

Clayton said that in addition to appearing to be in control, you "have to be assertive. That's essentially how you gain respect. I mean it's almost like a currency." He went on, "If you're not able to kind of disagree and stand up to the person who's supervising you, like that person probably . . . won't be supervising you. You'll be another couple layers down. You have to be able to say, 'No, I think you're wrong, and here's what I think is the answer,' or, 'This sounds like a really bad idea.' And if you're not able to do that, you just won't be in the room for very long, because you're not valued." He upped his language here, adding, "I think it tends to be people who are quite aggressive. And opinionated." This brings us to dominant cultural ideas about who gets to be aggressive and opinionated and have those qualities seen as positive, not negative. The valued political persona of firm decisions made without second-guessing, the strong opinions and decisive actions, that persona again points to the "natural fit" of privileged White men in powerful roles.

The cultural assumptions that benefit men, on top of the nearly un-limited number of hours required of politicos during campaigns, dispro-portionately limit women's access to high-level roles. Sophia explained that the dearth of women in politics was partly due to the same forces that apply in nearly all careers that require people to be "type A, totally career-driven" and were designed around the expectation that the em-ployee was a man with freedom from reproductive and household labor. If you're a woman in a career like that, Sophia pointed out, "There's no one there that is like doing their laundry and cooking and whatever else they need to get by, so they have to pay to have someone do that." Sophia had recently had a baby when we spoke and was considering moving out of political work. She told me, after I assured her I wouldn't make her recognizable because she didn't "want to burn bridges there at all," that her "firm had a horrible maternity leave policy, offensive for a progressive firm" that talked a lot about electing women as part of its mission. But "it was really terrible and made me question my ability to go back, having kids." So, she concluded with a resigned laugh, "I don't think it's about politics. I think it's about, like, America."

Sophia worked for a firm dedicated to shifting politics toward an America with the kinds of social welfare policies that would allow people with children to balance careers and home. But the firm itself, like so many organizations across all sectors, did not make that possible. Beyond that, though, some of what Sophia thinks makes it difficult for women politicos shows up differently in politics, or at least is especially bad in campaigns: "Culturally, the campaigns themselves at the highest levels are still back rooms, you know, like drinking and smoking." And women are "not on an equal footing in that kind of scene." Although women are at least as good as men and are taken seriously in organizing roles, "It's hard for women to break through and be taken seriously at the top levels."

Sarah, the Democratic field strategist, said, "It's definitely an old boys' network, still. And there's definitely a piece where you have to fight through to be kind of considered part of that. Like, the go-to guys are the guys," although a few women "consultants are emerging."

Susan, a White Democratic strategist, agreed: "I think to be a campaigner, you have to be . . . fairly self-confident"—so self-confident, in
fact, that you can "walk into a room and say two and two is five and believe
it. And I think men just do that better than women. I don't think that men
are necessarily better at the job than women are, but"—she faltered for
a bit, laughed a little—"men just have a natural confidence that women
don't have, and that is a huge impediment to your being successful in
this business." I would argue that that kind of confidence is learned, not
innate, but it is men, especially White men from privileged backgrounds
who are taught to display that kind of bluster and are rewarded when
they do so.

This take accords with the few studies that have been done specifically
about women in professional politics. Sarah Brewer wrote her dissertation
on gender in American politics. She found that both men and women
consultants believe women are at a disadvantage in political consulting.[8]
A few academics have noted, like Sophia and others, that political campaigns tend to have an overtly masculine atmosphere.[9] Some of this may
be shifting in recent years, at least on the Democratic side, but it is still
an issue.

It is nearly impossible for campaign professionals to objectively evaluate the impact they or their colleagues have had on election outcomes.
Instead, when they need to make judgments about who is a good campaign professional and what is a good campaign decision, they rely on
their acquired gut feeling of what makes for good campaigning. That can
make the people "in the room where it happens" unwilling to take in information from outside the room.

I often heard about the split between the national office and the local and state staff on presidential races. David Plouffe recounts an instance of this from his perspective as Obama's campaign manager, where
they wanted to approach the primary in South Carolina without going
through the usual power brokers. Plouffe and the inner circle wanted to
run their campaign a different way, focusing on on-the-ground organizing and turning out new voters. The staff who knew the state told them it
wouldn't work there, warning, "If you don't do it our way, you will lose."[10]
That time the national-level managers turned out to be right, and Obama
went on to win South Carolina decisively. But in the Clinton campaign

in 2016, listening to local staff might have alerted the national-level inner circle to problems with their models.

I heard about a similar dynamic in the Sanders 2020 campaign. As in the Obama '08 campaign, the top-level staff were committed to running a different way and turning out every voter they could. One person I spoke with told me, "Bernie's narrative was, like, we're going to turn out so many new people in the primary—that's how we're going to win this." But "all people wanted to talk about on the doors was like, which of these nominees is going to beat Donald Trump, and Bernie did not make that story compelling enough." The usual approach to voters is to focus on only those who are already likely to vote. Instead, Sanders and his campaign managers wanted to focus on identifying new potential voters. This staffer was hearing from people on the ground that persuasion of likely voters needed to be a bigger part of their strategy, and tried to convey that to those in the Sanders campaign's inner circle, but was rebuffed. They were committed to their vision of whom Sanders should target and what they should focus on. Although both Sanders campaigns were unconventional in many ways, in this instance the national campaign was as closed to bottom-up information as any other major campaign, and didn't win the nomination for their candidate.

The informality and arbitrariness of how politicos judge each other, combined with the goal of being in the "inner circle" and the overall intensity of campaign work, partly explain why it is incredibly difficult for outsiders and newcomers to gain meaningful roles in campaigns. Strategic decision-making roles on the inside, let alone in the "inner circle," are heavily restricted to those who have put in their time on campaigns, have shown themselves to be valuable, or have close relationships with the candidate, although none of these is necessarily a guarantee of gaining access to that elite status. This is made clear to volunteers and lower-level staff who want to get more involved in a campaign.

Politicos judge one another on the basis of the personas they project, the dedication they show, their 24–7 availability, and an intuitive judgment of their campaign outputs and practices, from the content of speeches to voter targeting and field strategy, media plans, and event schedules. Although they might not put it this way themselves, conforming to partially shared, often unarticulated standards and traditions of campaign practice is crucially important for their career success. These kinds of informal and subjective measures of merit are almost guaranteed to benefit people whose race, gender, class origin, education, and other characteristics resemble other staffers already in place. This is homophily in action.

One reason this is a problem is fairness and equity—ideally, anyone who wants to work in politics and is willing and able to do the work ought to have an equal shot at a career. Ideally, there would be clear paths to entry and criteria for good work (and reasonable working hours, while we're at it) so that people from all walks of life might be able to make their living in politics if they're moved to do so. That ideal applies equally to any field, really.

But politics is special, because politics by its nature affects all of our lives. It makes a difference to all of us what campaigns do, insofar as what they do matters for who participates and how, and how people see and understand politics and politicians and government. If campaigns are making ads that speak primarily to people like their staff, or even actively generate hostility against people unlike them, that affects us all. If campaign staff advise candidates that certain policies will never fly, or that they should tone down their feminism or play up their machismo, that constitutes a large part of American political cultural content. If campaign teams believe that the White working class loves racism and hates redistribution (they actually, on the whole, like both), or that nonvoters will never vote (when they can in fact be effectively mobilized), then they will craft campaigns based on those beliefs.[11] When the people running campaigns are so different from the rest of us, chances are that many people will continue to see politics as something for "other people."

$\star$ $\star$ $\bigstar$ $\star$ $\star$

CHAPTER 5

THE PRODUCTION OF POLITICS

I met Ken, a very senior Democratic media consultant, in early 2017 in the offices of his political and communications consulting firm. Between walking in the door and finally meeting him I went through the building receptionist, the receptionist for his firm, and his personal assistant, who took my water order very seriously (bottle or glass? ice or no ice?) as she ushered me to an upstairs conference room with a view out over the water. When I started my conversation with Ken, he asked what my working theory was. It was probably a strategic error, but I told him: a lot of what happens in campaigns is about conventional wisdom, and political professionals are often constrained from innovating too much in the strategies they use to connect with voters. He disagreed emphatically, at least in reference to politicos "working in a major senate or gubernatorial or certainly a presidential campaign" and those "actively involved all the time and thinking about campaigns and how the world is changing and how we communicate in different ways." If you're among that elite in the campaign world, said Ken, "You are looking for all sorts of different ways to understand the electorate, to activate the electorate, to communicate with the people you need to communicate with." Over sixty-five, White, and a veteran of nearly every Democratic presidential campaign since Bill Clinton's in 1992, Ken told me, "When I look at a campaign of four years ago, eight years ago, certainly ten years ago, I think the landscape has changed radically." There was a "sea change [from] Obama '08 to Hillary '16." Moreover, he said, "how we interface with voters has changed pretty radically as well. With a big asterisk: Yes, we still communicate on television.

Yes, we still have people who go door to door." But "the tools and how we do it and who we're focused on targeting—those kinds of things have changed in pretty fundamental ways." Campaign text messages now feel like an entirely normal part of political life, even though mass texting has only been part of politics for relatively few years.

Although other campaign professionals I'd spoken with agreed with me—in fact had given me this understanding in the first place—I clearly offended Ken by telling him my working theory honestly, especially in the wake of Clinton's loss, which we discussed at length and which everyone from moderate Republicans leftward was still reeling from. It is true, as Ken says, that the technology campaigns use has changed radically, but the fundamental way campaigns work has not.

Why hasn't the new media and technological landscape transformed politics into an entirely new beast? As Ken pointed out in our chat during the Trump administration, a lot of things in our cultural and political environment have changed in just the last decade: "In 2012, I think we sent out . . . a tweet. And now [we have] a president who can't stop [doing] it. And that drives news, it drives coverage, more broadly, in terms of social networks." Still, the people who produce politics haven't changed much, and the way they talk about and talk to voters has changed even less.

Scholars and journalists alike tend to approach campaigns as fairly straightforward attempts to persuade voters. But campaigns are highly produced sets of cultural objects, and they can be understood alongside other kinds of cultural production as the result of both analysis and intuition, data and creativity. However much they aim to influence voters, campaign tactics are not, and cannot be, entirely determined by predicting their potential effects. It is not possible to know for certain how any given voter or set of voters will react to particular messages; neither testing or experimentation can tell politicos the best possible path to victory. Furthermore, campaign outputs need to communicate with multiple audiences, including the media, funders, and political operatives inside and outside the campaign. Undoubtedly a lot of data analysis goes into creating political content, yet it remains a fundamentally creative, uncertain endeavor.

Chris, the Republican communications consultant, was among the many interviewees who explicitly compared creating a campaign to creating a Hollywood film or a breakthrough technology. He described political outreach as "a craft," continuing, "Much the way that people who produce TV shows are always looking for the new kind of *Lost*, people who produce movies are always looking for the new kind of *Shrek*. People who produce technology are looking for the new iPod or the new iPad. You need to be looking for a new way to hone your craft and get better, and advance sort of new things."

Chris may have been thinking about the mass-market appeal of each of those items, but his analogy is also telling in that cultural productions are always as much a story about the judgments and organizations of people in Hollywood, Silicon Valley, or New York as they are about the tastes of regular consumers.[1] Filmmakers, whether they are trying to make blockbusters or something for more "highbrow" audiences, respond to trends and ideas within Hollywood about what makes for "good" or "big" films. Similarly, the creative content of campaigns, from ads to mailers to new microtargeting strategies, is about what is happening inside the field of campaign work as much as or more than what, objectively, moves voters. In other words, political production is not just instrumental and rational, it is the outcome of a particular set of implicit beliefs and the expected practices and dynamics of competition in this field.

Another similarity between campaigns and other sites of cultural production is evident in the norms, practices, and rituals that characterize these hidden worlds. Where Hollywood celebrates itself with the Academy Awards and the advertising world hands out Webby and Clio Awards, the campaign world has *Campaigns & Elections* magazine (formerly *Politics*), which publishes an annual accounting of consulting firms' win-loss records as well as a list, "Rising Stars," of promising politicos under age forty. The American Association of Political Consultants (AAPC) and *Campaign & Elections* both host yearly awards ceremonies in which they honor campaigns, campaign outputs, and outstanding campaign managers and consultants. At the AAPC's annual Pollie Awards ceremony the organization recognizes promising politicos in its "40 under 40" list (evenly divided among Democrats and Republicans), hands out Campaign Excellence awards, one for each party, for the best campaign manager in a statewide or local race, and confers political advertising Gold, Silver, and Bronze awards in categories like "Best Use of Opposition Research—Republican."

As with every other way of measuring politicos' true value aside from their own personal intuition, my respondents were largely unconvinced that these awards are informative. One person interrupted my question about the Pollies to say they are "complete bullshit," and quite a few described the awards as a racket dependent on factors like connections to judges. Another interviewee who served on a committee deciding on awards told me, "Half the time I see the nominations and I read the nominations, and I have no clue about that campaign. So I have to take the advice of what was perceived to be an upset, or what was perceived to be a well-run campaign. And part of it is science, part of it is . . . you know, license to be creative and the like, but it's very hard to make that judgment of what was a good campaign and what's a bad campaign." Nonetheless, the awards are attended by many politicos every year, and consultants use their wins to sell their services to future clients.

Just as regular audience members' opinions of films don't determine Oscar winners, the views of people outside the politics industry don't matter much for who wins Pollies. They matter less than you might think for politicos too. Their understanding of voters would seem incredibly important for their work. Yet, in terms of their identities, their career paths, and much of their day-to-day work, they are quite disconnected from people outside the world of politics. When I asked politicos about what makes someone successful in their world, they talked about networks, putting in the hours, and having a competitive attitude. This is, of course, how basically all professionals describe what makes someone good at their jobs. See, for just one example, the hedge fund high-rollers, described by sociologist Megan Tobias Neely, who were self-sorted through networks and homophily in similar ways, brought into a similarly insular club, and imbued with a sense of almost mystical knowledge, when really it was often the wealth of their personal social networks that determined their success.[2] Many politicos also emphasized having a long-standing love of politics, or a good "sense" about politics generally, as important to success. But almost no one explicitly mentioned the people who ought to be the audience for their work: Voters. Regular people. The electorate.

Nonetheless, campaigns and politicos do try to make sense of voters and figure out how to get them to vote the way they want—that's how elections are won, and however much campaign professionals are aware that their ability to affect the outcome is limited, they try to make as much difference as they can. To do that, they need to have some way of understanding voters. As Rick Ridder, a Democratic political strategist, put it in his irreverent book about his work in politics, *Looking for Voters in All the Wrong Places*, "'All for one and one for all' is a good mantra for guys with capes and curls and cutlasses, but it is a lousy campaign strategy." Nobody can appeal to everyone. "So, 'divide and conquer' is a far better modus operandi for a candidate. It is called targeting. But you need to know whom to divide and whom to conquer."[3] Campaigns figure out which potential voters they want to aim to win over, turn out, or keep home through polls and voter databases.

Polling is a fairly straightforward way for campaigns to try to understand their electorate: campaigns can simply ask potential voters for their views. The ability to get a random sample of the electorate to tell a campaign directly what's important to them, how they plan to vote, and what might sway them may seem like a magic bullet for designing campaign strategy. However, polling has a number of limitations. The journal *Public Opinion Quarterly* and countless scholarly tomes are full of studies documenting the ways poll results can vary depending on subtle changes in the wording of questions, the possible answers offered, and even the order in which questions are asked. As sociologists Colin Jerolmack and Shamus Khan point out in their article "Talk Is Cheap," people's reports about their own attitudes and beliefs are not a great way to understand their actions.[4] The proportion of people who tell researchers that they voted in the last election, for example, is consistently about ten percentage points higher than actual turnout.[5]

What campaigns want to know from polls is who is persuadable and how to persuade them. Politicos tend to think of the electorate, of potential voters, of people, as collections of attributes that can predict voting behavior. This is how a lot of scholars of political science and sociology and economics think about or at least treat people, too, in what critics have called "variables-based" social science.[6] It's an appealing idea that we can know something we want to know about a person by putting together aspects of them that we can measure. And it's not entirely wrong, either—this kind of sociology and other social sciences have given us any number of useful insights into the social world. It works better, however, for describing overall patterns than for predicting what any given person, or even small numbers of people, will do.

Campaign professionals talk a lot about using polls along with other forms of data to identify the constituencies that will be key to electoral victory. This is the kind of analysis that generates the talk we hear in every big election about groups like "soccer moms" or "NASCAR dads." So Cameron, a terse Democratic communications consultant, seemed a bit appalled when I started to ask how he thought about "communications that are targeted at the general public—at voters." He interrupted before I even finished my question, saying, "No such thing. Millions of people in this country, there's no such thing as a general public." I said, "Okay. So how do you think about it then, if you're not—" and he interrupted again: "There's Latino, noncollege men thirty to forty [years old] in suburban Albuquerque with families, blue-collar—that's an audience." I asked, "So you're crafting a message specifically for that?" And after his "Yeah," I said, "So there's a lot of research that goes into that." But, he said, "most people we work for don't have the cash to do the research. So they basically got to intuit it. Deduce and intuit it."

Cameron is describing what sounds like an "objective" endeavor—figuring out a "fulcrum demographic" and then designing a message specifically for that group. But the granularity of his example is not really available to most pollsters. A campaign pollster generally contacts maybe five hundred voters, then adjusts using weighting and makes inferences from there. Even if you're just polling in New Mexico, even if you can get 500 randomly selected respondents, only about 125 will be Latino men, only about 30 of those will be age thirty to forty, and maybe if you're lucky, 10 of those will be blue-collar workers living in the suburbs of Albuquerque with their families. And then what you're able to ask them in a poll is a set of questions such as "On a scale of one to five, with five being will definitely vote for him, how likely are you to vote for this candidate?" Or, "What issues are most important to you?" Or, "Would you be more or less likely to vote for someone" who espoused a particular position? That's not no information, but it's not enough to definitively inform crafting a message that will move all the other Latino blue-collar family men in the suburbs of Albuquerque, let alone everyone else in New Mexico or whatever place you're trying to win.

Ken, the senior Democratic media and communications consultant, pointed out the problem: "We can do a laundry list of ten issues that come back in a poll and the top three are Social Security and Medicare and quote-unquote 'jobs' and whatever. But if that's interpreted by people as 'Oh, my God, it's just another blah, blah, blah, I've been hearing the same stuff for years,' they're going to shut down on you." So again, polls are not as powerful for informing campaign strategy as their proponents might like to believe, in part because polls almost always have limited numbers of respondents.

Data analytics, on the other hand, promise the potential to find patterns in data on nearly *everyone*. Jason, a Republican who works in this area, explains how voter data is used: "The idea is we take the data we have about a specific individual and we use that data to come to some informed judgment about who they're gonna vote for, how likely they are to vote, what sort of issues they care about. It's predictive analytics." Data firms like Jason's collect as much information as they can about voters, and then use "statistical modeling, algorithms, data mining" based on those whose political preferences they know in order to make inferences about the voters for whom they have less information. Jason and firms like his can put together data from a pollster whom I told I am a strong Democrat, from my CVS discount card that reveals I buy a lot of Ben & Jerry's, and from my voting record indicating I vote every time. Looking at other people for whom they have the same or comparable data, they might see that nearly everyone who bought a lot of Ben & Jerry's also reported being a strong Democrat. From there, they can infer that there's a good likelihood that other CVS shoppers with a love of Chocolate Chip Cookie Dough ice cream are strong Democrats as well.

As Jason put it, "Ultimately, it means that, even though I haven't talked to you, I may have talked to somebody like you, or to a group of people like you." Armed with the data about the people they might contact, whether through mail, phone, door-knocks, online targeting, or cable advertisements, "You can customize your appeal to the person you're talking to, which is really what any good politician wants to do." But instead of having to meet someone in person and say, "'What's on your mind, what do you care about?'" and respond appropriately, "we just cut out that step of having to ask that person—having to actually meet the person and ask the person about that." The promise of data analytics, for Jason, is that it further reduces the need for campaigns to hear from voters directly.

On the Democratic side, the main way campaigns and allied political organizations such as PACs and advocacy groups access voter data is through an interface known to Democratic operatives and experienced volunteers as "The VAN" (originally standing for Voter Activation Network; MiniVAN is the app used to access this data on mobile devices). The underlying databases, provided by companies such as Catalist, include all registered voters as well as some people who aren't even registered to vote, compiled from publicly accessible voter registration data and other sources. They usually contain scores calculated the way Jason described, for every potential voter. People in the database have a score indicating the predicted likelihood that they will vote or the estimated probability that, if they vote, they will vote for Democrats. These scores are guesses based on modeling that uses demographic information, past voting behavior, and data collected from consumer marketing firms. Almost always, the database has information on a registered voter's age and gender, and sometimes it has reliable race and ethnicity data. It tells you where that voter lives, the characteristics of their neighborhood, and how often they've voted over the last four election cycles. It then matches the individual data with the characteristics of people who have reported to pollsters that they will or will not vote, will or will not vote Democrat, are or are not "very liberal," and the like.

In his book *Hacking the Electorate*, Eitan Hersh makes two major points about the kind of data accessed through the VAN and, by extension, other similar political databases. First, campaign professionals think about these data as real information about real voters—as directly "perceived voters." But they're really perceiving modeled or best-guess versions of voters. There are a lot of layers of guesswork and indirect correlations between, say, Jane Smith, sixty-three, of West Philadelphia, and the row of data that represents her. In real life, Jane Smith is a person with all kinds of experiences with politicians, and policies, and government. But the Jane Smith in the database is based on a model that compiles a few facts, like her voting record (she votes in every election) and party registration (Democrat) and address; matches her with other types of available data about Jane Smith, sixty-three, at her address (maybe, for example, that she has a subscription to *Newsweek* and is a member of the American Association for Retired People and the Sierra Club); and, finally, predicts a whole lot of other things campaigns might want to know about her. The database's "Jane Smith" includes the real Jane Smith's name and gender marker, but Hersh's book shows that the system will be wrong fairly often about her political opinions, to the extent it can even model them at all.

Put another way, campaigns "see" voters in their databases, but they are only perceiving a representation of Jane Smith based on some more or less informed guesswork. There's a good chance the databases are wrong about pretty much everything about Jane Smith except her name, birthday, and address. Meanwhile, the two biggest predictors of whether Jane Smith is going to vote Democrat or Republican in any given election are her party affiliation and racial identity. And Hersh found that when algorithms are used to guess either of these attributes, they're often wrong. If they have both of these pieces of information, any additional data about Jane Smith adds extremely little to the database's capacity to predict her voter behavior.

People who sell access to this proprietary consumer data make a big deal out of their algorithms' comprehensiveness and power to add important data to the model, but the algorithms usually add very little to their prediction. For instance, if you know that I'm a White man in my mid-forties, your best guess—and a data model's—is that I'm a Republican. If I add some more information—say, that I live in one of the most Democratic neighborhoods in the country, West Philadelphia—you should probably guess I'm a Democrat. Knowing that I also buy a lot of Ben & Jerry's at CVS doesn't actually add much predictive power, nor does it tell you how you might persuade me to do anything different from what people like me almost always do: vote for the Democrat.

This means that even with enormous financial resources and sophisticated data analytics, campaigns, like pollsters and survey researchers outside campaigns, can get their information wrong. Ken, my interviewee from the top of the Clinton 2016 campaign, said, "We clearly have a problem right now that I hope gets solved, where when we try to determine who our different voter groups are, who the targets are, and what they think, we've got a research problem." Some researchers, he said, "think, 'This is a modeling issue, there are techniques that we can use to do a better job of understanding the electorate and getting their views'—but a million things impact that: mobile phones, land lines, shy Trump voters, all the social stigma that might be in play in these different places, that are really affecting the judgments you are about to make, in making the really critical decisions about where are you going and who you're talking to."

A more recent approach to understanding voters, A/B testing, might seem like it could yield important campaign insights. This means running experiments using two different options (A and B) such as two different-sized buttons on a website or two different wordings in an email. Analysts look at which option gets more clicks, or donations, or sign-ups, or whatever the campaign is trying to do. This can help with fine-tuning to select the more effective design or wording for a text message or a mailer, but it can't design a message from scratch—that still requires politicos' knowledge and gut instinct.

Contemporary polling, modeling, and targeting techniques can give politicos guidance about messaging, ad placement, and other aspects of campaign strategy, but no amount of technology can actually tell them what strategy will most reliably influence any particular person's or group's behavior on Election Day. Moreover, each of these is only as good as the questions they ask, the answers people give, and the representativeness of their sampling. If any of those things are off, and they almost always will be to some extent, campaign decision-making is still largely guesswork and intuition at best, and misguided at worst. Matt, a White Republican who's been the political director on a number of national races, told me, "This business is figuring out who is truly available, who is not already for you or against you. That is the science. And the art is what exactly do you say to them, to motivate them to your cause." Polling and data analysis are the science, but this kind of science is never perfect.

At the end of the day, it is really hard to figure out what people intend to do, and harder still to make them do what *you* want. But you have to have some theory of how to do that if your job is trying to win elections. Because campaign professionals cannot and do not know which strategies or tactics will be the most effective, and because they therefore cannot be evaluated by others in their field on that criterion, they end up using a number of shortcuts or proxies for quality.

Most politicos I talked with barely mentioned voters when I asked what made for good campaigning, but Ken, the Democratic communications consultant, was one of very few exceptions. When I asked Ken about his rubric for judging whether someone was good at campaign work, he was emphatic: "I think what's really important in campaigns is being able to see and hear the people you're trying to communicate with, and to pay attention to their lives and the forces that are impacting them every day." You have to look for "different techniques for understanding what people are feeling and how they're looking at the world," try to "understand where they go for their information and what the world is like that they interact in." So you need to figure out "who are those influencers? Who are the people that they are going to pay attention to?" In practice, this means that a "good" campaign professional, first and foremost, has an "openness" to identifying, understanding, and connecting with "the people who are going to determine the election."

More commonly, however, when campaign power brokers spoke about potential voters, they revealed a belief that the everyday American doesn't care about politics, doesn't pay attention, and needs to be told what to believe and whom to support. Chris, the Republican communications consultant, explained that although *he* cares about policy, he is unusual: "Everybody's like, 'Oh, well, the American people, once they learn what's in this bill, they're going to like it.'" But "the American public has never ever learned what's in a bill. They want—they were supportive of the Homeland Security Bill, because it had Homeland and Security in it. They didn't know that there was an internet-gambling-enforcement act in there. They had no idea." He went on, putting emphasis on each word: "They don't know and they never will know. They'll never figure that out. Maybe two percent of the public knows that that thing was larded as a vehicle to supposedly help social conservatives."

Almost all my respondents, the speakers at the trainings I attended, and the campaign management handbooks I read shared these foundational beliefs about regular people. This view of potential voters informs nearly every campaign decision and colors everything people hear about politics during elections.

The campaign wisdom is that the three ingredients of a successful campaign "product" are consistency, simplicity, and attention capture. The messages should be relatable, but also "cut through" voters' day-to-day concerns in order to grab and hold their attention. As Kevin, a Democratic communications consultant, explained, "You've got precious few moments" in a campaign, and if you're not communicating in a "compelling, persuasive, easily understood way, you've missed your opportunity and you really don't get that many of them."

Campaign pros repeatedly used physical metaphors to describe this work of producing politics. Jeff, who designed some of the best-known web and TV ads for a major Republican presidential campaign, told me you have to "touch voters" with your message "repeatedly, and hit them over the head. You know, you're just trying to burn a message into their brains." Alison, a young Republican campaign manager, described making decisions about messaging as "We gotta come up with something creative to pound this in," and Leon, another Republican, said his mission in creating a campaign website is to "give 'em the message, hit 'em over the head with action items they can take, and make it easy for them to understand." Jennifer, a Democrat, told me, "The more unpredictable you can be [with your ads], the better. And that's what makes them successful." When asked why she said, "There are a million different messages during campaign season that get out there, so you need to be able to penetrate and distinguish your client from the pack."

Somehow forcing voters to pay attention was one of the only specific requirements for good campaign communication that people described, despite a good deal of probing on my part. The politicos' comments clearly communicated their image of potential voters as passive, uninterested, and unmotivated. Jeff's view was typical: "The rest of the world is not focused on politics. They are focused on junk TV and MTV and reality TV and what the new movies are, or viral video mash-ups on YouTube."

This is the view that drives a lot of the content of campaign communications that voters and political analysts actually flag as disturbing. If your only way to connect with voters is by "hitting them over the head," your messages will necessarily tend toward simple and emotional rather than analytical. "It has to be catchy, and that can either be shocking or humorous or fact-driven," said Candice, a Republican who worked in fundraising and mail. But making messages surprising or penetrating in some way is what often results in negative ads. Chris told me that to motivate voters you have to "make the sort of choices that people face in politics more relatable," but, he noted, "oftentimes I think that happens by appealing to people's worst instincts, . . . why they should hate something, hate the alternative or hate the other choice." Nick, a Republican who worked in research and web design, told me he could tell if a campaign ad was good according to whether "it pulls at the heart strings" in order to "motivate somebody," or it serves "to shock them so much that they remember your message." Later he equated effective campaign messages with "a sense of urgency," saying of voters, "You want to scare 'em a little bit."

Both Republicans and Democrats talked about voters as not paying much attention and their own need to somehow cut through and connect with them. Republicans were more likely to mention wanting to incite fear or anger with their messaging. This makes sense given the differences in the two parties' bases, as the political scientist Davin Phoenix discusses in his book *The Anger Gap*. Because White anger is viewed differently from Black anger (the former legitimate, the latter destabilizing), Black people and other people of color are less likely to express anger publicly and to be moved to political action through anger. This means Republicans can rely on messaging like "I'm mad as hell" to get their White supporters mobilized; people of color are less likely to be motivated by this kind of rhetoric. Phoenix argues that this asymmetry partly explains the gap in political participation between White people and people of color.[7]

Nonvoters are disproportionately poor or working class, and Black, Latinx, Asian American, or Native American. The prevailing idea among politicos about this group is that they are hopeless targets for campaigns. Barry, who held leading roles in the campaigns of major Republican presidential candidates in 2012 and 2016, summarized: "If they've just not taken the time to vote . . . if they haven't voted in a presidential or a midterm over the course of two of each of those, then it's highly unlikely that there's going to be something that motivates them to vote."

Almost everything I heard about why people don't vote, how you motivate people to vote, was about "regular people" not caring, being occupied with other things. And the things most politicos thought were occupying people, instead of politics, were trivialities and entertainment. Few mentioned distractions from politics such as "paying the bills" or "trying to survive"—even though that's especially likely to be true of politically unengaged people. Matt, the Republican political director, went so far as to say that nonvoters were actually entirely content with their lives, saying, "if they're so disinterested as to not vote, that's because they're fundamentally happy, as opposed to fundamentally not happy. You don't see big spikes in voter turnout unless people are unhappy."

No one else told me that nonvoters are "happy," but aside from a few from the Bernie Sanders campaigns, most politicos were not that interested in increasing turnout. Matt did say something a few others echoed or hinted at, though: "The less people vote, the happier I am, right? 'Cause the smaller the voter pool, the less votes you need, the easier it is to figure out the math." He prefaced this comment by saying, "This is probably something you will never hear again, and please don't quote me, 'cause it could be the end of my career." Tony, who specializes in working for insurgent, nontraditional candidates, said something similar: "People may say, 'Oh, we want more people coming out to vote. Oh we want more people to run for office.' A lot of that stuff is just not true. The more people that come out to vote, the less of a—the less control you have over the outcome of a campaign." In fact, Tony laughed as he said, "If only three people vote and one of the candidates knows for sure that two of them are voting for him or her, that's great!"

Jimmy, a Republican campaign manager, was outright opposed to increasing political participation: "I think it should be tougher to vote, not easier." Not because he wanted to keep Democrats home but because he was "dumbfounded by people a week before the election who are undecided voters. How the hell are you undecided at that point in time?" He didn't think uninformed people should weigh in: "Look, if you don't know, don't vote!" He was incensed by "this MTV crap," that was telling people, "If you don't vote, you don't matter. It's not true. You're not informed, you don't matter. If you vote and you're not informed, you're just an idiot. And so, I'm for less new voters."

Only Jimmy, Matt, Tony, and a few others expressed active hostility to increasing turnout. But even if politicos did think increasing voter turnout would be desirable, almost all of the ones I spoke with were convinced that getting new voters to the polls is nearly impossible, or at least not worth the cost in time and effort and uncertainty. This despite research showing that talking to nonvoters can substantially increase the chances that they vote.[8]

Taken together, the incentives and disincentives of the campaign world, along with the prevailing wisdom, may contribute to skewing the democratic process. Campaigns' tendency to focus on motivating occasional voters while ignoring nonvoters increases inequality in political participation, because people who vote intermittently are richer on average than people who never vote. These better-off occasional voters who campaigns spend their field resources on are then more likely to turn up on Election Day than those potential voters who were not contacted.[9]

In addition, campaigns budget much less of their resources to field efforts, the work of one-on-one contacts with potential voters, than they do to advertising. Every election cycle, vast sums are spent on ads that people mostly don't notice or don't like, and that don't do much to influence how or whether people vote.[10] Campaign ads may be turning more people off of politics. Political scientists Richard Lau, Lee Sigelman, and Ivy Brown Rovner conducted a meta-analysis of research on negative advertising in 2007. They read essentially every study that had been published up to that date, and concluded, "The research literature does not bear out the proposition that negative political campaigns 'work' in shifting votes toward those who wage them."[11] It also doesn't directly reduce turnout, despite some observers' fears; people don't stay home just because of campaign attack ads. But Lau, Sigelman, and Rovner found that campaigns' negativity does make people feel less like their voice matters in politics and lowers their trust in government.

Many politicos I spoke with were somewhat defensive about the need for negative advertising and stretching the truth in campaigns. Kerri, the Democratic operative, was dismissive of politicians who have such concerns: "There are a lot of people who want to run for office, and they are firmly convinced that the problem in America is the way campaigns are run, and that may be true," but if you run a kinder, gentler campaign, "you're not going to win." Kerri is sure of what she's doing; she says she would absolutely not "do these things if it didn't work."

Jeff made a similar point about voters' responses: "Some people, it's like, 'Oh, we hate negative ads.' . . . You see these dial tests" where potential voters are asked to record their reactions by spinning a dial—positive or negative—in real time as they watch ads, and "they always score these negative ads low." Nonetheless, says Jeff, these ads are "effective because you're trying to reinforce some sort of central message that gets that person thinking in a subconscious way. 'Oh, I don't know about them all on spending.' You know? 'I don't know if I can trust this person.'" Jeff concludes, "What people say their reaction is, I completely believe is not what their reaction is."

Many politicos love negative ads, even though they know most other people say they don't. Leon told me, "One underlying characteristic with a lot of political operatives that seems to be pretty consistent [is that] a lot of us generally enjoy negative campaign ads." He doesn't even mind which side it's coming from; he enjoys ads that "our campaign will wage, or that wage back at us" because "we like to fight. I mean, that's the whole point of it, you know." He understood that "people really don't enjoy negative ads," and even that "it can cheapen the political process." But for Leon, and for most politicos, a campaign is a competition between their team and the other guys' team: "At the same time, it is a fight, and if you're being paid to wage a campaign, you can't be the person that seeks to—that's the candidates' job, to stay above it all. The staff is those guys that are willing to fight for the candidate and, you know, do anything to help them win."

This approach to campaigns as a fight between two opposing teams, or armies, is key for making sense of a lot of what campaigns do. The sociologist Matthew Mahler conducted an ethnographic study of a small campaign in which he recounted how campaign staff followed the news of their opposition's "hits" against them. He chronicled how deeply invested, emotionally and almost physically, the campaign team was in the fight.[12] It's hard to get the feeling of having landed a good hit from a report indicating your canvassers are making their targets—even if that's what research indicates is most likely to matter for the election's outcome. But ads are visible to everyone—your own team and your opponents', the media, and millions of viewers. Part of why so many politicos love and believe in negative ads is because they tend to get more media coverage than positive ones, which means they get more feedback about them.[13]

In no small part because they experience campaigns as a battle, many consultants also feel justified in stretching the truth, while most still insist that they have strong moral standards and would never, as Kerri put it "completely bald-face-lie about somebody." She told me emphatically, "I won't do that. But that does work." Curtis, a Republican direct-mail and general consultant, said, "Almost everyone takes liberties in a campaign in terms of how they spin the facts out there, but I do get resentful sometimes of people saying, 'All this stuff is lies, you're just lying.'" He continued: "I think I'm very edgy and can be very tough with campaign stuff, but I also am very serious about being fair in that—maybe fair is the wrong word—I'm very fact based. The person receiving it, who's the target of the hit, may say that was really unfair," but staying within the facts "to me, that's a big thing." Curtis, like so many others, believes that "you have to be combative in campaigns" but he also believes that "what you say has to be true. If it's not, the negative will fall apart."

Not everyone even agrees on this; Democratic strategist Rick Ridder's book of campaign rules includes rule number 4: "Personal integrity is not necessarily a qualification for office." He tells a story of a candidate who always told the truth no matter what reporters asked her, including saying she hated "Southern accents" when she was running for office in the South. He insists in his advice to campaign professionals: "Lying is good. Lying is fine. Lying is strategic."[14]

There is little evidence that attack ads and tear-jerkers and sticky, overly simplified messages have much impact on election outcomes at all, but politicos believe in them and enjoy them—even though they clearly fall short of both voters' and scholars' aspirations for what democracy could and should be.

Campaign professionals insisted they knew good campaign messages and materials when they saw them. They also tended to believe that they themselves produce good ads, speeches, polls, strategy, and advice (though some admitted to giving some campaigns their B or C product rather than their A product), but that some other politicos mostly put out low-quality campaign products. The common refrain I heard about bad products or bad decisions (including some that my interviewees had themselves participated in) was that "risk-averse" strategies lead to "cookie-cutter" outputs.

Adrian, a Democrat who works in data and targeting, explained how the "power of conventional wisdom" incentivizes reusing campaign content and strategies and disincentivizes innovation—at least, marked innovation: "The way the incentives end up working," he said, "is that in that small world of people going back and forth between party committees and consulting firms, there's basically less risk in losing using the conventional strategy that everybody would have used than trying something that actually might work to win. Yeah. Like, if you win that way, I suppose you're probably fine, but if you lose that way, . . . there's some danger of being sort of kicked out of the circle."

Tony, the insurgent-candidate specialist, put it this way: "You know, nobody wants to be the consultant that went out and did something crazy and lost the election." But, he noted, "it's not likely that the election was lost just because of that one thing, but they don't want to be the—the competitors can then say to potential candidates, 'Well, those are the people that did this.'"

Even though they know that win-loss records are a poor measure of anyone's actual skills or campaign contributions, politicos also know that the outcome of their last race or their cumulative win-loss record can nonetheless affect their chances of landing their next jobs. So they worry that if they do something unusual and therefore memorable (to other politicos) and lose, they will receive disproportionate blame for that loss. If, instead, you do what is considered standard and your campaign loses, it is less likely that the blame will fall to you individually.

Jerry had been a Democratic operative for many years when I met him but was moving out of political work to focus more on consulting for businesses. A New Yorker through and through, he described campaign operatives' risk aversion more colorfully: "There's a pervasive cover-your-ass mentality in politics, as well as government. And it's incredibly limiting." He recalled discussing the use of a new tactic in one campaign but seeing it ultimately quashed: "It was risky. Right? They looked at all the things that could go wrong, right? And there was no sure payoff, right? So in the strategic calculus that is rife in most campaigns, it was sort of like, 'Well, all these things could go wrong, so therefore we shouldn't do it.' And without necessarily fairly calculating what's the cost of inaction. Right? And so, you know, the default, unfortunately, is inertia." He told me campaigns "seem so cookie-cutter" because "it's the same people over and over again using the same methods and techniques."

James, a Democrat who worked for a polling firm, also suggested that other campaign professionals could get so busy "covering their asses" that they refused to stick their necks out: "My sense is that, from the campaign perspective, there are sort of just standard things that they want to do to cover themselves. From the beginning they're told, 'Okay, this is how things are done.' You don't want to take a chance on not doing what everyone does."

The power of conventional wisdom to make campaigns repetitious and conservative was a recurring theme. Sam, a long-serving White Democratic operative, said there are many "people who just say something because, you know, that's the way we always do things. Your 'I know and don't question it.'" Sarah, a Democrat, told me, "A lot of times I just tended to fight with certain people who say, 'This is the way it works in all these cases,' and they're very cookie-cutter." Alison, a Republican, explained, "Campaigns have a hard time being too creative, 'cause they think it's, like, 'We don't want to go that far out of the box.'" Jennifer, a Democrat, said, "When you've been doing this for as long as I have, and you're inside the Beltway, you tend to sort of, just—it's all groupthink." Candice, a Republican, said, "When do you ever see something *really* outside the box and different, right? If you took a political mailer and just dropped in an old White guy, it's the same thing. And that same campaign is running in 435 congressional districts across the country."

A few people offered some justification for the persistence of conventional wisdom. Susan, another Democrat with a lot of experience running field operations, decried the "new people coming on the scene, throwing tons of money at a race with new style, who totally bomb." She said, "With the old way of—not the 'old way,' but the traditional model of organizing, I tend to believe that if it isn't broken, don't fix it." Sophia explained that the "consulting business model, it works because it's repetitive, right? Like, because you can take the same model and apply it to all these different campaigns." She was disappointed that "it's not really as creative as I expected it to be." To show that she wasn't the only one who feels this way, she told me about a pollster who was the principal of a well-respected firm who is "just very successful, but the job's boring" because "the campaigns, they're just—I don't know, there's not that much variation, and that's how all these businesses work. Like, McKinsey, whatever—like, any consulting firm, you want to replicate your product elsewhere and just tweak it. But that makes for something that's not really that stimulating."

Nearly half of my interviewees mentioned "cookie-cutter" campaigning, either using the phrase itself or discussing, usually disparagingly, the practice of political consultants and campaign managers recycling the same strategies, slogans, and images, across many campaigns in different locations or different cycles. Regardless of their normative evaluations of repetition and conservatism in campaign strategies, my interviewees made it clear that campaign outputs and campaign professionals are judged primarily against the status quo. This only allows for small, incremental changes in campaign practice over time.

Jimmy picked up on this, discussing his work for one of Trump's strongest competitors in the 2016 primary. He told me that his primary campaign kept focusing on their candidate's experience, even when "clearly the problem we had is too much experience, not that it wasn't enough." He pointed out that the top finishers in 2016 were ranked in inverse order of political experience: Trump came out on top with no experience at all. I asked why people might have made that strategic error, instead of emphasizing something else during the campaign. He said, "I think everybody with any common sense knew that that was right. But it's easy to get into this groupthink, plus you had a candidate that they just wanted to please, right? He really believed that you need an adult." Jimmy tended to agree with his candidate—he clearly despised Trump, though he would not say so publicly for fear of losing political opportunities in Republican politics. But "it isn't what voters care about. Voters think that you should burn this town [Washington, DC] down. And don't take my word for it, look who the fuck they voted for."

Jerry discussed Democrats' messaging, finding it equally disconnected: "Democrats constantly recycle the language, 'I'm gonna fight for you.' And it's horribly clichéd and hackneyed and most of all ineffective." When voters have "heard ten people say the same exact thing," it will just make them think you "don't have an original idea in your head and you have no grasp of what's happening in the country right now and what we need to do about it." Moreover, this kind of messaging is "cheap and easy and cynical and I think a lot of voters—not all—but a lot of voters pick up on that. And those, to me, are the voters that decide elections."

It's not that campaign professionals mindlessly apply the same formulas to every campaign they work on; especially in big or close races, they look at the best polling data they can, they work out their candidates' and opponents' strengths and weaknesses and try to figure out how best to frame those, and they try their best to communicate a compelling message to potential voters. They do all that with limited knowledge of how those potential voters, most of them far outside their own social and professional world, will react to their efforts. Instead, they work with extensive knowledge of and peer feedback from politicos who share their world and worldview, and what they believe they know about which kinds of efforts they think will be most effective.

The pull of inertia, tied to the professional norms of the campaign field, makes campaigns slow to adapt new techniques, even when there is evidence that they are highly effective. When it's hard to know for sure what effects campaigns' efforts have on outcomes, and continued success in the field depends on being thought of as "having good instincts" by others, there's real danger in trying to introduce something new. For example, one of the key tenets of received wisdom about campaign strategy is that there is no point in trying to sway "unlikely" voters to show up at the polls. At the same time, there is strong evidence that even a single direct contact can dramatically increase the turnout of these voters.[15]

The Victory Lab: The Secret Science of Winning Campaigns, Sasha Issenberg's account of the increasing use of experimental methods in campaigns, tells the story of some campaigners' reluctance to adopt new strategies or use experimental methods to understand the effectiveness of campaign strategies.[16] It follows the proponents of data-driven campaigning from both academia and campaigns as they carry out their research and hails the increasing use of these methods as shepherding in a new era of campaign effectiveness.

But there is reason to be somewhat skeptical of this account: journalists' campaign retrospectives have a habit of creating dramatic tension from even mild conflicts between the old guard and upstart new guard, and campaign operatives who speak to journalists have a deep interest in coming off as cutting-edge strategists in order to impress their next clients and colleagues. The changes they make are rarely as radical as the iconoclasm they describe to reporters, often because any new technique they advocate has to be "legible," or recognizable, to the cohort of operatives ahead of them and around them, who judge their merit as the next campaign staffs up.

Sociologists have shown that in the art world, the avant-garde of a given moment tends to have a particular relationship to the previous generation's avant-garde, straying far enough to gain attention but not so far as to become entirely inexplicable to the dominant group.[17] It is no different in campaigns. *The Victory Lab* is cast as a battle between "geeks" and "gurus," between conventional-wisdom-bound older campaigners and a new generation of data-driven analysts. But this is nearly identical to the story told in *The Election Men* by David Rosenbloom, written nearly forty years earlier, about the new "professional campaign managers" who saw themselves as skilled professionals, bringing "scientific, or at least objective, views into an arena long dominated by myth and incompetence."[18] It is true that campaigns continually make increasing use of data and analysis; less clear is whether these methods provide a "secret science of winning campaigns," as the book's subtitle promises.

Issenberg recounts some politicos' excitement about studies done by two political scientists, Alan Gerber and Donald Green, showing how much personal contact with voters could increase turnout. He seems to imagine campaigns radically shifting their resources toward these methods that have been identified as so effective, away from the campaign ads whose effects fade nearly immediately. Instead, with the partial exception of the Obama campaigns (before and just after Issenberg was writing), the portion of spending on field compared with media and advertising has hardly shifted at all. The political scientists David Broockman and Josh Kalla reported that only 5 percent of campaign budgets go to field in a 2014 blog post headlined "Experiments Show This Is the Best Way to Win Campaigns. But Is Anyone Actually Doing It?"[19] The "best way to win" was focusing on voter contact instead of advertising. Is anyone actually doing it? The answer was, and remains, no.

Microtargeting, also called predictive analytics, is the practice of using models to predict which voters to target for persuasion or turnout; it was the hot new trend in campaigns in the early 2000s and is now standard practice. Jason, an early advocate of the technique, explained how hard it was to get it into the standard arsenal: "We ran into a lot of resistance when we first brought the product to market, because everybody says they want to be innovative until they're actually faced with innovation. Fortunately, I think the RNC had their minds fairly open about this," but they had campaigns test it for a few years in a few races before it became widely accepted. When 2004 came around, "thankfully people like Karl Rove and Ken Mehlman and Matt Dowd were extraordinarily complimentary about our product. They credited microtargeting, actually, with the victory—which is great for us. [But] there are still doubters. I think there are people who are used to doing it in a certain way; they find it hard to believe that we can predict without talking to people [about] how they'll vote. And they don't quite understand the idea behind it. Of course, with predictive analytics, you're inevitably going to have false positives and false negatives, and, you know, people love nothing more than pointing out those false negatives and false positives. There are some people who simply prefer to talk to a smaller, purer list of people who are hard IDs, rather than talking to people that there's some uncertainty about." Two of the political scientists profiled in *The Victory Lab* as proponents of innovation, Alan Gerber and and Donald Green, according to Jason. He told me that Gerber and Green "don't seem to think this works very well. You know, [they] bring up a few good points, [but] I think they have the luxury of being in academia, and not being actually out in the field."

· · ·

So is "disruption," even just real change, possible? What are the circumstances that lower the bar for adopting a new strategy? An unexpected
loss can make new approaches a better bet, and the "mutually assured
destruction" principle that operatives described in other chapters means
campaigns will be far more likely to try something new if their opponent
is already trying it; this neutralizes some of the risk, but ultimately makes
campaigns uniform in new ways.

Daniel Kreiss, a communications scholar, explains how and why
change happens in campaigns in his book *Prototype Politics*.[20] Each party is
most open to new ideas when they have just lost an election they expected
to win. Kreiss tells the story of the adaptation of online mobilization tools
by the Democrats in Obama's 2008 campaign and concludes that just
because something is effective doesn't mean campaigns will necessarily
adopt it. Even if it is used successfully outside politics, campaign professionals don't necessarily bring it in to their arsenal, and rarely if ever do
so quickly.

But if one side adopts something, it's likely the other side will do so
too, writes Kreiss. So change also happens in one party if the other party
has started using a technique that is getting credit for helping them win.
Will, a Democratic pollster, concurred: "I think that what happens is
there's kind of a leapfrog effect. You know, in 2004, Bush's reelect, they
clearly did a better job, it was the first time Republicans had done it,
where they did a better job on field and touching their people on the
ground, right? And in 2008, the Obama campaign kind of revolution-
ized the grassroots side of it. And so this is kind of what happens a lot of
times"—the two sides essentially copy each other.[21]

Whether or not it is good for a campaign's success, many politicos believe that following conventional campaign wisdom, at least up to a point,
is essential for their career success. A substantial minority of my respondents were concerned about the ways that the campaign world evaluates
politicos and political output. Jerry really brought it home. Hiring based
on reputations and networks "breeds institutionalized mentalities and per-
petuates sort of like this formulaic thinking, which I think is one of the
death knells and why people hate politics, is again, it's this recycling of the
same bullshit rhetoric on both sides and it's incredibly stifling to anything

that's creative or innovative." Like so many others I spoke with, he told me, "There's a premium on being safe and conventional in national politics," which he thinks is not only ineffective but "leads to, you know, running really mediocre campaigns." He also thinks "it's bad for the larger democratic system," which is at least as important for Jerry, and for the rest of us.

Because politicos are judged by their peers' perceptions of their campaign skills, they are reluctant to innovate too much, even when they think it might significantly improve their candidate's chances. We see similar campaign ads and themes year after year, such as candidates walking with men in construction gear and saying they will "fight for working families" or pictured with their own family in a living room saying they "share your values." There are also broad similarities in campaign strategies, such as who is and is not considered worth the effort to try to influence. For instance, campaigns almost always focus their GOTV efforts on occasional voters while ignoring those who have never voted.

Campaign professionals absolutely want to win campaigns whenever, and however, they can. But they also want to be seen as smart, reasonable, politicos with a keen "gut sense" of how to do politics. Consequently, consciously or unconsciously, they mostly stick to what those around them consider "tried and true" strategies. Moreover, the most reliable feedback they can get during a campaign is not about how they're affecting their odds of winning but about how other politicos in their own campaign see their work, how the opposing campaigns reacts, and how the press covers it.

A number of commentators, including Adam Sheingate in his incisive book on the history of political consulting, *Building a Business of Politics*, have hypothesized that financial incentives keep campaigns from making the choices political science says they ought to.[22] I think it is simultaneously much more complicated and much simpler than that. More complicated because, although ad consultants in particular stand to gain from continued high spending on ads, they certainly are not the only decision-makers when it comes to campaign spending. Most of the rest of the people involved with a campaign don't earn more or less depending on how much money is spent on ads and how many are run, but all of them want their campaigns to win and most believe that ads are effective.

Simpler because, if campaign professionals see themselves as being in a fight, they want to experience the fight and have the other side experience it too. No one except the people whose doors are being knocked on will be included in that aspect of the fight. Some substantial part of the ongoing investment in television and online ads and sophisticated analytics and so on, and the relative underinvestment in field and other proven forms of voter contact, is about adhering to conventional wisdom in order to stay "in the circle," and about visibly and experientially being in the fight. But as Jason pointed out, it's also about "mutually assured destruction"—if one side is doing it, the other can't stop entirely.

We might like to believe that political professionals working for candidates and parties we support are using all the research and evidence available to them, but in fact much of what campaign professionals believe about how to run campaigns effectively is essentially folklore handed down from one campaign to the next. They know about, and sometimes conduct, experiments on the relative efficacy of various messages or tactics, and they use data on voters to shape their messages and outreach strategies. But at the end of the day, most decisions—ranging from what the campaign theme should be ("Stronger Together" or "Build Back Better" or "Make America Great Again") to how much to spend on various kinds of outreach (television, the internet, mail, or in-person communication) to whether and where to hold rallies—reflect politicos' best guess or gut sense of what will get them the win. That gut sense, those guesses, are formed through working in campaigns with other campaign professionals; in other words, campaigners learn the conventional wisdom of campaigning and adhere to it, both because of the incentives in their work world and because there is no perfect science for winning campaigns.

Campaign decision-makers create political content not primarily by calculating its effect on vote share or on their pay but by drawing on acquired, practical knowledge, a "political practical sense" about what makes for good campaign material. They, like political scientists, are deeply uncertain about whether, when, and how much any particular campaign strategy will matter.

This is an odd situation: On the one hand, elections almost always end with an unambiguous result—a win for one side and a loss for the other—which journalists and pundits inevitably ascribe to the acuity or lapses of the opposing campaigns. On the other hand, a nearly infinite array of forces can affect citizens' ultimate decisions about whether and for whom to vote; and many of these, from the weather and the economy through candidates' flubs, are entirely outside the power of campaign operatives to influence.

There are many possible solutions to this problem of matching uncertain means to usually overdetermined ends, but within the field of electoral production the primary strategy is reliance on a campaign's internal conventional wisdom or institutional knowledge. Campaign professionals generally believe that good campaign strategy is a combination of natural political instinct and on-the-job learning; they eschew scholarly work on campaigns and generally place little faith even in schools dedicated to the art and science of campaign management. Because of the short-lived nature of campaign organizations and the lack of objective criteria for evaluating particular tactics or messages, political operatives get work primarily through their relationships and reputations with one another and with candidates. Thus the most important audience for a campaign's output may be other politicos rather than voters. Unconventional strategies are generally frowned upon, and those who deploy unconventional approaches risk being seen by their peers as having poor instincts or just not "getting it." While a win to which unorthodox means may have contributed might help a campaign professional's career prospects, a loss using the same tactics would be quite likely to damage their reputation. These factors combine to encourage what many of my respondents called "cookie-cutter" campaigning: the stifling of innovative approaches in favor of the reproduction of the kinds of tactics that drive both voters and scholars to despair about the democratic process.

My interviewees often described politics as a sort of hobby, or a game, in which they're the professional athletes, some people are fans, and some people just aren't part of the picture. Many potential voters are ignored, while others feel hounded or harassed. Politicos try their best to understand what will get people out to vote for their candidates, but they have trouble moving beyond the limited insights provided by polls, databases, and the received wisdom of the campaign practitioners who came before them and generally look just like them. This means they end up doing things that perpetuate cynicism about politics and inequality in who participates.

CHAPTER 6

DEMOCRATIC IMPACTS

The political scientist and sociologist Theda Skocpol begins her book *Diminished Democracy: From Membership to Management in American Civic Life* with an account of the gravestone of a fairly unremarkable man, Warren Durgin, who was born in 1839 and lived until 1929.[1] Skocpol was struck by the number of civic association memberships Durgin or his family found important enough to engrave on his tombstone, alongside his role in Abraham Lincoln's funeral and the names of some of his family members. Skocpol points out that in Durgin's time, it was not at all unusual for White men to be part of voluntary organizations like the Grange, the Independent Order of Odd Fellows, and the Grand Army of the Republic. These associations spanned class boundaries while maintaining racial and gender ones. Durgin was a "backwoods farmer, lumberman, and spoolmaker," but he was also a member of groups that included Maine's US senators and representatives and "elites in and out of government all over the United States."[2] By the late twentieth century, though, this "civil society once centered in nationally active and locally vibrant voluntary membership federations" had all but disappeared. Instead, "professionally run advocacy groups and nonprofit institutions now dominate civil society, as people seek influence through a very new mix of largely memberless voluntary organizations."[3]

The shift Skocpol traces in her book is part of a larger shift in the organization of US society overall, and in politics specifically, since the middle of the twentieth century. The political scientist Robert Putnam outlines the decline in people's participation in organized social clubs and

activities in *Bowling Alone*, in which he argues that our decreasing con-
nectedness spells trouble for our democracy.[4] Political parties have also
suffered a decrease in the depth and breadth of their organizational infrastructure and power over the last century; the way campaigns are run is
inseparable from that story.

For as long as there have been democratic elections or even leaders
who depend in some way on being seen as legitimate by their citizenry,
there have been "campaigns" to convince people to support one leader
over another, and political advisors who make it their business to help
those leaders make their case and win or hold on to power. For our pur-
poses, what is interesting and important is how campaigning has worked
in the United States and why we have the kinds of campaigns we do.

We can trace much of contemporary campaigning to the end of the
era of "machine politics" in US politics, roughly from the nineteenth
century to the early part of the twentieth. During that time, many big
cities were controlled by political machines that tied government benefits
to support for the local party boss. If you've seen the show *Boardwalk
Empire* and the movie *Mr. Smith Goes to Washington*, you have some idea
of how this system worked. Political machines, such as Tammany Hall
in New York City, ran on deep connections with particular communities, usually specific groups of relatively recent immigrants doing mostly
working-class jobs, such as Irish or Italians. The party bosses controlled
access to political power, city contracts, and civil service jobs; those who
voted for them got to enjoy these benefits. There were myriad problems
with this system, most notably all kinds of corruption and little political
voice for those outside it, but it's worth noting some of the possibly positive aspects as well.

Political machines were the opposite of memberless organizations.
Instead, like the early civic organizations Skocpol describes, they were
based on a hierarchical organizational structure that connected individual
residents of the city to the city's leaders. The exact details varied from city
to city and across time, but in neighborhoods and ethnic groups that were
part of the machine, there could be a representative of city leadership
assigned to every block, every church, every workplace. The work of political staff in that era entailed corralling votes for their party *and* knowing
a particular set of people or small community. Information flowed in both
directions, from communities inward to the political establishment and

outward from the political establishments and the halls of power to communities; ordinary people were in many ways meaningfully members of the party whose machine ran their city.[5]

Progressive Era reformers opposed these machines; their explicit concerns had to do with the exclusion, trading of favors, and lack of transparency that came with machine politics, but they were also opposed to the concentration of power in the hands of immigrants from Ireland and from Eastern and Southern Europe; political scientist Seth Masket concludes that "it is difficult in this time period to distinguish the desire for 'clean' government from common bigotry."[6] Progressives of the time were successful in instituting a number of changes to our electoral system in an attempt to make it more transparent and more accessible to people outside the machines' circles of influence. These reforms paved the way for many of the aspects of politics we take for granted today, from the secret ballot to primary elections. And, as the sociologist Andrew Perrin points out, they also made voting and our democracy less about community and connection and more about isolated individual preferences. Perrin writes that although the "Progressive reforms certainly made American democracy fairer," they also "made political participation less exciting—no more party carnivals and social events—and much more confusing." Moreover, by "insisting that each campaign be run separately instead of as a party operation, the reforms also increased the cost of campaigning." Perrin argues that "two of the thorniest issues of our current democracy—voter turnout and campaign finance—have their origins in the reforms Progressives championed to bring about fairness in the electoral system."[7]

Another shift happened, somewhat later, in how candidates were chosen. It used to be, as is still the case in most democracies, that political parties chose the candidates who would represent them in the general election through a process open only to active party members. This ensured that the candidate on the ticket aligned with the values of the party they were elected to represent but had the disadvantage that those not involved with the party organization had no say in choosing the candidates. This system would have prevented Donald Trump, who was strongly disliked by most party insiders, from being president, and would also have made it impossible—instead of just difficult—for a party outsider like Bernie Sanders to win the Democratic nomination.

Whatever you think of those outcomes, the Progressive Era reforms along with other changes substantially weakened parties' control of politics. By the 1970s, parties were no longer the employers of most professional political staff and were no longer in charge of most aspects of most campaigns.[8] As the political scientists Daniel Schlozman and Sam Rosenfeld put it, "Today's parties are hollow parties, neither organizationally robust beyond their role [of] raising money nor meaningfully felt as a real, tangible presence in the lives of voters or in the work of engaged activists."[9] Instead, the work that used to be handled by party hierarchies is carried out by journeyman campaign staff and political consultants, working directly for the candidates and the campaign organizations formed to elect them.

The shift in the organization of campaigns opened the way for an increasing business of politics. Since the middle of the twentieth century, the number of people making their living as political consultants has exploded. Clem Whitaker and Leone Baxter, who founded the firm Campaigns, Inc. after World War II, are widely believed to have been the first political consultants to make their living by providing services exclusively to political clients or causes; their accomplishments included defeating proposals for universal health care.[10] There were few other full-time political consultants until sometime in the 1960s, when advertising firms mostly ceased offering their services to political candidates. By the 1980s, observers were decrying the fall of parties and the increasing role of the consultants, which they saw as both the cause and consequence of that decline. Consultants were often criticized for manipulating voters using sophisticated new techniques, and for being more interested in making money than in the values or success of the parties they worked alongside.[11]

In reality, parties did not lose power primarily because of consultants. Most consultants are just as dedicated to their party's ideology as those who work directly for parties themselves, and they are at least as committed to their side winning elections and holding power.[12] What has changed is that many of the two-way channels for communication between elites and regular people—from machine politics to organizations like the Grange to formal bowling leagues—are gone. Perrin argues that "democracy is best understood as the back-and-forth interactions among citizens and institutions of government."[13] One of those institutions is the modern campaign, but it no longer fosters that kind of back-and-forth.

Or, as Adam Sheingate puts it in *Building a Business of Politics*, the work of campaigning to win votes has shifted "away from the party agent who mobilized armies of partisans at the local level and toward the political consultant who crafts images and messages."[14] Over the second half of the twentieth century, political campaigns increasingly came to resemble mass consumer marketing campaigns. This parallels what happened in the memberless advocacy groups Skocpol studied: These changes came about in large part because elites figured out that they could affect the changes they wanted—or at least make a good stab at lobbying politicians to get those changes—without a mass base of the type that had previously been necessary. If they could use professionals, funded by grants and donors, to produce reports or get people to sign petitions, they didn't need to spend the time going from town to town to drum up support in person. Mass media, direct mail, and, now, email, social media, and other techniques require money, but not necessarily relationships. So if you can find a source of funds, whether that's a rich benefactor or "grassroots" fundraising, you only need a one-way connection with your members: you can send messages *to* people even if you're not hearing *from* them beyond donations or petition-signing.

This is a consequential change in how politics is done in the US, one that shapes campaigns and that campaigns in turn perpetuate. Parties are now best thought of not as unitary hierarchical organizations but as networks of different organizations and individuals that include political consultants, political action committees (PACs), think tanks, and campaign staff.[15]

· · ·

That network is hard to miss when I look at my data on the careers of campaign professionals. Over 40 percent of Democratic and close to half of Republican operatives who had worked on at least one race in 2010 or earlier had spent at least some time working with one or more organizations that make up what political scientists call the "extended party network" or "expanded party."[16] These include party organizations, PACs (which raise and give limited amounts of money to candidates, parties, and other PACs) and super PACs (which can raise and spend unlimited amounts of money to elect their preferred candidates, as long as they don't coordinate with the campaign itself), and partisan-aligned organizations like think tanks and advocacy organizations.[17] Republicans were much more likely to have worked for one of their party organizations than their Democratic counterparts, though substantial portions of politicos from both parties had passed through them. About 35 percent of Republicans have worked for state or national party organizations like the Republican National Committee or the National Republican Senatorial Committee at some point, compared with only 24 percent of Democrats in the Democratic National Committee or similar.[18] This is likely a reflection of differences in organization and culture of the two parties, with the Republicans tending to be more hierarchical and centralized.[19]

The reverse is true for advocacy or partisan organizations outside the formal party organizations: more Democrats (24 percent) have worked for these groups than Republicans (16 percent). In total, about one out of five long-running politicos in my database had worked for unions, partisan groups, think tanks, or advocacy organizations by 2020. Groups Democrats had worked for included Emily's List, the ACLU, and the SEIU (Services Employees International Union). On the Republican side, politicos had worked in organizations such as the Heritage Foundation and Citizens United, the latter the lead plaintiff in the (in)famous US Supreme Court case.

The politicos I trace tend to have had high-level jobs in political organizations outside campaigns, moving, for example, from being the northeast regional director for American Majority to being the senior advisor for corporate relations at the Heritage Foundation, or working as the campaign director for America Votes and then as the political director for the Sierra Club.

Young people who hope to move into politics often find themselves at a dead-end at the bottom of these organizational hierarchies, at least on the Democratic-aligned side of politics. In her book *Activism Inc.*, the sociologist Dana Fisher documents how the professional "grassroots fundraising" firms promise idealistic young college graduates a chance to make a difference on issues dear to Democrats, like protecting the environment and LGBTQ rights.[20] Instead, they send these young people on grueling canvassing operations in unfamiliar neighborhoods to knock on people's doors and try to get them to give money and to sign up for a "membership" in the kind of advocacy organizations Skocpol described, which still mostly means sending money. Organizations such as the Human Rights Campaign and the Sierra Club pay for these canvasses, which generate enough on-paper memberships and one-time and ongoing donations to pay off financially. But these kinds of sign-ups don't foster any meaningful participation from newly enrolled members. Worse, most of the young people brought into these grassroots fundraising operations give up on organized political activism after a short time, as they don't see that they're making a difference in any direct way and are doing often miserable and low-paid work.

That makes one similarity to entry-level canvas jobs in campaigns, but with even less chance to advance and no excitement of an impending election and a win or loss. Fisher points out that "motivated young people on the left" have fewer opportunities to participate in politics than those on the right, that Republican-aligned organizations have better on-ramps to careers in politics and activism than their Democratic counterparts.[21]

In both parties, though, politicos who succeed in entering political work—whether through campaigns or partisan groups—can see their career paths expand outward and upward. Many politicos move from primarily managing politicians' and parties' quest for power to wielding it themselves, often through working in government. Some politicos run for office and even win—Terry McAuliffe was a Bill Clinton aide and DNC (Democratic National Committee) chair long before he ran for governor of Virginia—but many more follow the candidates they helped elect, working as advisors and staff and in positions in government agencies at the local, state, and federal level. Jen Psaki was candidate Joe Biden's communications director in the 2020 campaign; in 2021, she became President Biden's press secretary. Karl Rove was a key advisor to George W. Bush during both his campaigns and his presidency, serving the administration as deputy chief of staff and in a number of other White House positions.

In the months following my work on Barack Obama's 2008 campaign, I received a number of calls asking whether I wanted to be considered for federal government jobs in the new Obama administration. The callers weren't interested in me because of my previous experience in a nonprofit or my recently earned master's in sociology from Berkeley or my future PhD. In fact, I didn't get the sense they were interested in me, personally, at all—they were working their way down a list. But I was on that list because I'd worked on the campaign. People above me had passed my name along, and I was offered opportunities I wouldn't have otherwise had. (I never took them up on it or I probably wouldn't be writing this book, though it was certainly appealing to be offered the chance to continue to be part of the Obama team.)

I wasn't by any means the only person offered such an opportunity— many Obama campaign staff were offered the chance to apply for jobs in his administration. My boss in the Oakland Obama office took a job in the Labor Department and moved with her family from California to DC. After the election, one person I interviewed was appointed to a job in the US Department of Energy, and another had taken a post as a senior policy advisor in the White House. Over half of the Obama 2008 staffers and consultants in my campaign-careers database held White House or other administration jobs in 2010: the lower-level, lesser-known ones held positions such as senior advisor to the Office of the United States Trade Representative, communications director for the White House's Domestic Policy Council, and assistant director for the Office of Intergovernmental Affairs. Almost certainly there were more Obama campaign staffers who ended up working for his administration, but if they had ground-level positions like mine they may not have been included in my campaign-careers database.[22] This is not the only path, of course, to a presidential appointment or a government hire, but it's a common one, for those in both parties.

The approaches that people in the politics industry take to campaigning have an enormous influence on our democracy while they are working in campaigns, and that alone warrants making an effort to understand them and their approach to voters. But campaign professionals don't only work in campaigns and other political or government organizations. Former campaign professionals, including ones whose names don't make the press, suffuse government and other power structures at every level. Many go on to work in powerful positions in the nonprofit and foundations worlds, the corporate world, in finance and tech, and in lobbying and communications firms. This is a part of the political mechanism in the US that I wasn't really aware of until I started getting those calls from Obama administration staff.

Of the people in my database who had at least one campaign job before 2010, a little under half (45 percent of Republicans and 47 percent of Democrats) had held a position in government by 2020. Many of them, like Jen Psaki and Karl Rove, wielded substantial influence in the White House and federal agencies; a few, like Terry McAuliffe and Rahm Emanuel, went on to hold office themselves. Most worked directly for elected officials: in the Senate and House and in governors' and mayors' offices as spokespeople and chiefs of staff and directors of outreach.

As both candidates and holders of elected office, politicians are surrounded by these kinds of staff members guiding and supporting their work. The ultimate responsibility for any political decision rests with the officeholder, but most of what goes into making those decisions passes through political staff. People in these kinds of positions facilitate and mediate everything that our representatives do in office, from meeting with lobbyists, advocacy groups, and individual constituents to communicating with voters and researching policy positions. They tell politicians what polls and databases say about their constituents, advise them on how to present their initiatives to the press and the public, gather information about key players' positions on important issues, and more. If you send a letter or email to your congressperson in the House of Representatives, a member of their staff will decide whether your representative sees it or, more likely, will simply add it to a tally of constituents' positions on issues. If you hold a protest outside their office, their staff will advise them on how best to respond. Political operatives, then, are key intermediaries between people and politics, not only during campaigns but also in the halls of power. Half of Trump's ten initial appointees to the White House staff and half of Biden's initial fourteen had served on their respective campaigns.

Because so many of these people worked in campaigns, the same kinds of logic that dominate in campaigns will inform big swathes of government and our broader politics. Political operatives who speak the language of politics, who treat voters as terrain to be won more than people to be heard, and who have made their careers by fitting in and impressing other politicos take the approaches that have worked for them in campaigns into other positions of power.

Politicos also inform politics from outside government. Whatever kind of organization they are working for, former and current campaign operatives are all over the media during campaigns, giving their expert or insider analyses as pundits on cable and network news, in Substack newsletters, and as guest columnists in the *New York Times*, *Wall Street Journal*, and other news outlets.

Meanwhile, very few sociologists and other academics are regularly quoted in major newspapers, despite their high level of expertise (Tressie McMillan Cottom and Zeynep Tufekci are two laudable exceptions—both now have regular opinion pieces in the *New York Times*). The same is true for political scientists, with a few exceptions—the crew at the *Washington Post*'s excellent *Monkey Cage* blog is one. You might think that having spent a decade or more analyzing politics would qualify more of us to help the media and audiences make sense of political happenings, but it is fairly rare that television news shows and other major media ask an academic to opine on voters, politics, or policy.

Much more often they ask campaign professionals to comment. For example, of CNN's political contributors in the summer of 2020, sixteen of the thirty-four guests had worked on a campaign in some form; only two were scholars. Most people who have worked in politics a while accrue a long list of media appearances and often profiles and other write-ups. Another example: eight out of twenty politicos I randomly selected from the top ranks of the 2016 campaigns had been a guest on at least one major news program by 2020. The omnipresence of campaign professionals as commentators, pundits, interviewees, guests and even hosts in media coverage of politics means that the campaign-centered view of politics colors the national conversation.

Major media outlets tend to cover debates—even those about the content of substantive bills—with a focus on the fight, the players and the personalities, and the tactics more than on the actual issues and stakes. They are much more likely to talk about how a policy proposal will be received than about how it will affect people—politics as a fight, politics as a contest, voters as the prize. The goal is often to score a point against the other side—sometimes in the guise of analysis, sometimes as straight-up campaigning—thus motivating "your" base and demobilizing the other side's. This "game frame" approach to covering politics, used by journalists and campaigners in discussions of both campaigns and legislation, has been shown to lead to higher levels of cynicism about politics and to reinforce the perception that politics is a game played by elites with regular people as the prize.[23]

As much as campaign professionals love their work, only a few work solely in campaigns; campaign work is not a lifestyle that's sustainable for most people, especially as staff. Jimmy told me over lunch in spring of 2017 that he was "not doing campaigns anymore. I'm done with it; it just takes too much out of you. Twenty years, every single election cycle, I've been involved in a campaign. It's just exhausting." Sophia told me, "I haven't figured out my next steps yet. I just need some more balance. I can't see myself following the pace of my boss. He travels way too much. There's months that he's on the road, four days, five days a week. And I just can't live with that lack of boundaries." So nearly 85 percent of the 1,723 people who worked in a national-level campaign in 2008 or earlier (and whose trajectories I could trace) have held at least one position in a noncampaign organization. Many campaign staff move into political consulting, and many political consultants branch out into advising corporations as well as campaigns. Former and intermittent campaign staff work for all kinds of powerful organizations beyond the party network: Fortune 500 corporations, wealthy foundations, lobbying firms, and PR consultancies.

One lucrative destination for politicos is to offer their expert political advice as public affairs consultants, lobbyists, or experts in "strategic communication." About 30 percent of politicos with over a decade in politics had worked in one or another of these types of consulting firms at some point, and the rates of Democrats and Republicans with consultancy experience are essentially identical. Some of these are doing exactly what was described in the preceding chapters of this book: working for US politicians' campaigns as pollsters, media producers, and data providers. Others work in firms that also provide their services to politicians internationally, or help major corporations achieve their goals, whether tax breaks or regulatory policy or in public perception of their brand.

When they work as consultants, their relationships with other consultants become even more important for getting and keeping clients. Derek described making hiring decisions for his firm on the basis of the connections someone could bring with them: "that field director may know candidate X, who's running for Congress, and have a very good relationship with him, and maybe also knows lieutenant governor Y, because they worked with each other, and therefore, I'm going to hire that individual to be part of my firm, so I can get the account of future congressperson X, and lieutenant governor Y." Research has also shown that candidates benefit, at least in terms of fundraising, from having well-regarded consultants on their teams.[24]

Many political consultants take on at least a few clients that are not political campaigns. In 2020, politicos in my dataset were working with political consultancies and PR agencies and public affairs firms such as Axiom Strategies, Bully Pulpit Interactive, and Black Rock Group (Republican), and Blue State Digital and Hilltop Public Solutions (Democratic). Most of these are partisan firms, hiring and working only with people and causes aligned with one party or the other, including corporations, initiatives, and advocacy groups. Axiom Strategies is a Republican firm that features on its website its defeat of an initiative that would have hurt "small tobacco" by increasing the cigarette tax. Hilltop Public Solutions, which has employed at least six people in my database, claims that they can use their "national network of state public affairs professionals to ensure our clients are heard at the state and local levels."[25]

These kinds of services often work by generating political engagement from everyday citizens that looks bottom up and spontaneous while actually being orchestrated from above.[26] Sociologist Caroline Lee documents how firms who specialize in "participatory democracy" or public engagement organize town halls and other ways for people to "have their say" without necessarily actually having an influence.[27] Edward Walker, in his book on public affairs consultants, describes how "grassroots for hire" firms encourage "plug-in political participation" that "is facilitating the decoupling of participation from the cultivation of democratic citizenship."[28]

Finally, politicos also parlay their experience in politics into high-powered roles in the private sector, often working as internal lobbyists or strategists for megacorporations. This is in addition to the people who work in firms that provide lobbying and communications services to these kinds of companies. About 24 percent of Republicans, and 18 percent of Democrats had worked in the private sector at some point by 2020. Campaign workers in my database have gone on to hold jobs such as director of public policy and philanthropy at Twitter, senior vice president for communications at Walmart, and the vice president for strategy and advocacy at Boeing. They held similar positions at Uber, Airbnb, and JPMorgan Chase, and this is all just in 2020.

Politicos don't generally move from campaigns into only one other part of the political power structure, though. If you look at the numbers throughout this chapter, you may notice that the percentages of those who work beyond campaigns add up to way more than 100 percent: close to half of politicos in each party had held a position in government or working for an elected official, 40 percent of Democrats and 50 percent of Republicans had held jobs in party or partisan organizations, about 30 percent from each party had worked in consultancies of various sorts, a quarter of Republicans (and fewer Democrats) have worked in business, and a quarter of Democrats (and fewer Republicans) had worked in advocacy organizations. That is because most politicos I tracked have worked across multiple types of powerful organizations and positions. At least 44 percent had done two or more types of work outside campaigns: in a party organization and a public affairs consultancy, for example, or for both a private corporation and an advocacy group; 13 percent had worked in three types of organizations.

Sociologists have long been interested in elites, their networks, and how they hold on to and exercise power. At least since C. Wright Mills published *The Power Elite* in 1956 sociologists have tracked the relationships of corporate CEOs and major shareholders, their interlocking roles in corporate and foundation boardrooms, their shared memberships in exclusive country clubs and luxurious retreats.[29] They have argued about the extent to which the elites coordinate with one another, share interests, and determine our politics through backroom deals or large donations. Other disciplines have contributed by studying the revolving doors through which politicians move from elected office right into lobbying roles, peddling access to their former colleagues.[30]

But there is another way that elites are connected besides through their direct relationships with one another, and it is through the circulation of the people I've dubbed campaign professionals. They advise politicians, and then they advise big companies about how to influence those politicians, and then they work for those politicians again. Even though a few of them may become subjects of breathless human-interest pieces in major newspapers—usually if they have just been credited with winning a major race—most are not household names, even among hardcore politics-followers. But the ways they approach politics and voters—their beliefs about who is paying attention, what they care about, and how they can be moved—shape politics all year, every year, not only when they are working on campaigns. Politicos' movement through all kinds of sites of political power, from corporations to elected officials to advocacy groups, is part of an important story about how politics is organized and managed in the United States. Political revolving doors circulate people not only between elected office and lobbying or even between political staff and lobbying but also among all kinds of organizations, associations, and corporations seeking to influence the direction of law and policy in the United States.[31]

In other words, politics is in many ways a game elites play against each other in Washington, even when it is sometimes made to look as though regular people are involved, with the "backing" of petition-signers and donations-givers or with a carefully staged town hall or protest; sometimes just with the expertise of professionals crafting reports, or pollsters documenting public opinion. And with few or no institutionalized ways to facilitate communication in both directions—from people to politicians as well as the other way around—it's not surprising so many people seem to see it that way.[32]

Campaign professionals are one substantial part of a group of political intermediaries whose job it is to try to get the political outcomes they or their employers or clients want, whether electing a particular politician, securing their party's control of the House or Senate or in governorships or state legislatures, or winning a legislative or policy or public opinion victory for a corporate client or advocacy organization.

Most if not all of the people working in this world for one side or the other emphatically believe in much of what they do. But the campaign people I spoke with are largely not sure that most regular people care that much about the outcomes of their work. And so they see their job as fighting against the other side—Ds or Rs, liberals or conservatives, pro-choice or anti-abortion forces, and so on. They may do this by motivating regular people—getting them to vote or show up at a town hall or even volunteer to text or call other potential voters. But they are not in the business of making actual connections with people or bringing new people into politics. Ordinary citizens don't wield a lot of power in politics. A big portion of the power that everyday people have in a democracy is in voting for politicians who we believe will represent us, and letting those politicians know, once elected, what we'd like for them to do. Those of us who are more similar to the people already there, and the people working in campaigns—White, college-educated, well-off—are the most likely to do those things, and therefore also wield the most power. The role played by campaign professionals partly explains why that inequality in political participation exists, why people outside the world of politicos use, or don't use, available democratic channels.

CONCLUSION

I n *How Organizations Develop Activists: Civic Associations and Leadership in the 21st Century*, the political scientist Hahrie Han draws a distinction between organizing and mobilizing.[1] She notes that many people and organizations don't see the difference, but it's an important one: when an organization simply tries to get numbers of people to do something—sign a petition, attend a protest, call their congressional representative—they are mobilizing, but not necessarily organizing. Mobilizing is transactional: it engages people who already are at least minimally motivated to be involved and gives them an action to take. It often accomplishes its goals. But mobilizing doesn't develop political engagement in people who weren't already there—that takes organizing. Organizing is not just channeling people who already want to do something into an outlet to express themselves; it means moving people who might not yet be ready into action as well. It's increasing the numbers of people who care and want to be involved, not just moving those people around.

Han's book is about citizen advocacy organizations, groups that are governed by some form of member democracy and seek to influence policy in Washington—the organizations that haven't been as hollowed-out as political parties and most of the associations Skocpol described in *Diminished Democracy*.[2] These are not the same as campaigns, but they are a type of organization many campaign staff move in and out of in their careers. Han finds that many of these organizations do not do organizing; some focus purely on mobilization, while others are what she terms "lone wolves" who simply hope that the information they put out into the world will itself get people to act.

Most campaigns at best mobilize people who are already engaged. One analyst suggests even the word "mobilization" is too strong, and "activation" is a better term for a style of politics aimed mostly at turning out just the right people to secure a victory.[3] We see the results of this "activation" in low turnout in US elections. The elections of 2018 and 2020 set records for their high turnout compared to recent trends, but still just over two-thirds of eligible voters showed up in 2020, and barely half did in 2018; even smaller fractions vote in off-year state and local contests. Campaigns don't pay much attention to the people they call "low-propensity voters," those people who have rarely or never voted, and who are also disproportionately lower-income and Black, Native American, Latinx, and Asian American. Campaigns pay less attention to those voters than to higher-likelihood voters who are more likely to be White and richer, which continues to widen the participation gap.[4]

With a few exceptions, campaigns are rarely involved in organizing in Han's sense. The Obama '08 campaign did some of this type of outreach; Han has also written about how the Obama campaign "transformed campaigning in America."[5] Obama's campaign organizations approached volunteers differently than most modern campaigns before or since, giving them more autonomy, organizing them to some extent rather than simply trying to mobilize them. Han and others, including me, hoped that this new approach, and the credit it got for helping Obama win both his national elections, might stick around. In his book on contemporary campaigning, Dennis Johnson, a longstanding scholar of professional campaign activities, predicted that Obama-style empowerment of enthusiastic supporters would characterize the twenty-first-century campaign. But despite Johnson's and Han's optimism, it doesn't look like the 2016 or 2020 general election campaigns did very much true organizing. Clinton's 2016 campaign had some very active supporters in independently organized groups, primarily on social media, such as Pantsuit Nation on Facebook, but did not do much to connect with local communities.[6] Trump excited a lot of people who had not been excited about an election before, but his campaigns, despite their unusual candidate, were not involved in unusual levels of organizing.

Today's campaigns, with few exceptions (Bernie Sanders's campaigns were the most notable), are not in the business of organizing people nor of otherwise connecting disengaged voters to politics. Their focus on one-way messages, prioritization of existing voters over new or occasional ones, and negative advertising—combined with their practitioners' distance from everyday people—actually turn many people off from politics. The 2020 election saw the highest turnout levels in decades, but it also evinced some of the most bitter partisan animosity this country has seen.

In the wake of that election and Trump's "big lie" that it was "stolen" we have weathered an attempted insurrection and seen a rise in efforts by Republicans to make voting more and more difficult for more and more people.[7] Huge swathes of the country, disproportionately Republicans, distrust public health experts and are resisting the vaccines needed to defeat Covid-19. There's a movement afoot to ban the teaching of critical race theory, which to its proponents means any discussion of the racist history of our country. The news about the climate catastrophe keeps getting worse, and political elites seem largely unable or unwilling to make the kinds of big changes we need to reduce our carbon output and mitigate the effects we're already seeing. And many people seem not to care.

A lot of that not-caring is a byproduct of how our campaigns are organized and who runs them. It's born of a sense among many people that politics is a game played by elites, one they are not invited to participate in.[8] When asked by survey researchers, about 26 percent of people strongly agree with the statement "Public officials don't care much what people like me think" and 24 percent with the statement "People like me don't have any say about what the government does." (Over 60 percent agree generally with each statement; I'm focusing here on the "strong" agrees.) Rates of strong agreement for both of these statements are much higher at the bottom of the income distribution than at the top: only 18 percent of people in households earning over $175,000 annually strongly agreed that public officials don't care, but the rate of strong agreement was over 33 percent in households with incomes under $30,000, and 30 percent in those earning $30,000 to $60,000. The pattern is very similar for not having any say: 27 to 29 percent strongly agree in the lower income brackets, but less than 18 percent strongly agree at the top.[9] People who have come to the conclusion that most political elites don't care about them and people like them—for whatever reason, including political messaging—may disengage completely or turn to "burn this town down" politics, as my interviewee Jimmy described it. We see this on the right in the form of

Trumpism and in some radical groups on the left as well. In the face of the sense that politics is overwhelming and out of their control, other people focus on problems they can frame as "close to home"—within their ability to make a difference.[10]

Two challenges for our contemporary politics are political disengagement on the one hand and extreme levels of partisan hostility and distrust on the other. These are actually two sides of one coin, both related to class position and race and campaigns. The highest levels of polarization are found among the relatively well-off and well educated; the least-engaged people are also generally poorer and less educated, and are the most likely to express moderate or neutral political positions.[11] Most partisans assume everyone in the *other* party is highly ideological and politically engaged; when they find out the truth—that most people with either partisan identity are actually fairly moderate and not that active—their hostility decreases substantially.[12] But that kind of symmetrical analysis is not the whole story. A substantial part of the distance between the two parties is entangled with race and racism: the Republican party is increasingly a party of White people, while the Democrats rely on a multiracial coalition.[13] The single best predictor of a vote for Trump in 2016 was hostility to Black people and other people of color; the next best was holding sexist attitudes.[14]

Many White Republicans, especially those in rural areas and without college degrees, increasingly see the Democratic Party as an alliance between White elites and poor and working-class people of color who get "free stuff" in return for their votes.[15] Many Democrats, not unsurprisingly but not entirely accurately either, in turn see the entirety of people who identify as Republican as irredeemably and virulently sexist, racist, nationalist, and, as Hillary Clinton notoriously put it in 2016, "deplorable."

These two features of our politics—hostile partisanship and class- and race-linked inequalities in participation—combine with campaigns to produce a vicious cycle: campaigns produce ads and speeches that play to hostility toward the other side (though again, this is not symmetrical). This stokes fear and hostility in some, and causes others to turn away from the entire spectacle. Those who still participate are more polarized; those who disengage are disproportionately disadvantaged already, and unlikely to be targeted by campaigns.

These might seem like intractable problems; there certainly are no easy solutions. But campaigns' activities are not determined by laws of nature or even good research on Americans' voting behavior. Campaign output cannot be fully understood just by looking at research on campaign effects or by speculating about political operatives' motivations in the abstract. Instead, campaigns' output is created within a culture of competition for status and recognition. Individual politicos want to be "at the table" on the next campaign; political consultants want to drum up business. In order to succeed in this field, they need to be perceived as having good political instincts, which largely means following or modestly improving on prevailing norms, without, of course, generally acknowledging that that is what they are doing. Campaign choices are not mostly the outcome of campaign decision-makers' cynical or rational or research-based ideas about what moves voters; this means that they also could be made very differently.

Political sociologists and political scientists pay great attention to questions of how individuals relate to politics—their positions on issues, beliefs about democracy and government, and how and why they vote or abstain. All these political positions are necessarily responses to the actual politics on offer, much of which is produced in campaigns.[16] And what campaigns do is largely driven by how politicos understand their work, each other, and voters. The internal dynamics of the campaign field are not the only reason campaigns look the way they do, nor are campaigns' strategies the only reason that American voter turnout is so low and unequal or that Americans are so polarized and racist. But these factors are a key part of the story, one that has been left out by many studies of campaigns and voters.

• • •

This is not the first book to point out that how campaigns and politics are run in the United States is not great for democracy, inclusion, or equity. But most of those books, I believe, misidentify the sources of that problem, in two ways.

First, they focus almost exclusively on political consultants, who are the most visible and the most highly paid people who work on campaigns.[17] But campaign staff without their own consulting firms are also key players in most campaigns and deserve at least as much attention. More importantly, the distinction between campaign staff and consultants is mostly a question of seniority: almost all consultants I spoke with had been paid campaign staff before "hanging out a shingle" of their own, and the few who hadn't worked in campaigns wished they had. Thus, getting rid of the business of political consulting or otherwise shifting how campaign work is organized wouldn't on its own fundamentally reshape how American politics works. Consultants want their party and candidate to win just as much as campaign staff do; they're mostly not in it simply to line their pocketbooks, despite the concerns about the increasing influence of consultants, raised especially in the late twentieth century.

Second, many critiques of our current campaign system tend to focus on the enormous amounts of money flowing through campaigns. This is one of the main things we hear about the problems with US democracy, and there is indeed a lot of money involved. In 2020, over $5.7 billion was spent by the presidential campaigns alone, and total spending in federal elections exceeded $14 billion.[18] Barack Obama was so concerned about the Supreme Court's decision in *Citizens United*—which struck down campaign finance laws to allow unrestricted spending in elections by corporations, unions, and interest groups—that he criticized the ruling in a State of the Union address, an unusual measure for a sitting president. National organizations like Public Citizen and Common Cause, and figures such as Michael Moore and Lawrence Lessig, have argued that the first step to improve the quality of American democracy must be to dramatically reduce the role of money in politics. Indeed, campaign finance laws have an enormous effect on how much money flows through politics, and from which sources. The amounts determine the scope of activities that campaigns can engage in, and there is some indication that politicians, when elected, are inclined to try to stay in the good graces of their donors (though these effects are less overt than many critics fear).[19]

However, the amount of money flowing through campaigns is not the main problem. At least as important is how those campaigns and other partisan organizations spend all that money, and that is up to the people working in them. Campaign professionals—consultants, a campaign manager, and so forth—designed, executed, and approved ads like the infamous racist one featuring Willie Horton in the 1988 race between George H. W. Bush and Michael Dukakis, and the more recent xenophobic anti-China ad for Joe Biden. More generally, the particular form of campaigning in the US—who is contacted, through what media—and the content and tone of speeches, ads, call scripts, and more are not determined by how much money is available or who gives it. We might be less concerned about the scale of campaign spending if billions of dollars were being spent to fund longer-term political infrastructure to connect regular people to politics and government, instead of only to try to win the next election.

Efforts to curtail campaign spending also have unintended consequences. Even in the post–*Citizens United* landscape, the laws governing political donations and spending are so complex that groups without the resources to retain an election law expert should be wary about getting involved. Similarly, regulations restricting the political activity of registered 501(c)(3) nonprofits dissuade many from engaging in politics at all, even within the bounds of what the law allows. In part because of attempts to limit or at least shed light on the sources of political donations, engaging in electioneering is mostly restricted to large political organizations and campaigns.

· · ·

Of course, any number of factors beyond the beliefs and composition of campaign professionals do affect the broad strokes of campaign strategy in the United States. The fact that almost all elections in the United States are run on a winner-takes-all, one-member-per-district basis means that 100 percent of the politicians representing a given neighborhood—in the city council, in the state legislature, and in Congress—might be from the same political party, even if only 60 percent of people who live there vote for that party. It also means there are countless uncontested elections across the country each year, because there is little point in a candidate running in a single-member district where a sizable majority of voters are in the other party. Gerrymandering those districts can further lock in one party's advantage, and, as in the Electoral College, can result in election outcomes that don't match the popular vote. Other electoral systems, such as those with proportional representation and multimember districts, can resolve some of these issues.

Campaigns' choices are also affected by the size and distribution of the population, the media environment, and the role of money in determining who can run for office in the first place. These kinds of structural features of our democracy shape the parameters within which campaigns operate, but if we try to understand the problems with American politics only by looking at its structure, we miss all the things that could be different even within those constraints.

If you zoom out a bit from the campaign professionals in this book, you get to the question of whether American democracy can ever be truly representative, given what we know about the history and presence of White supremacy and capitalism in this country. The country was founded on the labor of enslaved Africans and the displacement and genocide of Native Americans. Until well into our history, participating in democracy required that you be White, a man, and own property. Removing each of these requirements took struggle. It was only in 1965 that the voting rights of African Americans were secured, and they are under attack again in 2021. There are many who argue, with reasonable evidence, that politicians are simply in the service of wealthy White elites, whatever their public stances and speeches might be, whatever their party affiliation.

It is probably true that elites will tend to wield an outsize influence as long as they control outsize proportions of the economy and its rewards—to use Marxist terminology, as long as they control the means of production. A number of studies demonstrate that the better-off are the most likely to express their political voices through voting, contacting elected officials, and involvement in campaigns, along with making donations. Politicians are more likely to pass laws that have the support of richer people.[20] This is true across the board, but the amount of inequality, in wealth as well as in political voice, varies substantially over time and across countries, as the French economist Thomas Piketty has shown.[21]

The fundamental inequality inherent in capitalism and the intractability of White supremacy are problems beyond the scope of this book. But democratic processes and choices can affect the levels of inequality, the degree of suffering, and the extent of White dominance, and those all have real consequences for the quality of people's lives. How and whether politics solves or exacerbates problems has a lot to do with how politics is produced.

Campaigns are potential sites for political figures to connect with regular people. But they are run by people who are markedly different from and largely cut off from the rest of us. When I met Ken I went through not one, not two, but three people working for him or his building before I reached him. But he does believe it's important to be able to really connect with regular people. He designs ads to make those connections in his extremely nice office suite in Washington, DC. Or there's Chris, whose first experience with campaigns was very local and grassroots and connected, handing out flyers to neighbors on his paper route, who now lobbies Congress to advance the ideas of the foundation that employs him.

It's not that what these two and other politicos are doing is wrong. They are genuinely trying to advance a vision of society that they think is right. But they are unquestionably disconnected from everyday voters and people, earning incomes higher than almost everyone else, and engaging primarily with others in similar roles. At least as important, it's nearly impossible for regular people—people who aren't White men, from rich families, who've loved politics since elementary school—to join their ranks, to be part of the processes that shape our laws and policies or even that shape what campaigns look like.

Moreover, those who do become campaigners learn to see the world through the lens of their peers, which shapes how they think about politics, themselves, and voters.

Politicos are wrong to assume that regular people don't care about politics. Many people who don't vote, or don't vote regularly, do absolutely care about the issues that are determined by laws and policies. They just aren't convinced that which party holds the presidency, let alone their senator's or state representative's seat, is going to make a big difference in their lives. It's also true that many, perhaps most regular people—especially those who haven't attended college and also haven't been brought into some kind of political or social movement—don't spend a lot of time thinking about what social policies could do to improve their lives and wishing that someone would implement them. Many are too bogged down in the realities of navigating the challenges those policies have created in their lives, such as, for example, securing health care, well documented by the political scientist Jamila Michener in her book on Medicaid recipients.[22] Many citizens frame problems that seem insoluble as not "close to home," as the sociologist Nina Eliasoph put it—and therefore neither their responsibility nor their concern.[23] They cultivate political indifference because they've come to the conclusion, consciously or not, that there's not much they as individuals can do about the problems in their communities. These kinds of disengagement and cynicism may manifest as seeing electoral politics as uninteresting or irrelevant, but that is not necessarily the same as genuinely not caring what politicians do with their power.

Even people who are interested in politics get a lot of their analyses and ideas about potential solutions from their church or union, from campaigns themselves, or from other forms of elite or political-group persuasion or signaling. It is most often middle- and upper-middle-class people with college degrees or more who have strong ideological positions and independently seek out ways to influence politics. Poor and working-class people are far more likely to get involved in social movements or politics when someone they already know or who has important things in common with them invites them in.[24]

For many of us, our sense of identity, including the party we feel closest to, shapes how we understand the world, and when powerful actors from our side give us signals about what is happening in the world, we follow them. For example, partisan identity colors perceptions of the economy: Republicans think it's worse when Democrats are in charge, and vice versa.[25] More pernicious, Trump's tweets about the theft of the 2020 election convinced many of his supporters that the election was illegitimate.[26] In other words, politics and politicians shape people's opinions rather than just representing them.

Ken put it perfectly: "So campaigns impact people; they have a huge effect on how people see not just the campaign, but also see the world, see America. It's more than just a function, or a reflection on a campaign. It's: Are we positive about America, are we positive about our economic future, or did a campaign convince everybody that things are terrible—'We're gonna make America great again,' or whatever."

Campaigns' messaging isn't the only thing that matters for people's political views, of course. Public opinion has often changed for the better after political processes have played out: majority support for racial integration developed after it became the law of the land; public opinion on gay marriage seems to have followed its legalization. Medicare and Social Security, programs that profoundly reduced poverty and suffering among senior citizens, are now often called the third rail of American politics because they are so popular—especially among a group, older people, who vote reliably—that no one can touch them. More recently, Obamacare has mostly gotten more popular since it was enacted a decade ago.[27] As the sociologist Lane Kenworthy argues in *Social Democratic America*, we might get a more equitable US just by implementing policies one by one when there's an opening; they become popular as people appreciate their benefits, and then they're very hard to repeal.[28] The fact that Obamacare survived all of Trump's and his Republican congressional majority's attempts to repeal it was a great example of this. Part of how you change hearts and minds is by giving people things they might not even know they want.

So politics can alter people's political beliefs both through campaign messaging and through the actions of Congress, the president, and the Supreme Court. A progressive who wants to see more equitable policy might take a look at the recent history described above and conclude that Democrats just need to win more elections, rather than shift how campaigns work. But even though elite action sometimes produces desirable results and shifts in public opinion, policies decided only by elites are a problem for democracy, even when they're good decisions.

First off, a political arena where the players are predominantly White, highly educated, and well-off, is unlikely to generate outcomes that are truly good for those who are shut out of the process. But more than that, democracy itself is a really good idea, even if it has yet to work fully the way democratic theorists imagine it could, through reasoned debate and all voices having an equal seat at the table.[29] If people believe politics is a game elites are playing without them, if they have a sense that there is no relationship between their basic needs and desires and the actions of politicians, then the legitimacy of the entire enterprise is threatened. This is more or less the message of the book that coined the term "meritocracy." *The Rise of the Meritocracy* is speculative fiction about a dystopian future where everything is run by the smartest and most capable people, and even though they are trying to do good, the regular people get sick of being at the bottom—even if they "deserve it"—and revolt.[30]

Right now, such a development looks more and more possible. Trump has continued to mobilize a lot of people, mostly through top-down communication from himself in tandem with conspiracy theories like those of QAnon, propagated through social media. He and the Republican Party are, as sociologist Dana Fisher put it, "waging an attack on our democracy at the state level—and getting away with it." They have been fighting for, and often passing, laws to make protesting essentially illegal and to roll back voting rights; the Brennan Center for Justice reported that nineteen states passed laws restricting voting in 2021, including S.B. 1 in Texas, which outlawed innovations such as drive-through voting and twenty-four-hour voting.[31] Taken together, these two efforts are aimed at making it harder for people to be engaged in politics, especially low-income people and people of color, the very groups most likely to vote against Republicans. Many Democratic politicians and politicos are fighting this onslaught, but the outcome for our democracy, like the questions about how we will handle climate change, rising inequality, and racial injustice, is far from resolved.

At the end of our interview, I asked Angela, a Democratic pollster, whether there was anything else she wanted me to know. She said, "I think that public service in general and political consulting in particular are really suffering in terms of hiring millennials, because I think the millennials want to reflect their values. Most of the people I know in the business are pretty darn committed to what they do, and they work very hard to make this country a better place." But a lot of younger people, especially on the left side of the political spectrum, don't see electoral politics as a place to live out their values. "So," she continued, "I worry about the recruitment of the next generation, because I think both public service and political consulting are getting such bad raps, and it's a very, very important vehicle for social change."

I think Angela is right: if you believe this country could and should be better, you should get into political work. My hope is that work in politics, especially on the side that tries, however imperfectly, to represent the interests of a multiracial, cross-class coalition, might become more accessible and more sustainable. Work in politics ought to be a viable path even for people without the financial support to weather unpaid internships, or the willingness to work so much that you miss family weddings and newborns' first months. If you feel like your community is ignored by politics, like the ads on television don't really speak to you, like there is so much more that could be done, why not work for a candidate or organization you believe in?

There are a number of organizations that are working to include more people in the democratic process and to organize specifically in poor and working-class communities and among people of color. Stacey Abrams's organization and organizers in Georgia have been working tirelessly for years, and were able to turn out just enough new voters to turn the state blue in 2020. In the wake of Trump's election in 2016, Indivisible, spearheaded by two politicos, and other resistance groups around the country got many new people involved in politics, though many of them were the type—older, educated, White—who are most likely to get involved to begin with.[32]

If you don't want to make a career of politics, then figure out how to actually influence outcomes yourself in other ways. Connect with other people and organizations that share your values. Contact politicians, volunteer, and figure out how to build power.[33] Don't do what so many ideologically committed people do: just armchair-quarterback what the politicos and politicians ought to do. Get involved in making political change happen.

Our democratic process is conducted largely through people in the politics industry who, given the impossibility of knowing for sure what will move voters, rely on conventional wisdom, working ridiculous hours, and the anticipated reactions of other politicos and the media in order to create "good" campaigns. They try their hardest to figure out how to activate the voters they need to win elections, but they are not in the business of connecting communities with politics. More and more people seem to be coming to the conclusion that democracy is not working for them. Some of those are the White people without college degrees and with a lot of hostility toward people of color who support Trump; others are the Black and Brown and working-class and poor people who might broadly agree with Democratic Party policy positions, but have too often been ignored by Democratic politicians.

Campaigns should work to make connections between potential voters and the political sphere, but in fact they do a number of things that may turn people away from politics instead. They see their job as transmitting a message from their candidate to voters rather than as being any kind of conduit between people and politics. And they see voters as fairly passive, unengaged receptacles for their messaging, with bundles of attributes that make them more or less likely to receive the messages they send. So they drown some voters in mailers, telephone calls, advertisements, and door-knocks while ignoring others. They create content designed to appeal to people's basest fears and prejudices or to excite the media or anger the opposition, with little actual insight into how that content will affect voters. These tactics feel right to campaign professionals but they have not been proven effective by systematic research.

The one tactic that has been shown again and again to make a real difference in voting is having meaningful conversations with people, in person. Studies have shown that canvassing, especially when done by people with some social connection or similarity to the people they're talking with, can move nonvoters to vote for the first time, and increase the odds that occasional voters will in fact vote. "Deep canvassing" is the political-world name for the practice of having honest, open conversations with people, rather than just asking a few questions and spouting a few talking points. It is one of the few tactics campaigns might use that has been shown to sometimes persuade people to vote differently than they might have, and to change people's opinions on everything from transgender rights to immigration. When we take the time to really talk with and listen to people, change can happen.[34]

This kind of voter contact is time consuming and not at all glamorous: the opposing team is unlikely to see what you're doing, and the media are less likely to talk about it than they would a controversial or creative ad. It's also hard to measure: when campaigns do person-to-person outreach they tend to focus on the numbers of knocks and contacts rather than on the quality of conversations. So it's not surprising that deep in-person conversations have not been a mainstay of recent political campaigns. This is unfortunate, and it could be different.

A few national-level campaigns have made efforts to reach out to people who don't normally vote, or to use the "deep canvass" technique; Bernie Sanders's campaigns got some attention for making this effort in the primaries, though it is not clear that they were able to consistently increase turnout.

Even without any transformation in our election laws, changes in the approaches taken by campaigns could profoundly improve the quality of our democracy. At most 67 percent, and usually between 50 and 60 percent, of eligible voters have voted in recent presidential elections. Many of those who stay home as well as a substantial portion of those who vote see politics as a contest between elites who aren't interested in them or their problems. As long as campaign professionals approach their mission the way they do, that idea won't be entirely wrong. In the course of this book, I have shown how the dynamics of the politics industry constrain what campaigners can do, but I also have attempted to make the point that they could very well do things differently, and I hope that they will.

Making politics more communicative and connected to regular people won't change the fundamental dynamics of White supremacist modern capitalism in the US. But it could help to shift the balance of power, and therefore the distribution of goods and services and the policies of the state, more toward regular people. If political parties were composed of people more reflective of the electorate, if they facilitated two-way conversation, if they focused on connecting people to politics for the longer term rather than aiming every year to do just whatever it takes to get to 50 percent + 1, more regular people would feel more connected to politics, and be more connected, and see more channels through which to work to get their needs met. And we could have a profoundly better democracy in this country.

ACKNOWLEDGMENTS

This book started with research for my dissertation in the Sociology Department at UC Berkeley in 2008. In the course of nearly fifteen years it has gone through many iterations with the help of more people than I fear I'll be able to recall. I find writing acknowledgments really difficult; it feels both dangerously close to bragging to list all the resources and support I am so privileged to have, and also impossible to express sufficiently how much that support means to me. Ultimately, my writing is both entirely my own responsibility and inextricably the product of my relationships and conversations with family, friends, and colleagues. In other words, writing a book—like pretty much everything else people do—is fundamentally the product of both an individual and their social world; the point of acknowledgments, then, is to counterbalance the lone author name on the cover with some indication of the social part of research and writing. So, in roughly chronological order, here is an accounting of the myriad individuals and institutions that facilitated the writing of this book.

First, my appreciation for my mom as both a parent and a role model is why I dedicated this book to her. I benefited enormously from the way she lived her values: while I didn't like the seemingly endless Sunday mornings our family spent at protests against South African apartheid when I was little, I'm now proud that we were there. She unreservedly embraced and supported me both times I came out to her, first as a queer kid in 1992 and then as a transgender man in 2005; over the course of my teenage years, she was an unofficial foster parent to a dozen or so other kids who needed to get away from homophobic or otherwise less-than-ideal parents. When I was in college, she finished her own college degree while working full time, so that she could be a social worker and spend her days with recently homeless people who were coping with addictions and severe mental and physical health problems. She was diagnosed with early-onset Alzheimer's in 2012. I also owe a lot to my brother Jonathan, who agreed to care for her when I had the opportunity to move to London. I don't think either of us fully grasped how hard that would be at the time.

In my grown-up life, I am incredibly lucky to have the best partner and co-parent I could ever have dreamed of. Thank you, Hannah, for forgiving the dalliance with campaign work that started this book, for encouraging me to schedule days and even a whole week outside our house (in a pandemic!) to concentrate entirely on writing and editing, and for all the years in between. I am also deeply grateful to my kids, Ingrid and Charlie, who deserve appreciation and praise just for being the awesome, brilliant, funny, kind, and creative humans that they are and continue to grow into. I'm thrilled to get to be your "Powy" and to have you as my kids. I am also very grateful to have a best friend who is really family; thank you, Eliza Manoff, for all the late-night Catan games, talking about all the things, and always cheering me on.

Moving to intellectual community, I benefited enormously from working directly with four of the renowned researchers at Berkeley who served on my dissertation committee: Mike Hout, Loïc Wacquant, Marion Fourcade, and Laura Stoker. Thank you all for supporting me to do this research, for all I learned in your classes and office hours, and for your incisive feedback on my imperfect dissertation. More specifically, thank you to Mike for shepherding me through all the bureaucratic and administrative hurdles of graduate school and NSF funding; to Marion for being excited by my work but telling me not to come back to your office hours until I submitted a paper for publication; to Loïc for being a little bit (a lot) intimidating and always willing to tell me where I was smart as well as where I needed to think more clearly and carefully; and to Laura for being willing to endorse the project while being skeptical of some of my more sociological intuitions. I was also privileged to learn from many other brilliant and often also kind professors in the UC Berkeley Sociology Department; people in both categories included Ann Swidler, Jerry Karabel, Sandra Smith, and (for the first few years I was there) Dawne Moon.

It is not just the faculty who made Berkeley such a rich place to begin my academic career. Other students in my cohort, as well as those ahead of me, helped me make sense of the department and of sociology as a discipline and academia as a profession, and provided both emotional and intellectual support from the beginning of this process to now. Among many others, I am especially grateful to get to call Dawn Dow and Hana Brown friends and mentors.

Beyond Berkeley, many sociologists, political scientists, and other scholars have at some point read some part of what eventually became this book, and have generously given me both criticism and encouragement. Michael McQuarrie probably read more early drafts of this than anyone. Andrew Perrin and the UNC Cultural and Political Sociology workshop invited me to talk to them and came out (in a snowstorm!) to help me see which parts of this story were most interesting to other people. Dana Fisher, Ella Foster-Molina, Daniel Kreiss, Stephen Medvic, Dan Hirschman, and Eitan Hersh all gave me feedback, and all have done work that informs much of my understanding of the US political landscape.

I have had what I consider to be an embarrassment of riches in terms of both research and financial support for this book, as well. At Berkeley, the Undergraduate Research Apprenticeship Program, URAP, matched me with twenty-six undergraduate research assistants over the course of three years. They each toiled six or more hours a week, across one or more semesters, finding and organizing data on campaign professionals' careers—all for the reward of a few course credits. Maria Buxton, Sean Diament, Calias Dull, Steve Edelstone, Alessandra Gangone, Jerry Gorin, Jason Joffe, Ashlyn Kong, Gonzalo Lozano, Willie Marquez, William Qiu, Katie Schiff, Ben Schwartz, and Heewon Suh each dedicated one semester to the project. Kelly Kyungyoul Chae, Joe Krammer, Emma Levine, Nick Lopez, Youngeun Na, Carli Raben, and Una Shin each spent two semesters with me. Those who worked with me longer contributed even more, both in terms of time and also their own insights and observations. These included Sophie Ha and Tommy Kedar, who worked on this for three semesters; Claire Hwang and Sowmya Ramanathan, who contributed four semesters each; and last and most, Vincent Yung, who spent three full academic years working with me before heading to grad school himself. I could not have done this without these students, many of whom are now professors and researchers and/or doing many other kinds of important work.

I am also grateful for the financial support I received at Berkeley: the Sociology Department itself, the Center for Race and Gender, and the Institute for the Study of Social Issues all gave me funding, and I was lucky to receive a National Science Foundation Dissertation Improvement Grant (SES-1003809), which supported my travel to conduct interviews and paid for transcription of those earlier interviews. The Nelson W. Polsby fellowship supported me in the last few years of work on my dissertation, and Linda Polsby met with me about my work and helped facilitate key connections to other scholars and political professionals (including James Thurber and Jeff Biggs), who in turn opened the door to many of the interviews I was able to conduct.

I say more about this in the body of the book, but I do want to highlight how glad I am that I got a chance to be part of the 2008 Obama campaign, and to thank my colleagues on that campaign—especially Pam Coukos—for all I was able to learn from you.

And, of course, this book would not have been possible without all the politicos who agreed to sit with me for interviews. I hope you can recognize in this book my appreciation for the work you do and the motivations that drive you, and see that most of my criticisms are about the system in which you work. Thank you for sharing your time, knowledge, and professional networks with me.

I am extremely grateful to Mike Savage at the London School of Economics for supporting me in the post-doc that gave me the time to do enough good work to get a good job, to Sam Friedman for being my collaborator and coauthor in much of that work, and then to Swarthmore College for hiring me as an assistant professor. Since I arrived, I have had the privilege of teaching incredibly smart and enthusiastic students, and working with inspiring and insightful colleagues. I have also had access to a lot of research support, both financial (through my startup funds as well as grants from the Lang Center and the Hungerford fund) and human. Thank you to my undergraduate research assistants on this project at Swarthmore: Angus Lam, Laura Wilcox, Jimmy Pham, and Annie Zhang, all of whom did excellent work that helped this book along.

Most recently, thank you to readers of the penultimate draft of this book: Annie Zhang, Beau Weston, Dana Fisher, Ella Foster-Molina, Hannah Laurison, Kevin Reuning, and Rebecca Subar. They all read complete drafts and told me where I was being obtuse, vague, contradictory, or excessively wordy—though, of course, any remaining errors, infelicities, and logical flaws are all my own. A special thank-you to Letta Page for reading the first (and later) drafts and streamlining my often verbose approach to explanatory text. Finally, Beacon's copyediting team did a truly excellent job, further increasing the clarity and flow of the manuscript I gave them.

It might have taken even longer for this very long-running project to become a book contract and then a book if it weren't for my agent, Lauren Sharp of Aevitas, who talked me through what an agent does, and then did it; thank you for that, and for so many great conversations about what this book could be. And it wouldn't have been *this* book if my editor, Joanna Green, at Beacon hadn't taken it on: thank you for your patience with me as I figured out how to write it (in a pandemic!) and for seeing it through. Thank you also to all the staff at Beacon, in all the departments, for the work that I do and don't see that goes into turning a text document on my computer into a book out in the world.

Finally, thank you to Nicole Pepe, Mariko Wirth, and Beth Blum for helping me keep my physical self in more-or-less working order despite way too much time with my computer, and for checking in about how "our" book was coming along. Thank you to Elizabeth Corbett for being a constant friend and cheerer-on. Thank you to so many people, friends and acquaintances, academics and otherwise, on Twitter and other social media, for being, individually and collectively, an academic reference library, a political bellwether, a cheering squad, and a place to talk about the vicissitudes of parenting and academia. Last but not at all least, thank you to the Anapatters for being a constant source of love and advice on all things.

I think that's roughly everyone and everything I can identify without which this book might not have happened or might not have been however good it turns out to be. I am tempted to list a number of other people and institutions that I just plain like and/or that I recognize contribute broadly to my well-being and capacity, but this is already very long; hopefully it will suffice to say I also appreciate so many other connections I have, as well as both the luck and privilege that got me to this point. I know there are many, many people who could do work at least as good as mine but have not had the resources and opportunities to do so.

NOTES

INTRODUCTION

1. Dennis W. Johnson, *Campaigning in the Twenty-First Century: A Whole New Ballgame?* (Florence, KY: Taylor & Francis Group, 2010); Elizabeth McKenna, Hahrie Han, and Jeremy Bird, *Groundbreakers: How Obama's 2.2 Million Volunteers Transformed Campaigning in America* (New York: Oxford University Press, 2015).

2. See, for example, "Obama's Inner Circle Shares Inside Story," *60 Minutes*, CBS, Nov. 7, 2008, https://www.cbsnews.com/news/obamas-inner-circle-shares -inside-story.

3. The appropriate usage and meanings of terms for both social class and race are frequently contested. Here I use "upper middle class" to mean families where at least one parent had a fairly high-level professional or managerial job. Throughout the text, I capitalize "White" and "Black," along with all other terms for racial and ethnic groups, because all of these terms, whether or not they refer to a particular geographic origin, are equally the product of social, cultural, and political struggles. The preferred names for each racial-ethnic group (with the partial exception of "White") have also shifted along with our country's near-constant battles between greater racial equality and persistent White supremacy, and as racialized groups have organized themselves into more or less connected communities and movements. I use the terms people use for themselves when I know them. When referring to the entire set of people in the United States who are not racialized as White, I mostly use the "people of color." Perhaps the most contested question of racial-ethnic nomenclature at the moment concerns people who are referred to as Latinx, Latino/a, or Hispanic. Many people in this group prefer to be called Latino or Hispanic (these two terms are not necessarily synonymous), but I use Latinx because of its increasing prominence among younger people, and because I try to use gender-neutral language wherever possible. A great example of this usage is in Rocio García, "Latinx Feminist Politicmaking: On the Necessity of Messiness in Collective Action," *Mobilization: An International Quarterly* 25, no. 4 (December 2020): 441–60, https://doi.org/10.17813/1086-671X-25-4-441. On the use of "Latinx," see G. Cristina Mora, Reuben Perez, and Nicholas Vargas, "Who Identifies as 'Latinx'? The Generational Politics of Ethnoracial Labels," *Social Forces* (February 24 2021), https://doi.org/10.1093/sf/soab011. For a deeper dive into the question of terminology, see Michael Rodríguez-Muñiz, *Figures of*

the Future: Latino Civil Rights and the Politics of Demographic Change (Princeton, NJ: Princeton University Press, 2021), 26–27; for more on the history, see G. Cristina Mora, "Cross-Field Effects and Ethnic Classification: The Institutionalization of Hispanic Panethnicity, 1965 to 1990," *American Sociological Review* 79, no. 2 (April 2014): 183–210.

4. There is an abundance of excellent work demonstrating that, as the sociologist Glenn Bracey put it, the US state has always been in some sense a "tool created, maintained, and used by whites to advance their collective racial interests." Glenn E. Bracey, "Toward a Critical Race Theory of State," *Critical Sociology* 41, no. 3 (May 2015): 553–72, 558, https://doi.org/10.1177/0896920513504600. See also W. E. B. Du Bois, *Black Reconstruction in America (The Oxford W. E. B. Du Bois): An Essay Toward a History of the Part Which Black Folk Played in the Attempt to Reconstruct Democracy in America, 1860–1880* (New York: Oxford University Press, 1934); Charles W. Mills, *The Racial Contract* (Ithaca, NY: Cornell University Press, 1999); Nikole Hannah-Jones and the *New York Times Magazine, The 1619 Project: A New Origin Story*, ed. Caitlin Roper, Ilena Silverman, and Jake Silverstein (New York: One World, 2021); Adam Dahl, *Empire of the People: Settler Colonialism and the Foundations of Modern Democratic Thought* (Lawrence: University Press of Kansas, 2018). There is a similar abundance of feminist scholarship on the founding principles of the United States; a few examples: Nancy F. Cott, *The Bonds of Womanhood: "Woman's Sphere" in New England, 1780–1835*, 2nd ed. (New Haven, CT: Yale University Press, 1997); Linda K. Kerber, Alice Kessler-Harris, and Kathryn Kish Sklar, eds., *U.S. History as Women's History: New Feminist Essays* (Chapel Hill: University of North Carolina Press, 1995); Carol Pateman, *The Sexual Contract* (Stanford, CA: Stanford University Press, 1988); Dorothy Roberts, *Killing the Black Body: Race, Reproduction, and the Meaning of Liberty* (New York: Vintage, 1998).

5. Pew Research Center, "With a Month to Go, Nearly Half of Voters Say They Have Been Contacted by 2016 Campaigns," *U.S. Politics & Policy* (blog), Oct. 6, 2016, https://www.pewresearch.org/politics/2016/10/06/with-a-month-to-go -nearly"-half-of-voters-say-they-have-been-contacted-by-2016-campaigns; Howard Homonoff, "2020 Political Ad Spending Exploded: Did It Work?," *Forbes*, Dec. 8, 2020, https://www.forbes.com/sites/howardhomonoff/2020/12/08/2020-political -ad-spending-exploded-did-it-work.

6. C. Wright Mills, *The Sociological Imagination* (1959; Oxford: Oxford University Press, 2000), 187.

7. Drew DeSilver, "Turnout Soared in 2020 as Nearly Two-Thirds of Eligible U.S. Voters Cast Ballots for President," Pew Research Center (blog), Jan. 28, 2021, https://www.pewresearch.org/fact-tank/2021/01/28/turnout-soared-in-2020-as -nearly-two-thirds-of-eligible-u-s-voters-cast-ballots-for-president.

8. Max Greenwood, "Democratic Pollsters Acknowledge 'Major Errors' in 2020 Surveys," *The Hill*, April 13, 2021, https://thehill.com/homenews/campaign /547876-democratic-pollsters-acknowledge-major-errors-in-2020-surveys; Eitan D. Hersh, *Hacking the Electorate: How Campaigns Perceive Voters* (Cambridge: Cambridge University Press, 2015). Hersh shows that campaigns' databases are regularly flawed, to the point of getting even voters' race and party identification wrong.

9. David Broockman and Joshua Kalla, "Experiments Show This Is the Best Way to Win Campaigns. But Is Anyone Actually Doing It?," *Vox* (blog), Nov.

13, 2014, http://www.vox.com/2014/11/13/7214339/campaign-ground-game; Joshua L. Kalla and David E. Broockman, "The Minimal Persuasive Effects of Campaign Contact in General Elections: Evidence from 49 Field Experiments," *American Political Science Review* 112, no. 1 (Feb. 2018): 148–66, https://doi.org /10.1017/S0003055417000363.

10. Sasha Issenberg, *The Victory Lab: The Secret Science of Winning Campaigns* (New York: Crown, 2012).

11. David Axelrod, *Believer: My Forty Years in Politics* (New York: Penguin, 2016); Karl Rove, *Courage and Consequence: My Life as a Conservative in the Fight* (New York: Threshold Editions, 2010).

12. This dataset includes every person working in a named role on a primary or general election presidential campaign in 2004, 2008, and 2020 and on general election contests for the US Senate in 2006 and for president in 2012 and 2016. Names and positions were found primarily through Eric M. Appleman's incredibly thorough and invaluable Democracy in Action project (https://democracyinac- tion.us), which we supplemented and confirmed with news reports and archived campaign websites. Appleman's site often includes biographies of staff sourced from news reports; we used these in concert with news reporting on campaign staff, their LinkedIn pages, and biographies posted on firms' websites. The dataset comprises 4,406 entries; for 2,169 of these, or just under half, we were able to identify at least one additional position the politico held beyond the one for which they were included in the database. We focused our efforts on those in higher-level positions on the campaign we initially found them in. To identify race and gender, we made a number of assumptions that will not be perfectly accurate, but we are confident give a reasonable estimate. Gender was assigned on the basis of the usual gender associated with the first name. Where this was unclear or ambiguous, we looked at pronouns used in biographies or news reports. Race was identified wherever possible through explicit mentions of racial group identity. Where no mention of race was made, my research assistants and I used photographs to make our best guesses, cross-referenced with politicos' career history (for example, almost all directors for African American voter outreach are African American). This is not at all a perfect system, but I am reasonably confident that when I report percentages by racial group, I am if anything understating the Whiteness of the field. This is because many people had no mention of race and no photograph online, and so are not counted in estimates of racial composition; these are likely to be disproportion- ately White people (because Whiteness so often goes unmarked whereas people of color often have their race identified in biographies and news stories). I hope future research will ask campaign professionals to self-identify their race, gender, class, and other important characteristics, but for now this is the only systematic attempt I know of to identify the entirety of people in national-level campaign staff and consulting roles across years. A few scholars have put together datasets covering some part of the field of political professionals: Daniel Kreiss, *Prototype Politics: Technology-Intensive Campaigning and the Data of Democracy* (New York: Oxford University Press, 2016), covers tech and digital staff. Richard M. Skinner, Seth E. Masket, and David A. Dulio, "527 Committees and the Political Party Network," *American Politics Research* 40, no. 1 (Jan. 2012): 60–84, https://doi.org/10.1177 /1532673X11420420, looks at 527 staff's networks but not their demographics.

A number of studies from the late 1990s to the early 2000s look at consultants only. See James A. Thurber, *The Battle for Congress: Consultants, Candidates, and Voters* (Washington, DC: Brookings Institution Press, 2001); James A. Thurber and Candice J. Nelson, *Campaign Warriors: Political Consultants in Elections* (Washington, DC: Brookings Institution Press, 2000); David A. Dulio and Candice J. Nelson, *Vital Signs: Perspectives on the Health of American Campaigning* (Washington, DC: Brookings Institution Press, 2005).

13. All interviews were conducted following federal guidelines for human-subjects research, and with approval from institutional review boards at each of my home institutions when this research was conducted. Interviewees received consent forms explaining that I would do everything I could to maintain their anonymity, which I hope I have done. They signed the forms, acknowledging that they understood the risks and benefits of participating. All but three interviews were recorded and transcribed. Quotations from interviews are from these transcriptions, with occasional small changes for grammar and consistency. Most interviews took place in September 2009, June 2010, and from March to May 2017. I conducted a few additional interviews in early 2021. Almost all the interviews were conducted in person in Washington, DC, most often at respondents' offices or in nearby coffee shops. A few others were done in Oakland or over the phone (in 2009 and 2010) or video conferencing (in 2017 and 2021). I interviewed twelve people twice; some of those individuals had moved out of working in campaigns by the time I interviewed them and were instead doing lobbying or public affairs work, or were working for advocacy or nonprofit organizations. Interviewees had worked in nearly every aspect of campaigns: as campaign managers and consultants and staff (often both at different times); in communications, fundraising, polling, field, phones, direct mail, voter file data, microtargeting, media buying, ad production, political departments, and more.

14. Of the seventy-two people I interviewed, there were fifty-three men and nineteen women, and sixty-five White people and seven people of color. When I began this project I was not thinking as much as I wish I had been about racial representation, and there were also even fewer Black, Latinx, and Asian American political operatives. For more on the experiences of Black people in politics, an excellent book is Donna Brazile, Yolanda Caraway, Leah Daughtry, Minyon Moore, and Veronica Chambers, *For Colored Girls Who Have Considered Politics* (New York: St. Martin's Press, 2018).

15. James N. Druckman et al., "(Mis-)Estimating Affective Polarization," *Journal of Politics* 83, no. 3 (June 2021), https://doi.org/10.1086/715603; Doug McAdam and Karina Kloos, *Deeply Divided: Racial Politics and Social Movements in Postwar America* (Oxford: Oxford University Press, 2016).

16. On how campaigns ignore nonvoters, see Ryan D. Enos, Anthony Fowler, and Lynn Vavreck, "Increasing Inequality: The Effect of GOTV Mobilization on the Composition of the Electorate," *Journal of Politics* 76, no. 1 (2014): 273–88. On nonvoters, see "The 100 Million Project: The Untold Story of American Non-Voters," Knight Foundation, released Feb. 19, 2020, "Executive Summary" at https://knightfoundation.org/reports/the-100-million-project. The years 2018 and 2020 saw the highest turnout rates of the twenty-first century: 50 percent for the 2018 midterm and 67 percent for the 2020 general. See Michael P. McDonald,

"2018 November General Election Turnout Rates," 2018g—United States Elections Project, last updated Dec. 14, 2018, http://www.electproject.org/2018g.

CHAPTER 1: DO CAMPAIGNS REALLY MATTER?

1. Jake Tapper and Betsy Kulman, "The Macaca Heard Round the World," *ABC News*, Aug. 17, 2006, https://abcnews.go.com/Nightline/story?id=2322630&page=1.

2. A Lexis-Nexis search for "Allen" and "Macaca" between the day the story broke and the election returned over two thousand stories.

3. All direct quotes in this book are from my anonymized interviews with politicos unless otherwise sourced. See introduction, note 13, for more details.

4. John Sides and Lynn Vavreck, *The Gamble: Choice and Chance in the 2012 Presidential Election* (Princeton, NJ: Princeton University Press, 2013); Lynn Vavreck, *The Message Matters: The Economy and Presidential Campaigns* (Princeton, NJ: Princeton University Press, 2009); E. C. James, "The Fundamentals in US Presidential Elections: Public Opinion, the Economy and Incumbency in the 2004 Presidential Election," *Journal of Elections, Public Opinion and Parties* 15, no. 1 (2005): 73–83.

5. Bruce E. Keith, *The Myth of the Independent Voter* (Berkeley: University of California Press, 1992).

6. Christopher Ingraham, "Somebody Just Put a Price Tag on the 2016 Election. It's a Doozy," *Washington Post*, Apr. 14, 2017, https://www.washingtonpost.com/news/wonk/wp/2017/04/14/somebody-just-put-a-price-tag-on-the-2016-election-its-a-doozy; Open Secrets, "2020 Election to Cost $14 Billion, Blowing Away Spending Records," Oct. 28, 2020, https://www.opensecrets.org/news/2020/10/cost-of-2020-election-14billion-update.

7. "Presidential Election Results: Biden Wins," *New York Times*, Nov. 3, 2020, https://www.nytimes.com/interactive/2020/11/03/us/elections/results-president.html; "2016 Presidential Election Results," *New York Times*, Aug. 9, 2017, https://www.nytimes.com/elections/2016/results/president.

8. Donald P. Green, Bradley Palmquist, and Eric Schickler, *Partisan Hearts and Minds: Political Parties and the Social Identities of Voters* (New Haven, CT: Yale University Press, 2004); William G. Mayer, ed., *The Swing Voter in American Politics* (Washington, DC: Brookings Institution Press, 2008); Lynn Vavreck, "The Myth of Swing Voters in Midterm Elections," *New York Times*, Apr. 22, 2014, http://www.nytimes.com/2014/04/23/upshot/the-myth-of-swing-voters-in-midterm-elections.html.

9. Shiro Kuriwaki, "Cumulative CCES Common Content," Harvard Dataverse, Apr. 6, 2021, https://doi.org/10.7910/DVN/II2DB6 (my analysis of the data).

10. John Herbert Aldrich, *Why Parties: The Origin and Transformation of Political Parties in America* (Chicago: University of Chicago Press, 1995); W. J. Crotty and G. C. Jacobson, *American Parties in Decline* (Boston: Little Brown, 1980); R. J. Dalton and M. P. Wattenberg, *Parties Without Partisans: Political Change in Advanced Industrial Democracies* (New York: Oxford University Press, 2000); M. P. Wattenberg, *The Decline of American Political Parties, 1952–1996* (Cambridge, MA: Harvard University Press, 1998); Larry Sabato, *The Party's Just Begun: Shaping Political Parties for America's Future* (Glenview, IL: Scott, Foresman/Little, Brown College Division, 1988); Richard S. Katz and Peter Mair, "Changing Models of Party

Organization and Party Democracy: The Emergence of the Cartel Party," *Party Politics* 1, no. 1 (Jan. 1995): 5–28, https://doi.org/10.1177/1354068895001001001; David M. Farrell and P. Webb, "Political Parties as Campaign Organizations," in Dalton and Wattenberg, *Parties Without Partisans*, 102–28.

11. Adam Sheingate, *Building a Business of Politics: The Rise of Political Consulting and the Transformation of American Democracy* (New York: Oxford University Press, 2016), 222. For more on my database, see note 12 to the introduction.

12. David L. Rosenbloom, *The Election Men: Professional Campaign Managers and American Democracy* (New York: Quadrangle Books, 1973), 27.

13. Larry Sabato, *The Rise of Political Consultants: New Ways of Winning Elections* (New York: Basic Books, 1981).

14. Christopher Wylie, *Mindf*ck: Cambridge Analytica and the Plot to Break America* (New York: Random House, 2019).

15. Jonathan Allen and Amie Parnes, *Shattered: Inside Hillary Clinton's Doomed Campaign* (New York: Crown, 2017), 394.

16. John Sides, Michael Tesler, and Lynn Vavreck, *Identity Crisis: The 2016 Presidential Campaign and the Battle for the Meaning of America* (Princeton, NJ: Princeton University Press, 2018), 198–99.

17. Kris-Stella Trump, "Four and a Half Reasons Not to Worry That Cambridge Analytica Skewed the 2016 Election," *Washington Post*, Mar. 23, 2018, https://www.washingtonpost.com/news/monkey-cage/wp/2018/03/23/four-and -a-half-reasons-not-to-worry-that-cambridge-analytica-skewed-the-2016-election.

18. Gary C. Jacobson, "How Do Campaigns Matter?," *Annual Review of Political Science* 18, no. 1 (2015): 31–47, https://doi.org/10.1146/annurev-polisci-072012 -113556.

19. On turnout, see, for example, Lisa García Bedolla and Melissa R. Michelson, *Mobilizing Inclusion: Transforming the Electorate Through Get-Out-the-Vote Campaigns* (New Haven, CT: Yale University Press, 2012); on persuasion, see, for example, Joshua Kalla and David E. Broockman, "The Minimal Persuasive Effects of Campaign Contact in General Elections: Evidence from 49 Field Experiments," *American Political Science Review* 112, no. 1 (Feb. 2018): 148–66, abstract at https://doi.org /10.1017/S0003055417000363. For a counterpoint on the effect of advertising, see John Sides, Lynn Vavreck, and Christopher Warshaw, "The Effect of Television Advertising in United States Elections," *American Political Science Review* (Nov. 2, 2021): 1–17, https://doi.org/10.1017/S000305542100112X.

20. See, for example, Alan I. Abramowitz, "Forecasting the 2008 Presidential Election with the Time-for-Change Model," *PS: Political Science and Politics* 41, no. 4 (Oct. 2008): 691–95; Alan Abramowitz, "Forecasting in a Polarized Era: The Time for Change Model and the 2012 Presidential Election," *PS: Political Science and Politics* 45, no. 4 (Oct. 2012): 618–19, https://doi.org/10.1017/S104909651200087X; James E. Campbell, "Polls and Votes: The Trial-Heat Presidential Election Forecasting Model, Certainty, and Political Campaigns," *American Politics Research* 24, no. 4 (1996): 408–33; Peter K. Enns and Julius Lagodny, "Forecasting the 2020 Electoral College Winner: The State Presidential Approval/State Economy Model," *PS: Political Science and Politics* 54, no. 1 (Oct. 2020): 81–85, https://doi.org/10.1017 /S1049096520001407.

21. Ruth Dassonneville and Charles Tien, "Introduction to Forecasting the 2020 US Elections," *PS: Political Science and Politics* 54, no. 1 (Oct. 2020): 47–51, https://doi.org/10.1017/S104909652000147X.

22. Michael Bang Petersen, Rune Slothuus, and Lise Togeby, "Political Parties and Value Consistency in Public Opinion Formation," *Public Opinion Quarterly* 74, no. 3 (2010): 530–50, https://doi.org/10.1093/poq/nfq005; Shawn Treier and D. Sunshine Hillygus, "The Nature of Political Ideology in the Contemporary Electorate," *Public Opinion Quarterly* 73, no. 4 (Dec. 2009): 679–703, https://doi.org/10.1093/poq/nfp067.

23. Meredith Rolfe, *Voter Turnout: A Social Theory of Political Participation* (New York: Cambridge University Press, 2012); Jennifer Sherman, *Those Who Work, Those Who Don't: Poverty, Morality, and Family in Rural America* (St. Paul: University of Minnesota Press, 2009); Sarah K. Bruch and Joe Soss, "Learning Where We Stand: How School Experiences Matter for Civic Marginalization and Political Inequality," Washington Center for Equitable Growth, July 5, 2016, http://equitablegrowth.org/equitablog/learning-where-we-stand-how-school-experiences-matter-for-civic-marginalization-and-political-inequality.

24. Green, Palmquist, and Schickler, *Partisan Hearts and Minds*.

25. Peter K. Enns, Paul M. Kellstedt, and Gregory E. McAvoy, "The Consequences of Partisanship in Economic Perceptions," *Public Opinion Quarterly* 76, no. 2 (July 2012): 287–310, https://doi.org/10.1093/poq/nfs016.

26. Dina Smeltz and Lily Wojtowicz, "Public Opinion on US-Russian Relations in the Aftermath of the 2016 Election," *SAIS Review of International Affairs* 38, no. 1 (2018): 17–26, https://doi.org/10.1353/sais.2018.0002. One study even found that people may shift what we think of as fixed identities—their sexual orientation or ethnicity. Patrick J. Egan, "Identity as Dependent Variable: How Americans Shift Their Identities to Align with Their Politics," *American Journal of Political Science* 64, no. 3 (2020): 699–716, https://doi.org/10.1111/ajps.12496.

27. Richard M. Harley, "The Evangelical Vote and the Presidency," *Christian Science Monitor*, June 25, 1980, https://www.csmonitor.com/1980/0625/062555.html; Pew Research Center, "In Changing U.S. Electorate, Race and Education Remain Stark Dividing Lines," June 2, 2020, https://www.pewresearch.org/politics/2020/06/02/in-changing-u-s-electorate-race-and-education-remain-stark-dividing-lines.

28. Michael C. Dawson, *Behind the Mule: Race and Class in African-American Politics* (Princeton, NJ: Princeton University Press, 1995); Philip Bump, "When Did Black Americans Start Voting So Heavily Democratic?," *Washington Post*, July 7, 2015, https://www.washingtonpost.com/news/the-fix/wp/2015/07/07/when-did-black-americans-start-voting-so-heavily-democratic.

29. Desmond S. King and Rogers M. Smith, *Still a House Divided: Race and Politics in Obama's America* (Princeton, NJ: Princeton University Press, 2011); Paul Frymer, *Black and Blue: African Americans, the Labor Movement, and the Decline of the Democratic Party* (Princeton, NJ: Princeton University Press, 2011); Zoltan L. Hajnal, *Dangerously Divided: How Race and Class Shape Winning and Losing in American Politics* (Cambridge, UK: Cambridge University Press, 2020). There is some indication that this trend reversed slightly in the 2020 election, with Latinx and Asian

American people voting for Trump at slightly higher rates than they had in 2016; it is too early to tell what this means for the relationship between race and partisanship going forward.

30. James Druckman et al., "(Mis-)Estimating Affective Polarization," *Journal of Politics*, forthcoming; Lilliana Mason, *Uncivil Agreement: How Politics Became Our Identity*, illus. ed. (Chicago: University of Chicago Press, 2018).

31. For the percentage who identify with a party, see Pew Research Center, "In Changing U.S. Electorate, Race and Education Remain Stark Dividing Lines," June 2, 2020, https://www.pewresearch.org/politics/2020/06/02/in-changing-u-s -electorate-race-and-education-remain-stark-dividing-lines/. More people lean toward one or the other party, but the antipathy findings are about those who identify as a member of either party. See Pew Research Center, "Partisan Antipathy: More Intense, More Personal," Oct. 10, 2019, https://www.pewresearch.org/politics /2019/10/10/partisan-antipathy-more-intense-more-personal.

32. Kay Lehman Schlozman, Henry E. Brady, and Sidney Verba, *Unequal and Unrepresented: Political Inequality and the People's Voice in the New Gilded Age* (Princeton, NJ: Princeton University Press, 2018).

33. Keith, *The Myth of the Independent Voter*.

34. Geoffrey Skelley, "Just How Many Obama 2012–Trump 2016 Voters Were There?," *Sabato's Crystal Ball* (blog), June 1, 2017, https://centerforpolitics.org /crystalball/articles/just-how-many-obama-2012-trump-2016-voters-were-there.

35. Michael P. McDonald, "2020 November General Election Turnout Rates," United States Elections Project, last updated Dec. 7, 2020, http://www.elect project.org/2020g.

36. Sides and Vavreck, *The Gamble*; Sides, Tesler, and Vavreck, *Identity Crisis*.

37. For Romney's statement, see Molly Moorhead, "Mitt Romney Says 47 Percent of Americans Pay No Income Tax," *Politifact*, Sept. 18, 2012, https://www .politifact.com/factchecks/2012/sep/18/mitt-romney/romney-says-47-percent -americans-pay-no-income-tax/; Sides and Vavreck, *The Gamble*.

38. John Sides, "Did 'Macaca' Lose the 2006 Election for George Allen?," *The Monkey Cage* (blog), Dec. 24, 2007, http://themonkeycage.org/2007/12/24/did _macaca_lose_the_2006_elect.

39. Robert S. Erikson and Christopher Wlezien, *The Timeline of Presidential Elections: How Campaigns Do (and Do Not) Matter* (Chicago: University of Chicago Press, 2012).

40. Kalla and Broockman, "The Minimal Persuasive Effects of Campaign Contact," 148.

41. Vavreck, *The Message Matters*, 158.

42. Sides, Tesler, and Vavreck, *Identity Crisis*.

43. Sides, Tesler, and Vavreck, *Identity Crisis*, 193–94.

44. Alan S. Gerber and Donald P. Green, "The Effects of Canvassing, Telephone Calls, and Direct Mail on Voter Turnout: A Field Experiment," *American Political Science Review* 94, no. 3 (Sept. 2000): 653–63, https://doi.org/10.2307 /2585837; Donald P. Green and Alan S. Gerber, *Get Out the Vote: How to Increase Voter Turnout*, 3rd ed. (Washington, DC: Brookings Institution Press, 2015); García Bedolla and Michelson, *Mobilizing Inclusion*; Seth E. Masket, "Did Obama's Ground Game Matter? The Influence of Local Field Offices During the 2008 Presidential

Election," *Public Opinion Quarterly* 73, no. 5 (Jan. 2009): 1023–39, https://doi.org/10.1093/poq/nfp077.

45. Sides, Tesler, and Vavreck, *Identity Crisis*, 195.

46. Sides, Tesler, and Vavreck, *Identity Crisis*, 197.

47. Masket, "Did Obama's Ground Game Matter?"

48. David Plouffe, *The Audacity to Win: How Obama Won and How We Can Beat the Party of Limbaugh, Beck, and Palin* (New York: Penguin, 2010).

49. Whether and how much political advertising matters is a hotly contested topic in political science; while Kalla and Broockman in "The Minimal Peruasive Effects of Campaign Contact in General Elections" say their best estimate of advertising effects is zero, a recent article by John Sides and co-authors shows a fairly strong relationship between a party's advertising advantage and its vote share. John Lynn Vavreck and Christopher Warshaw, "The Effect of Television Advertising in United States Elections," American Political Science Review (Nov. 2, 2021): 1–17, https://doi.org/10.1017/S000305542100112X. They also say, though, that "this relative difference in advertising's effect does not mean that its effect is 'large' in some absolute sense or large enough to potentially change the outcome of an election. That would be most likely in close races where one party is able to muster a substantial advertising advantage. But we do not claim that this is a common occurrence" (14). See also Alan S. Gerber et al., "How Large and Long-Lasting Are the Persuasive Effects of Televised Campaign Ads? Results from a Randomized Field Experiment," *American Political Science Review* 105, no. 1 (2011): 135–50, https://doi.org/10.1017/S0003055410000047X; Jonathan S. Krasno and Donald P. Green, "Do Televised Presidential Ads Increase Voter Turnout? Evidence from a Natural Experiment," *Journal of Politics* 70, no. 1 (2008): 245–61, https://doi.org/10.1017/S0022381607080176; David E. Broockman and Donald P. Green, "Do Online Advertisements Increase Political Candidates' Name Recognition or Favorability? Evidence from Randomized Field Experiments," *Political Behavior* 36, no. 2 (June 2014): 263–89, https://doi.org/10.1007/s11109-013-9239-z.

50. Jacobson, "How Do Campaigns Matter?"

51. David Broockman and Joshua Kalla, "Experiments Show This Is the Best Way to Win Campaigns. But Is Anyone Actually Doing It?," *Vox*, Nov. 13, 2014, https://www.vox.com/2014/11/13/7214339/campaign-ground-game.

52. Sheingate, *Building a Business of Politics*.

53. Jerome Armstrong and Markos Moulitsas, *Crashing the Gate: Netroots, Grassroots, and the Rise of People-Powered Politics* (White River Junction, VT: Chelsea Green, 2008).

54. These analyses are based on a dataset provided to me by the authors: James A. Thurber, Candice J. Nelson, and David A. Dulio, "Survey of Political Consultants" dataset, from the "Improving Campaign Conduct" grant, funded by the Pew Charitable Trusts, Center for Congressional and Presidential Studies, American University, 1999. Results of these analyses are published in their book, James A. Thurber and Candice J. Nelson, eds., *Campaign Warriors: Political Consultants in Elections* (Washington, DC: Brookings Institution Press, 2000), and in a chapter I wrote: Daniel Laurison, "Positions and Position-Takings Among Political Producers: The Field of Political Consultants," in *Bourdieu and Data Analysis*, ed. Michael Grenfell and Frédéric Lebaron (Oxford: Peter Lang, 2014).

55. Gregory J. Martin and Zachary Peskowitz, "Agency Problems in Political Campaigns: Media Buying and Consulting," *American Political Science Review* 112, no. 2 (May 2018): 231–48, https://doi.org/10.1017/S0003055417000594. This study shows that political consultants are far more extreme in their ideological views (as indicated by their political donations) than the country at large and that firms tend to have ideologically homogenous employees.

56. Martin and Peskowitz, "Agency Problems"; Matt Grossmann, "Going Pro? Political Campaign Consulting and the Professional Model," *Journal of Political Marketing* 8, no. 2 (2009): 81–104, https://doi.org/10.1080/15377850902813352; Matt Grossmann, "Campaigning as an Industry: Consulting Business Models and Intra-Party Competition," *Business and Politics* 11, no. 1 (2009).

57. Sasha Issenberg, *Rick Perry and His Eggheads: Inside the Brainiest Political Operation in America; a Sneak Preview from the Victory Lab* (New York: Crown, 2011); Sasha Issenberg, *The Victory Lab: The Secret Science of Winning Campaigns* (New York: Crown, 2012).

58. This is an oversimplification of this theory and its deployment. For a more extensive discussion, see Donald Green and Ian Shapiro, *Pathologies of Rational Choice Theory: A Critique of Applications in Political Science* (New Haven, CT: Yale University Press, 1996).

59. Daniel Kreiss, *Prototype Politics: Technology-Intense Campaigning and the Data of Democracy* (New York: Oxford University Press, 2016).

60. See note 3 in introduction on racial-ethnic group terms.

CHAPTER 2: A FOOT IN THE DOOR

1. A significant majority of Americans agree with the statement "Who gets ahead in society is determined by hard work." See Jonathan J. B. Mijs, "Visualizing Belief in Meritocracy, 1930–2010," *Socius* 4 (Jan. 2018), https://doi.org/10.1177/2378023118811805. Almost all British people, when interviewed about their careers, pointed to their own hard work as key to their success. See Sam Friedman and Daniel Laurison, *The Class Ceiling: Why It Pays to Be Privileged* (Bristol: Policy Press, 2019).

2. Daniel Laurison, Dawn Dow, and Carolyn Chernoff, "Class Mobility and Reproduction for Black and White Adults in the United States: A Visualization," *Socius* 6 (Jan. 2020), https://doi.org/10.1177/2378023120960959.

3. This leaves aside the question of whether meritocracy is actually desirable as a system of allocating positions and rewards. The term "meritocracy" was actually coined in a dystopian novel by Michael Young, wherein "merit" was used to legitimate inequality and those deemed merit-less eventually revolted. Michael Young, "Comment: Down with Meritocracy," *Guardian*, June 29, 2001, http://www.theguardian.com/politics/2001/jun/29/comment; Michael Young, *The Rise of the Meritocracy*, 2nd ed. (New Brunswick, NJ: Routledge, 1994).

4. In 2018 the professoriate was about 75 percent White. See National Center for Education Statistics, "Fast Facts, Race/Ethnicity of College Faculty," https://nces.ed.gov/fastfacts/display.asp?id=61. In 2021 Congress was 77 percent White. See Katherine Schaeffer, "Racial, Ethnic Diversity Increases Yet Again with the 117th Congress," Pew Research Center, Jan. 28, 2021, https://www.pewresearch.org/fact-tank/2021/01/28/racial-ethnic-diversity-increases-yet-again-with-the

-117th-congress. According to my estimate, from 2000 to 2020, 70 to 80 percent of campaign staff were White.

5. For more on this database, see note 12 to the introduction.

6. These percentages are for the 2,169 people from both parties in my database for whom I have been able to find information on at least two positions that they've held, weighted by party. The racial composition percentages are for a subset of that group, the 1,733 people for whom I have been able to find some indication of their racial identity. I count people as having attended college if the name of a college or university appears in any biographical information I was able to find.

7. US Census Bureau, "QuickFacts: United States," https://www.census.gov /quickfacts/fact/table/US/PST045219.

8. John Gramlich, "What the 2020 Electorate Looks Like by Party, Race and Ethnicity, Age, Education and Religion," Pew Research Center, Oct. 26, 2020, https://www.pewresearch.org/fact-tank/2020/10/26/what-the-2020-electorate -looks-like-by-party-race-and-ethnicity-age-education-and-religion.

9. The denominator here is Republican politicos who meet the two criteria in note 6 above: I was able to find at least one role for them beyond the one for which they were initially included in the database, and I was able to find some indication of their racial identity. As I pointed out in the introduction, note 12, the people for whom I could not find any information about their race are even more likely to be White than those for whom I could, so the percentages given here may be underestimates of politicos' Whiteness and overestimates of their racial diversity.

10. For comparisons across years, I combine the 2004 and 2008 cycles and include only people who meet the criteria laid out in this chapter's note 6 *and* who were working in a national-level campaign in that particular cycle; for example, people who worked on a major campaign in 2018 but not in 2020, are not counted in 2020.

11. Percentages in this paragraph are calculated the same as for Republicans, as described in note 9 above.

12. Jonathan Allen and Joseph Williams, "Obama Camp Tries to Diversify," *Politico*, Apr. 18, 2012, https://www.politico.com/story/2012/04/wh-black-outreach -better-late-than-never-075323.

13. Sean J. Miller, "As 2020 Campaigns Diversify Staff, Some Strategists Worry Firms Still Aren't Doing Enough," *Campaigns & Elections*, July 10, 2019, https://www.campaignsandelections.com/campaign-insider/as-2020-campaigns -diversify-staff-some-strategists-worry-firms-still-aren-t-doing-enough.

14. Gramlich, "What the 2020 Electorate Looks like by Party, Race and Ethnicity, Age, Education and Religion."

15. Miller, "As 2020 Campaigns Diversify Staff, Some Strategists Worry Firms Still Aren't Doing Enough."

16. Ruth Igielnik, "Men and Women in the U.S. Continue to Differ in Voter Turnout Rate, Party Identification," Pew Research Center, Aug. 18, 2020, https:// www.pewresearch.org/fact-tank/2020/08/18/men-and-women-in-the-u-s-continue -to-differ-in-voter-turnout-rate-party-identification.

17. Kuriwaki, "Cumulative CCES Common Content" (my analysis of the data for validated registered voters).

18. US Census Bureau, "QuickFacts: United States." My analysis is for the people in my database for whom I could find information about their activities in at least two different even-numbered years. Some of those for whom I found a college listed may not have graduated, but the vast majority appear to have bachelor's degrees.

19. Raj Chetty et al., "Mobility Report Cards: The Role of Colleges in Intergenerational Mobility," Working Paper Series (Cambridge, MA: National Bureau of Economic Research, July 2017), https://doi.org/10.3386/w23618. For their reporting on the selectivity of internships in journalism, journalists at the Voices project of the Asian American Journalism Association compiled Chetty et al.'s list of colleges, their tiers, and other characteristics in a table. See Farnoush Amiri et al., "How America's Top Newsrooms Recruit Interns from a Small Circle of Colleges," Voices, Aug. 2, 2019, https://voices.aaja.org/index/2019/8/1/how-americas-top -newsrooms-recruit-interns-from-a-small-circle-of-colleges. For the table, see https://docs.google.com/spreadsheets/d/1QSIxs-doe_QOTS514jpbpMrXxem MJMTxzffM42Frh20/edit#gid=1430844554.

20. See also Introduction, note 12.

21. See, for example, Florencia Torche, "Is a College Degree Still the Great Equalizer? Intergenerational Mobility Across Levels of Schooling in the United States," *American Journal of Sociology* 117, no. 3 (Nov. 2011): 763–807, https://doi .org/10.1086/661904; Michael Hout, "A Summary of What We Know About Social Mobility," *Annals of the American Academy of Political and Social Science* 657, no. 1 (Jan. 2015): 27–36, https://doi.org/10.1177/0002716214547174; Laura T. Hamilton and Elizabeth A. Armstrong, "Parents, Partners, and Professions: Reproduction and Mobility in a Cohort of College Women," *American Journal of Sociology* 127, no. 1 (July 2021): 102–51, https://doi.org/10.1086/714850. Class origins matter across racial groups, but racism erects further barriers to social mobility for Black people and other people of color; see, for example, Enobong Hannah Branch and Christina Jackson, *Black in America: The Paradox of the Color Line* (Cambridge: Polity, 2020); Laurison, Dow, and Chernoff, "Class Mobility and Reproduction for Black and White Adults in the United States."

22. The scholarship and analysis establishing the ways that race, racism, settler colonialism, and White supremacy are part and parcel of the political development of the United States are the subjects of many excellent books and articles—too numerous to cite here. See, for example, W. E. B. Du Bois, *Black Reconstruction in America (The Oxford W. E. B. Du Bois): An Essay Toward a History of the Part Which Black Folk Played in the Attempt to Reconstruct Democracy in America, 1860–1880*, ed. Henry Louis Gates (1935; New York: Oxford University Press, 2007); Nikole Hannah-Jones, "America Wasn't a Democracy, Until Black Americans Made It One," *New York Times Magazine*, Aug. 14, 2019, https://www.nytimes.com/interactive/2019 /08/14/magazine/black-history-american-democracy.html; King and Smith, *Still a House Divided*; Dorothy Roberts, *Fatal Invention: How Science, Politics, and Big Business Re-Create Race in the Twenty-First Century* (New York: New Press, 2012); Michael L. Rosino and Matthew W. Hughey, "Who's Invited to the (Political) Party: Race and Party Politics in the USA," *Ethnic and Racial Studies* 39, no. 3 (Feb. 2016): 325–32, https://doi.org/10.1080/01419870.2016.1096413; Michelle Alexander, *The New Jim Crow: Mass Incarceration in the Age of Colorblindness* (New York: New Press, 2012); Crystal Marie Fleming, *How to Be Less Stupid About Race: On Racism, White*

Supremacy, and the Racial Divide (Boston: Beacon Press, 2018); Hana E. Brown, "Racialized Conflict and Policy Spillover Effects: The Role of Race in the Contemporary U.S. Welfare State," *American Journal of Sociology* 119, no. 2 (Sept. 2013): 394–443, https://doi.org/10.1086/674005; Adam Dahl, *Empire of the People: Settler Colonialism and the Foundations of Modern Democratic Thought* (Lawrence: University Press of Kansas, 2018).

23. Victor Ray, "A Theory of Racialized Organizations," *American Sociological Review* 84, no. 1 (Feb. 2019): 30, https://doi.org/10.1177/0003122418822335.

24. Joan Acker, "Inequality Regimes: Gender, Class, and Race in Organizations," *Gender and Society* 20, no. 4 (Aug. 2006): 441–64, https://doi.org/10.1177/0891243206289499; Friedman and Laurison, *The Class Ceiling*.

25. It might seem like everyone in DC is involved with politics in some way, but in reality many people who live there, just like in other major US cities, make their living in various parts of the service industry and live in segregated parts of the city. So it's not surprising that a working-class kid could grow up without knowing anyone in politics.

26. On elite firms' recruitment strategies, see Lauren A. Rivera, *Pedigree: How Elite Students Get Elite Jobs* (Princeton, NJ: Princeton University Press, 2015). There are groups like the College Republicans and the College Democrats on college campuses; the College Republicans tend to be much more active and directly connected to Republican Party and partisan organizations, and sometimes serve as a pipeline for young people interested in careers in politics. Some of my Republican interviewees got their first work in campaigns through this route, but most of them traced their careers to other kinds of connections, just like most Democrats I spoke with.

27. Daniel Laurison, "Social Class and Political Engagement in the United States," *Sociology Compass* 10, no. 8 (Aug. 2016): 684–97, https://doi.org/10.1111/soc4.12390; Sidney Verba, Kay Lehman Schlozman, and Henry E. Brady, *Voice and Equality: Civic Voluntarism in American Politics* (Cambridge, MA: Harvard University Press, 1995).

28. Eitan Hersh, *Politics Is for Power: How to Move Beyond Political Hobbyism, Take Action, and Make Real Change* (New York: Scribner, 2020).

29. Nicholas Carnes, *White-Collar Government: The Hidden Role of Class in Economic Policy Making* (Chicago: University of Chicago Press, 2013); Nicholas Carnes, *The Cash Ceiling: Why Only the Rich Run for Office—and What We Can Do About It* (Princeton, NJ: Princeton University Press, 2018). Percentages are for 2008 (Congress) and 2013 (US citizens).

30. US Census Bureau, "QuickFacts: United States"; Michael T. Nietzel, "The College Profile of the New Members in the 117th Congress," *Forbes*, Jan. 8, 2021, https://www.forbes.com/sites/michaeltnietzel/2021/01/08/the-college-profile-of -the-new-members-in-the-117th-congress.

31. Priscilla Murolo, *From the Folks Who Brought You the Weekend: A Short, Illustrated History of Labor in the United States*, later ed. (New York: New Press, 2003); Patrisse Cullors and asha bandele, *When They Call You a Terrorist: A Black Lives Matter Memoir* (New York: St. Martin's Griffin, 2020); Alicia Garza, *The Purpose of Power: How We Come Together When We Fall Apart* (New York: One World, 2020); Joan Maya Mazelis, *Surviving Poverty: Creating Sustainable Ties Among the Poor* (New

York: New York University Press, 2017); Frances Fox Piven, *Poor People's Movements: Why They Succeed, How They Fail* (New York: Pantheon Books, 1977).

32. Betsy Leondar-Wright, *Missing Class: Strengthening Social Movement Groups by Seeing Class Cultures* (Ithaca, NY: Cornell University Press, 2014).

33. Kimberlé Crenshaw, "Mapping the Margins: Intersectionality, Identity Politics, and Violence Against Women of Color," *Stanford Law Review* 43, no. 6 (1991): 1241–99; Patricia Hill Collins and Sirma Bilge, *Intersectionality* (New York: John Wiley, 2016); Patricia Hill Collins, "Learning from the Outsider Within: The Sociological Significance of Black Feminist Thought," *Social Problems* 33, no. 6 (1986): S14–S32, https://doi.org/10.2307/800672.

34. Vicki L. Crawford, Jacqueline Anne Rouse, and Barbara Woods, eds., *Women in the Civil Rights Movement: Trailblazers and Torchbearers, 1941–1965* (Bloomington: Indiana University Press, 1993).

35. Daniel Laurison, Hana Brown, and Ankit Rastogi, "Voting Intersections: Race, Class, and Participation in Presidential Elections in the United States 2008–2016," *Sociological Perspectives* (Dec. 9, 2021), https://doi.org/10.1177/07311214211059136.

36. There's a team of political scientists who have published multiple three-hundred-plus-page tomes on this topic, along with a number of articles. These include Henry Brady, Sidney Verba, and Kay Lehman Schlozman, "Beyond SES: A Resource Model of Political Participation," *American Political Science Review* 89, no. 2 (June 1995): 271–94, https://doi.org/10.2307/2082425; Kay Lehman Schlozman, Henry E. Brady, and Sidney Verba, *Unequal and Unrepresented: Political Inequality and the People's Voice in the New Gilded Age* (Princeton, NJ: Princeton University Press, 2018); Kay Lehman Schlozman, Sidney Verba, and Henry E. Brady, *The Unheavenly Chorus: Unequal Political Voice and the Broken Promise of American Democracy* (Princeton, NJ: Princeton University Press, 2012); Sidney Verba, Kay Lehman Schlozman, and Henry E. Brady, *Voice and Equality: Civic Voluntarism in American Politics* (Cambridge, MA: Harvard University Press, 1995).

37. Bernard L. Fraga, *The Turnout Gap: Race, Ethnicity, and Political Inequality in a Diversifying America* (Cambridge: Cambridge University Press, 2018); Janelle Wong, S. Karthick Ramakrishnan, Taeku Lee, and Jane Junn, *Asian American Political Participation: Emerging Constituents and Their Political Identities* (New York: Russell Sage Foundation, 2011).

38. Eline A. de Rooij and Donald P. Green, "Radio Public Service Announcements and Voter Participation Among Native Americans: Evidence from Two Field Experiments," *Political Behavior* 39, no. 2 (June 2017): 327–46, https://doi.org/10.1007/s11109-016-9358-4.

39. Constitutional Rights Foundation, "South Africa: Revolution at the Ballot Box," https://www.crf-usa.org/bill-of-rights-in-action/bria-12-2-a-south-africa-revolution-at-the-ballot-box, accessed July 7, 2021.

40. Matt Flinders, "Low Voter Turnout Is Clearly a Problem, but a Much Greater Worry Is the Growing Inequality of That Turnout," *British Politics and Policy at LSE* (blog), Mar. 13, 2014, http://blogs.lse.ac.uk/politicsandpolicy/look-beneath-the-vote/.

41. Rolfe, *Voter Turnout.*

42. On Black political organization, see Angela Behrens, Christopher Uggen, and Jeff Manza, "Ballot Manipulation and the 'Menace of Negro Domination': Racial Threat and Felon Disenfranchisement in the United States, 1850–2002," *American Journal of Sociology* 109, no. 3 (Nov. 2003): 559–605; Evelyn Nakano Glenn, *Unequal Freedom: How Race and Gender Shaped American Citizenship and Labor* (Cambridge, MA: Harvard University Press, 2004); Charles M. Payne, *I've Got the Light of Freedom: The Organizing Tradition and the Mississippi Freedom Struggle, with a New Preface*, 2nd ed. (Berkeley: University of California Press, 2007); Ari Bearman, *Give Us the Ballot: The Modern Struggle for Voting Rights in America* (New York: Picador, 2016); Kenneth T. Andrews, *Freedom Is a Constant Struggle: The Mississippi Civil Rights Movement and Its Legacy* (Chicago: University of Chicago Press, 2004); Kraig Beyerlein and Kenneth T. Andrews, "Black Voting During the Civil Rights Movement: A Micro-Level Analysis," *Social Forces* 87, no. 1 (2008): 65–93, https://doi.org/10.1353/sof.0.0095.

43. WTTW Chicago, *Dusable to Obama: Chicago's Black Metropolis*, "Power, Politics, Pride: Dawson's Black Machine," July 16, 2018, https://interactive.wttw.com/dusable-to-obama/dawsons-black-machine; Matthew J. Countryman, *Up South: Civil Rights and Black Power in Philadelphia*, illus. ed. (Philadelphia: University of Pennsylvania Press, 2007).

44. Donna M. Owens, "Jim Clyburn Changed Everything for Joe Biden's Campaign. He's Been a Political Force for a Long Time," *Washington Post*, Apr. 1, 2020, https://www.washingtonpost.com/lifestyle/style/jim-clyburn-changed-everything-for-joe-bidens-campaign-hes-been-a-political-force-for-a-long-time/2020/03/30/7d054e98-6d33-11ea-aa80-c2470c6b2034_story.html.

45. Donna Brazile et al., *For Colored Girls Who Have Considered Politics* (New York: St. Martin's Press, 2018).

46. Rolfe, *Voter Turnout*; Dawson, *Behind the Mule*.

47. Wong et al., *Asian American Political Participation*; Louis DeSipio, Natalie Masuoka, and Christopher Stout, "The Changing Non-Voter: What Differentiates Non-Voters and Voters in Asian American and Latino Communities?," Sept. 19, 2006, https://escholarship.org/uc/item/3n67v86t; Kim Geron, *Latino Political Power* (Boulder, CO: Lynne Rienner, 2005).

48. Carol Anderson, *One Person, No Vote: How Voter Suppression Is Destroying Our Democracy* (New York: Bloomsbury, 2018); Frances F. Piven and Richard A. Cloward, *Why Americans Still Don't Vote: And Why Politicians Want It That Way* (Boston: Beacon Press, 2000); Behrens, Uggen, and Manza, "Ballot Manipulation and the 'Menace of Negro Domination'"; Bridgett A. King and Laura Erickson, "Disenfranchising the Enfranchised: Exploring the Relationship Between Felony Disenfranchisement and African American Voter Turnout," *Journal of Black Studies* 47, no. 8 (Nov. 2016): 799–821, https://doi.org/10.1177/0021934716659195.

49. This doesn't mean there's no discrimination in the medical field. See Sabino Kornrich, "Entrepreneurship as Economic Detour? Client Segregation by Race and Class and the Black-White Earnings Gap Among Physicians," *Work and Occupations* 36, no. 4 (Nov. 2009): 400–31, https://doi.org/10.1177/0730888409346822; Adia Harvey Wingfield and Koji Chavez, "Getting In, Getting Hired, Getting Sideways Looks: Organizational Hierarchy and Perceptions of Racial Discrimination,"

American Sociological Review 85, no. 1 (Feb. 2020): 31–57, https://doi.org/10.1177 /0003122419894335.

50. Rivera, *Pedigree*; Adia Harvey Wingfield and John Harvey Wingfield, "When Visibility Hurts and Helps: How Intersections of Race and Gender Shape Black Professional Men's Experiences with Tokenization," *Cultural Diversity and Ethnic Minority Psychology* 20, no. 4 (2014): 483–90, https://doi.org/10.1037/a0035761.

51. Brian is not White, and he had a highly visible campaign job, so I am not describing him more fully so as not to identify him.

52. Friedman and Laurison, *The Class Ceiling*.

53. I wish I could say what kinds of jobs they might have left for, but I don't have much data on people who were briefly low-level staffers in campaigns and then left politics.

54. Miller, "As 2020 Campaigns Diversify Staff."

CHAPTER 3: THE HIDDEN WORLD OF CAMPAIGNS

1. Matthew Mahler, "Politics as a Vocation: Notes Toward a Sensualist Understanding of Political Engagement," *Qualitative Sociology* 29, no. 3 (Sept. 2006): 281–300, http://dx.doi.org.proxy.swarthmore.edu/10.1007/s11133-006-9032-y; Matthew Mahler, "The Day Before Election Day," *Ethnography* 12, no. 2 (June 2011): 149–73, https://doi.org/10.1177/1466138110392470.

2. Exact income data is hard to obtain; the Bureau of Labor Statistics doesn't have an occupational category for "political consultants" or "campaign staff." In Washington, DC, the average earnings of "public relations and fundraising managers," the job category a lot of political consultants would likely be in, is $204,270 a year. That's in the top 3 percent of earners nationwide. A survey of political consultants in 2000 found that over 27 percent reported earnings over $150,000/ year, which in 2000 put them in the 98th percentile of earners. For the survey results, see James A. Thurber, Candice J. Nelson, and David A. Dulio, eds., *Crowded Airways: Campaign Advertising in Elections* (Washington, DC: Brookings Institution Press, 2000). See also US Bureau of the Census, "Money Income in the United States: 2000," Sept. 1, 2000, table C. For more on campaign workers' pay, see also the discussion in chapter 1.

3. Terry McAuliffe and Steve Kettmann, *What a Party! My Life Among Democrats: Presidents, Candidates, Donors, Activists, Alligators and Other Wild Animals* (New York: St. Martin's Griffin, 2008), 289–90.

4. David Plouffe, *The Audacity to Win: How Obama Won and How We Can Beat the Party of Limbaugh, Beck, and Palin* (New York: Penguin, 2010).

5. Rasmus Kleis Nielsen, *Ground Wars: Personalized Communication in Political Campaigns* (Princeton, NJ: Princeton University Press, 2012).

6. For good overviews of the organization of contemporary campaigns, see Robert P. Watson and Colton C. Campbell, eds., *Campaigns and Elections: Issues, Concepts, Cases* (Boulder, CO: Lynne Rienner, 2003); Wayne P. Steger, Sean Q. Kelly, and J. Mark Wrighton, *Campaigns and Political Marketing* (New York: Haworth Press, 2006).

7. Moreover, when research focuses on consultants it often ends up including people who are essentially vendors of campaign-related services, such as those who mass-mail fundraising letters or produce signs with candidates' names on them, with little or no meaningful influence on how campaigns operate.

8. On party organizations see, for example, Jonathan Bernstein, "The Expanded Party in American Politics," PhD diss., University of California, Berkeley, 1999; Jonathan Bernstein and Casey B. K. Dominguez, "Candidates and Candidacies in the Expanded Party," *PS: Political Science and Politics* 36, no. 2 (2003): 165–69, https://doi.org/10.1017/S1049096503002014; Peter L. Francia and Paul S. Herrnson, "Keeping It Professional: The Influence of Political Consultants on Candidate Attitudes Toward Negative Campaigning," *Politics and Policy* 35, no. 2 (May 2007): 246–72, https://doi.org/10.1111/j.1747-1346.2007.00059.x; Brendan Nyhan and Jacob M. Montgomery, "Connecting the Candidates: Consultant Networks and the Diffusion of Campaign Strategy in American Congressional Elections," American Journal of Political Science 59, no. 2 (Feb. 1, 2015): 292–308, https://doi.org/10.1111/ajps.12143; Richard M. Skinner, Seth E. Masket, and David Dulio, "527 Committees and the Political Party Network," *American Politics Research* 40, no. 1 (Jan. 2012): 60–84.

9. Plouffe, *The Audacity to Win*, 64.

10. Green and Gerber, *Get Out the Vote*; Alan S. Gerber and Donald P. Green, "Do Phone Calls Increase Voter Turnout? A Field Experiment," *Public Opinion Quarterly* 65, no. 1 (2001): 75–85; Alan S. Gerber, Donald P. Green, and Ron Shachar, "Voting May Be Habit-Forming: Evidence from a Randomized Field Experiment," *American Journal of Political Science* 47, no. 3 (July 2003): 540–50, https://doi.org/10.1111/1540-5907.00038.

11. That was the year Republicans first attempted to use an app called ORCA, an effort that failed memorably. See Maggie Haberman and Alexander Burns, "Romney's ORCA Program Sank," *Politico*, Nov. 9, 2012, https://www.politico.com/story/2012/11/romneys-orca-program-cant-stay-afloat-083653.

12. Nielsen, *Ground Wars*, 90–91.

13. García Bedolla and Michelson, *Mobilizing Inclusion*.

14. Kay Lehman Schlozman, Sidney Verba, and Henry E. Brady, *The Unheavenly Chorus: Unequal Political Voice and the Broken Promise of American Democracy* (Princeton, NJ: Princeton University Press, 2012), 161.

15. Ryan D. Enos and Eitan D. Hersh, "Party Activists as Campaign Advertisers: The Ground Campaign as a Principal-Agent Problem," *American Political Science Review* 109, no. 2 (May 2015): 252–78, https://doi.org/10.1017/S0003055415000064.

16. Ryan D. Enos and Anthony Fowler, "Aggregate Effects of Large-Scale Campaigns on Voter Turnout," *Political Science Research and Methods* 6, no. 4 (Oct. 2018): 733–51, https://doi.org/10.1017/psrm.2016.21; Daniel E. Bergan et al., "Grassroots Mobilization and Voter Turnout in 2004," *Public Opinion Quarterly* 69, no. 5 (Jan. 2005): 760–77, https://doi.org/10.1093/poq/nfi063.

17. Andy Kroll, "The Best Way to Beat Trumpism? Talk Less, Listen More," *Rolling Stone*, Sept. 15, 2020, https://www.rollingstone.com/politics/politics-news/2020-presidential-campaign-tactic-deep-canvassing-1059531; Pema Levy, "The Secret to Beating Trump Lies with You and Your Friends," *Mother Jones*, Nov. 2020, https://www.motherjones.com/politics/2020/10/relational-organizing.

18. Sara Eckel, "Why I Love Political Canvassing," *Washington Post*, Oct. 25, 2018, https://www.washingtonpost.com/outlook/2018/10/25/why-i-love-political-canvassing.

19. Josh King, *Off Script: An Advance Man's Guide to White House Stagecraft, Campaign Spectacle, and Political Suicide* (New York: St. Martin's Press, 2016).

20. Olivia Nuzzi, "The Full(est Possible) Story of the Four Seasons Total Landscaping Press Event," *Intelligencer*, Dec. 21, 2020, https://nymag.com/intelligencer /2020/12/four-seasons-total-landscaping-the-full-est-possible-story.html.

21. Greenwood, "Democratic Pollsters Acknowledge 'Major Errors.'"

22. Courtney Kennedy et al., "An Evaluation of 2016 Election Polls in the U.S.," report prepared by the Ad Hoc Committee on 2016 Election Polling for the American Association for Public Opinion Research, https://www.aapor.org /Education-Resources/Reports/An-Evaluation-of-2016-Election-Polls-in-the-U-S .aspx?mod=article_inline.

23. Keith, *The Myth of the Independent Voter*; Pew Research Center, "Political Independents: Who They Are, What They Think," report, Mar. 14, 2019, https:// www.pewresearch.org/politics/2019/03/14/political-independents-who-they-are -what-they-think.

24. See Hakeem Jefferson, "The Curious Case of Black Conservatives: Construct Validity and the 7-Point Liberal-Conservative Scale," SSRN Scholarly Paper, July 6, 2020, available at https://ssrn.com/abstract=3602209 or http://dx.doi. org/10.2139/ssrn.3602209; Daniel Laurison, "The Willingness to State an Opinion: Inequality, Don't Know Responses, and Political Participation," *Sociological Forum* (Sept. 1, 2015): 925–48, https://doi.org/10.1111/socf.12202.

25. Pierre Bourdieu, "Political Representation: Elements for a Theory of the Political Field," in Language and Symbolic Power, trans. John B. Thompson, 171–202 (Cambridge, MA: Harvard University Press, 1991); Pierre Bourdieu, "Public Opinion Does Not Exist," in *Communication and Class Struggle*, vol. 1: *Capitalism, Imperialism*, ed. Armand Mattelart and Seth Siegelaub (Amsterdam: International General, 1979), 124–30; Adam J. Berinsky, *Silent Voices: Public Opinion and Political Participation in America* (Princeton, NJ: Princeton University Press, 2004).

26. Homonoff, "2020 Political Ad Spending Exploded."

27. Brad Adgate, "Targeting Households Using Addressable TV Advertising Is Being Tested," *Forbes*, Aug. 17, 2020, https://www.forbes.com/sites/bradadgate /2020/08/17/targeting-households-using-addressable-tv-advertising-is-being -tested.

28. Eitan D. Hersh and Brian F. Schaffner, "Targeted Campaign Appeals and the Value of Ambiguity," *Journal of Politics* 75, no. 2 (Apr. 2013): 520–34, https:// doi.org/10.1017/S0022381613000182.

29. Homonoff, "2020 Political Ad Spending Exploded."

30. Broockman and Kalla, "Experiments Show This Is the Best Way to Win Campaigns."

31. Rick Perlstein, "Exclusive: Lee Atwater's Infamous 1981 Interview on the Southern Strategy," *Nation*, Nov. 13, 2012, https://www.thenation.com/article /archive/exclusive-lee-atwaters-infamous-1981-interview-southern-strategy; Ian Haney-López, *Dog Whistle Politics: How Coded Racial Appeals Have Reinvented Racism and Wrecked the Middle Class* (New York: Oxford University Press, 2015).

32. America's Voice, "Searchable Database of Racist and Xenophobic Dog-Whistle Ads; 1092 Total Ads."

33. Zoltan L. Hajnal, *Dangerously Divided: How Race and Class Shape Winning and Losing in American Politics* (Cambridge, UK: Cambridge University Press, 2020).

34. Marie Gottschalk, "The Democrats' Shameful Legacy on Crime," *New Republic*, Sept. 11, 2019, https://newrepublic.com/article/154631/democrats-shameful-legacy-crime; Biden for President, *Unprepared*, video, Apr. 18, 2020, https://www.youtube.com/watch?v=PmieUrXwKCc.

35. Davin L. Phoenix, *The Anger Gap: How Race Shapes Emotion in Politics*, illus. ed. (Cambridge: Cambridge University Press, 2019).

36. Stephen Ansolabehere and Shanto Iyengar, *Going Negative* (New York: Free Press, 1997); Richard R. Lau, Lee Sigelman, and Ivy Brown Rovner, "The Effects of Negative Political Campaigns: A Meta-Analytic Reassessment," *Journal of Politics* 69, no. 4 (2007): 1176–1209, https://doi.org/10.1111/j.1468-2508.2007.00618.x.

37. Ken Rudin, "John Edwards' $400 Haircut Tip Came from Obama Campaign," *Political Junkie* (blog), NPR, Nov. 10, 2009, https://www.npr.org/sections/politicaljunkie/2009/11/john_edwards_400_haircut_tip_c.html.

38. Plouffe, *The Audacity to Win*, 57.

39. Sean Jeremy Westwood, Solomon Messing, and Yphtach Lelkes, "Projecting Confidence: How the Probabilistic Horse Race Confuses and Demobilizes the Public," *Journal of Politics* 82, no. 4 (Oct. 2020): 1530–44, https://doi.org/10.1086/708682.

CHAPTER 4: THE ROOM WHERE IT HAPPENS

1. Where in chapter 2 the denominator for these kinds of figures was *people*, here I'm looking at *positions*. Specifically, I'm looking at key roles on presidential, US Senate, governor, or US House campaigns in 2004 or later. I included all national-level and multistate positions, and director-level statewide positions (such as national political director, Midwest communications director, or Iowa state director). There are 3,077 rows in my database that meet these criteria. Of these, 987 are national, regional, or statewide campaign directors or managers or deputy directors; 1,757 are national, regional, or statewide *department* directors; and 333 have other key roles at the national level only. A national deputy communications director is included, but the deputy communications director for a statewide or House race or in a statewide role on a presidential campaign, is not included. The same individuals may be counted more than once because here my focus is positions, not individuals. Thus, if a White person in my dataset has been a campaign manager five times in their career and a Black person only once, that would contribute to the conclusion that campaign managers are more likely to be White. I have not been able to identify who held every role in every major national campaign in that time, but if someone who is in my dataset held one of those roles, they will be counted here.

2. Pierre Bourdieu, "The Forms of Capital," in *Handbook of Theory and Research for the Sociology of Education*, ed. J. Richardson (New York: Greenwood Press, 1986), 241–58, https://www.marxists.org/reference/subject/philosophy/works/fr/bourdieu-forms-capital.htm; Nan Lin, "Social Networks and Status Attainment," *Annual Review of Sociology* 25, no. 1 (Aug. 1999): 467–87, https://

doi.org/10.1146/annurev.soc.25.1.467; Ronald S. Burt, "The Contingent Value of Social Capital," *Administrative Science Quarterly* 42, no. 2 (June 1997): 339–65; Ted Mouw, "Social Capital and Finding a Job: Do Contacts Matter?," *American Sociological Review* 68, no. 6 (Dec. 2003): 868–98, https://doi.org/10.2307/1519749; Sandra Susan Smith, "'Don't Put My Name on It': Social Capital Activation and Job-Finding Assistance Among the Black Urban Poor," *American Journal of Sociology* 111, no. 1 (July 2005): 1–57, https://doi.org/10.1086/428814.

3. As discussed in chapter 3, campaign managers fall into two very different groups: relatively inexperienced young people who work for local and state and upstart candidates and are mostly bossed around by consultants and party committees; and very experienced people who work for presidential, gubernatorial, and US Senate races. Many consultants have clients in both kinds of races.

4. For a few examples of how this works, see Lauren A. Rivera, "Hiring as Cultural Matching: The Case of Elite Professional Service Firms," *American Sociological Review* 77, no. 6 (Dec. 2012): 999–1022, https://doi.org/10.1177/0003122412463213; Kevin Woodson, "Race and Rapport: Homophily and Racial Disadvantage in Large Law Firms," *Fordham Law Review* 83, no. 5 (Apr. 2015): 2557; Rosabeth Moss Kanter, *Men and Women of the Corporation: New Edition*, 2nd ed. (New York: Basic Books, 1993).

5. Jonathan Capehart, "Symone Sanders Has Something to Say—and Now She'll Speak for Kamala Harris," *Cape Up*, podcast, Dec. 8, 2020, https://www.washingtonpost.com/podcasts/cape-up/symone-sanders-has-something-to-say--and-now-shell-speak-for-kamala-harris.

6. See Ballotpedia, "Election Results 2020: Incumbent Win Rates by States," https://ballotpedia.org/Election_results,_2020:_Incumbent_win_rates_by_state. See also Gary W. Cox and Jonathan N. Katz. "Why Did the Incumbency Advantage in U.S. House Elections Grow?," *American Journal of Political Science* 40, no. 2 (May 1996): 478, https://doi.org/10.2307/2111633.

7. Hubert L. Dreyfus and Stuart E. Dreyfus, "Peripheral Vision: Expertise in Real World Contexts," *Organization Studies* 26, no. 5 (May 2005): 779–92, https://doi.org/10.1177/0170840605053102; Dale F. Whelehan, Kevin C. Conlon, and Paul F. Ridgway, "Medicine and Heuristics: Cognitive Biases and Medical Decision-Making," *Irish Journal of Medical Science* 189, no. 4 (Nov. 2020): 1477–84, https://doi.org/10.1007/s11845-020-02235-1.

8. Sarah E. Brewer, "Gender and Political Vocation: Women Campaign Consultants," PhD diss., American University, 2003. Though another study found that firms with women partners were not less likely to be hired onto campaigns: Costas Panagopoulos, David A. Dulio, and Sarah E. Brewer, "Lady Luck? Women Political Consultants in U.S. Congressional Campaigns," *Journal of Political Marketing* 10, no. 3 (2011): 251–74, https://doi.org/10.1080/15377857.2011.588103.

9. Kelly Dittmar, "Negotiating Gender: Campaign Practitioners' Reflections on Gender, Strategy, and Campaigns," paper presented at the annual meeting of the American Political Science Association, Washington, DC, 2010, abstract at http://papers.ssrn.com/sol3/papers.cfm?abstract_id=1669795; Matthew Mahler, "Politics as a Vocation: Notes Toward a Sensualist Understanding of Political

Engagement," Qualitative Sociology 29, no. 3 (Sept. 2006): 281–300, http://dx.doi.org.proxy.swarthmore.edu/10.1007/s11133-006-9032-y.

10. David Plouffe, *The Audacity to Win: How Obama Won and How We Can Beat the Party of Limbaugh, Beck, and Palin* (New York: Penguin, 2010), 66–67.

11. How we understand the politics of the "White working class" depends to a considerable extent on whom you categorize as working class. White Americans who are experiencing economic precarity are actually much more likely to identify as liberal and support Democrats; White Americans without college degrees but often with medium or even high incomes are much more conservative. See Martin Gilens, *Why Americans Hate Welfare* (Chicago: University of Chicago Press, 1999); Kevin Reuning, "Identifying the Working Class," *Data for Progress* (blog), Feb. 5, 2019, https://www.dataforprogress.org/blog/2019/2/5/identfying-the-working-class; Kevin Reuning and Sean McElwee, "The Precarious: How American Voters View the Working Class," *Politics, Groups, and Identities*, published online Apr. 1, 2021: 1–19, https://doi.org/10.1080/21565503.2021.1908149; On the effectiveness of turnout efforts, see García Bedolla and Michelson, *Mobilizing Inclusion* ; Ryan D. Enos, Anthony Fowler, and Lynn Vavreck, "Increasing Inequality: The Effect of GOTV Mobilization on the Composition of the Electorate," Journal of Politics 76, no. 1 (2014): 273–88.

CHAPTER 5: THE PRODUCTION OF POLITICS

1. Todd Gitlin, *Inside Prime Time* (Berkeley: University of California Press, 2000); Richard A. Peterson and N. Anand, "The Production of Culture Perspective," *Annual Review of Sociology* 30 (Jan. 2004): 311–34; Wayne E. Baker and Robert R. Faulkner, "Role as Resource in the Hollywood Film Industry," *American Journal of Sociology* 97, no. 2 (1991): 279–309; Clayton Childress, *Under the Cover: The Creation, Production, and Reception of a Novel* (Princeton, NJ: Princeton University Press, 2019); Pierre Bourdieu, *The Rules of Art: Genesis and Structure of the Literary Field* (Stanford, CA: Stanford University Press, 1996).

2. Megan Tobias Neely, *Hedged Out: Inequality and Insecurity on Wall Street* (Berkeley: University of California Press, 2022).

3. Rick Ridder, *Looking for Votes in All the Wrong Places: Tales and Rules from the Campaign Trail* (New York: Radius Book Group, 2016), 24.

4. Colin Jerolmack and Shamus Khan, "Talk Is Cheap: Ethnography and the Attitudinal Fallacy," *Sociological Methods and Research* 43, no. 2 (May 2014): 178–209, https://doi.org/10.1177/0049124114523396.

5. Matthew DeBell et al., "The Turnout Gap in Surveys: Explanations and Solutions," *Sociological Methods & Research* 49, no. 4 (Nov. 2020): 1133–62, https://doi.org/10.1177/0049124118769085.

6. Among numerous critiques of this kind of approach a key one is that treating race and other ascribed characteristics that are the product of historical and structural inequalities as simple variables often ends up attributing unequal outcomes to people's race (or other characteristics) in and of themselves, rather than to the racism and racist processes that produce unequal outcomes. See Tukufu Zuberi and Eduardo Bonilla-Silva, *White Logic, White Methods: Racism and Methodology* (Lanham, MD: Rowman & Littlefield, 2008).

7. Davin L. Phoenix, *The Anger Gap: How Race Shapes Emotion in Politics*, illus. ed. (Cambridge: Cambridge University Press, 2019).

8. Lisa García Bedolla and Melissa R. Michelson, *Mobilizing Inclusion: Transforming the Electorate Through Get-Out-the-Vote Campaigns* (New Haven, CT: Yale University Press, 2012); Green and Gerber, *Get Out the Vote*.

9. Ryan D. Enos, Anthony Fowler, and Lynn Vavreck, "Increasing Inequality: The Effect of GOTV Mobilization on the Composition of the Electorate," *Journal of Politics* 76, no. 1 (2014): 273–88.

10. Erika Franklin Fowler, Travis N. Ridout, and Michael M. Franz, "Political Advertising in 2016: The Presidential Election as Outlier?," *Forum* 14, no. 4 (2017): 445–69, https://doi.org/10.1515/for-2016-0040; Gerber et al., "How Large and Long-Lasting Are the Persuasive Effects of Televised Campaign Ads?"; Joshua Kalla and David E. Broockman, "The Minimal Persuasive Effects of Campaign Contact in General Elections: Evidence from 49 Field Experiments," *American Political Science Review* 112, no. 1 (Feb. 2018): 148–66.

11. Richard R. Lau, Lee Sigelman, and Ivy Brown Rovner, "The Effects of Negative Political Campaigns: A Meta-Analytic Reassessment," *Journal of Politics* 69, no. 4 (2007): 1183, https://doi.org/10.1111/j.1468-2508.2007.00618.x.

12. Matthew Mahler, "Politics as a Vocation: Notes Toward a Sensualist Understanding of Political Engagement," *Qualitative Sociology* 29, no. 3 (Sept. 2006): 281–300, http://dx.doi.org.proxy.swarthmore.edu/10.1007/s11133-006-9032-y.

13. Stephen Ansolabehere and Shanto Iyengar, *Going Negative* (New York: Free Press, 1997).

14. Rick Ridder, *Looking for Votes in All the Wrong Places: Tales and Rules from the Campaign Trail* (New York: Radius Book Group, 2016),

15. See, for example, García Bedolla and Michelson, *Mobilizing Inclusion*.

16. Sasha Issenberg, *The Victory Lab: The Secret Science of Winning Campaigns* (New York: Crown, 2012).

17. Pierre Bourdieu, *The Rules of Art: Genesis and Structure of the Literary Field* (Stanford, CA: Stanford University Press, 1996).

18. David L. Rosenbloom, *The Election Men: Professional Campaign Managers and American Democracy* (New York: Quadrangle Books, 1973), 99.

19. Broockman and Kalla, "Experiments Show This Is the Best Way to Win Campaigns."

20. Kreiss, *Prototype Politics*.

21. Paul J. DiMaggio and Walter W. Powell, "The Iron Cage Revisited: Institutional Isomorphism and Collective Rationality in Organizational Fields," *American Sociological Review* 48, no. 2 (1983): 147–60, https://doi.org/10.2307/2095101.

22. Adam Sheingate, *Building a Business of Politics: The Rise of Political Consulting and the Transformation of American Democracy* (New York: Oxford University Press, 2016)

CHAPTER 6: DEMOCRATIC IMPACTS

1. Theda Skocpol, *Diminished Democracy: From Membership to Management in American Civic Life* (Norman: University of Oklahoma Press, 2003).

2. Skocpol, *Diminished Democracy*, 3, 5, 6.

3. Skocpol, *Diminished Democracy*, 127.

4. Robert D. Putnam, *Bowling Alone: The Collapse and Revival of American Community* (New York: Simon & Schuster, 2001).

5. Andrew J. Perrin, *American Democracy: From Tocqueville to Town Halls to Twitter* (Malden, MA: Polity Press, 2014).

6. Seth E. Masket, "When Party Machines Turned Immigrants into Citizens and Voters," *Washington Post*, Dec. 16, 2014, http://www.washingtonpost.com/blogs /monkey-cage/wp/2014/12/16/when-party-machines-turned-immigrants-into -citizens-and-voters. Much of the social welfare policy that was developed during this time made life markedly better for poor and working-class White people, while excluding Black people and other people of color. See Cybelle Fox, *Three Worlds of Relief: Race, Immigration, and the American Welfare State from the Progressive Era to the New Deal* (Princeton, NJ: Princeton University Press, 2012); Thomas C. Leonard, *Illiberal Reformers: Race, Eugenics, and American Economics in the Progressive Era* (Princeton, NJ: Princeton University Press, 2017).

7. Perrin, *American Democracy*, 29.

8. John Herbert Aldrich, *Why Parties: The Origin and Transformation of Political Parties in America* (Chicago: University of Chicago Press, 1995); David H. Everson, "The Decline of Political Parties," *Proceedings of the Academy of Political Science* 34, no. 4 (1982): 49–60, https://doi.org/10.2307/3700968.

9. Daniel Schlozman and Sam Rosenfeld, "The Hollow Parties," in *Can America Govern Itself?*, ed. Frances E. Lee and Nolan McCarty (Cambridge: Cambridge University Press, 2019), 120–52, summary at https://doi.org/10.1017 /9781108667357.006.

10. Adam Sheingate, *Building a Business of Politics: The Rise of Political Consulting and the Transformation of American Democracy* (New York: Oxford University Press, 2016), 5.

11. Larry Sabato, *The Rise of Political Consultants: New Ways of Winning Elections* (New York: Basic Books, 1981); Dennis W. Johnson, *No Place for Amateurs: How Political Consultants Are Reshaping American Democracy* (New York: Routledge, 2001). For a more comprehensive history of campaign professionals, see the overview in the introduction to Jason Johnson, *Political Consultants and Campaigns: One Day to Sell* (New York: Routledge, 2011).

12. James A. Thurber and Candice J. Nelson, eds., *Campaign Warriors: Political Consultants in Elections* (Washington, DC: Brookings Institution Press, 2000).

13. Perrin, *American Democracy*, 12.

14. Sheingate, *Building a Business of Politics*, 4.

15. Richard M. Skinner, Seth E. Masket, and David Dulio, "527 Committees and the Political Party Network," *American Politics Research* 40, no. 1 (Jan. 2012): 60–84; Jacob Montgomery and Brendan Nyhan, "The Party Edge: Consultant-Candidate Networks in American Political Parties," *Paper 8*, Southern Illinois University, 2010, https://opensiuc.lib.siu.edu/pnconfs_2010/8; Jonathan Bernstein and Casey B. K. Dominguez, "Candidates and Candidacies in the Expanded Party," *PS: Political Science and Politics* 36, no. 2 (2003): 165–69, https://doi.org/10.1017 /S1049096503002014.

16. For this chapter's analyses of my database, I include politicos for whom I can identify at least one role on a campaign in 2008 or earlier and for whom I could find at least one additional position (whether on a campaign or not) other than the

one for which they were added to the database. For more on the party network, see note 15 above.

17. Each of these types of organizations is governed by different tax codes and levels of campaign finance regulations as to how much money they can raise, how much they have to disclose their donors, how they can spend that money, and the extent to which they can coordinate with an official campaign. This results in all kinds of bureaucratic and administrative contortions. Some organizations have different arms with different legal statuses, or they split their staff between a coordinated side that can share inside information from an official campaign entity and an independent expenditure (IE) side that cannot, with what is commonly called a firewall—but is actually just an agreement not to share information that can't legally be shared—between them.

18. These numbers should be understood as minimums; they are likely underestimates, as the structure of the data collection limited me to including only one organizational affiliation per two-year cycle. If someone worked for Obama's campaign in 2008, the DNC in 2009, and for a Senate candidate in 2010, their work at the DNC will not be recorded. However, this shouldn't affect the differences between parties that I note.

19. Seth E. Masket et al., "Networking the Parties: A Comparative Study of Democratic and Republican National Convention Delegates in 2008," paper presented at the annual meeting of the American Political Science Association, Toronto, Sept. 6, 2009, abstract at http://papers.ssrn.com/Sol3/papers.cfm?abstract _id=1451174.

20. Dana R. Fisher, *Activism, Inc.: How the Outsourcing of Grassroots Campaigns Is Strangling Progressive Politics in America* (Stanford, CA: Stanford University Press, 2006).

21. Fisher, *Activism, Inc.*, 108.

22. As noted earlier, I only record people's jobs every two years, so people who worked in the administration in 2009 but on a campaign or anywhere else by 2010 will not show up as having worked in the administration.

23. Claes H. de Vreese and Matthijs Elenbaas, "Spin and Political Publicity: Effects on News Coverage and Public Opinion," in *Political Communication in Postmodern Democracy: Challenging the Primacy of Politics*, ed. Kees Brants and Katrin Voltmer (London: Palgrave Macmillan, 2011), 75–91, https://doi.org/10.1057 /9780230294783_5; Rasmus Tue Pedersen, "The Game Frame and Political Efficacy: Beyond the Spiral of Cynicism," *European Journal of Communication* 27, no. 3 (Sept. 2012): 225–40, https://doi.org/10.1177/0267323112454089; Rasmus Tue Pedersen, "News Media Framing of Negative Campaigning," *Mass Communication and Society* 17, no. 6 (Nov. 2014): 898–919, https://doi.org/10.1080/15205436.2013 .858749.

24. Sean A. Cain, "An Elite Theory of Political Consulting and Its Implications for U.S. House Election Competition," *Political Behavior* 33, no. 3 (Sept. 2010): 375–405, https://doi.org/10.1007/s11109-010-9140-y.

25. On "little tobacco," see Axiom Strategies, Outside the Box Public Affairs, "Little Tobacco's Big Comeback," https://axiomstrategies.com/public-affairs; Hilltop Public Solutions, "Our Services—Public Affairs," https://hilltoppublicsolutions .com/services/#public-affairs.

26. Caroline W. Lee, Michael McQuarrie, and Edward T. Walker, *Democratizing Inequalities: Dilemmas of the New Public Participation* (New York: New York University Press, 2015).

27. Caroline W. Lee, *Do-It-Yourself Democracy: The Rise of the Public Engagement Industry* (New York: Oxford University Press, 2015).

28. Edward T. Walker, *Grassroots for Hire: Public Affairs Consultants in American Democracy* (New York: Cambridge University Press, 2014), 205.

29. C. Wright Mills, *The Power Elite* (New York: Oxford University Press, 1999); G. William Domhoff, *Who Rules America? The Triumph of the Corporate Rich*, 7th ed. (New York: McGraw-Hill Education, 2013); Mark S. Mizruchi, *The Fracturing of the American Corporate Elite* (Cambridge, MA: Harvard University Press, 2013).

30. Jeffrey Lazarus, Amy McKay, and Lindsey Herbel, "Who Walks Through the Revolving Door? Examining the Lobbying Activity of Former Members of Congress," *Interest Groups and Advocacy* 5, no. 1 (Mar. 2016): 82–100, https://doi.org/10.1057/iga.2015.16.

31. Jordi Blanes i Vidal, Mirko Draca, and Christian Fons-Rosen, "Revolving Door Lobbyists," *American Economic Review* 102, no. 7 (2012): 3731–48, https://doi.org/10.1257/aer.102.7.3731.

32. Nina Eliasoph, *Avoiding Politics: How Americans Produce Apathy in Everyday Life* (Cambridge: Cambridge University Press, 1998); Elizabeth Beaumont, "Promoting Political Agency, Addressing Political Inequality: A Multilevel Model of Internal Political Efficacy," *Journal of Politics* 73, no. 1 (2011): 216–31, https://doi.org/10.1017/S0022381610000976.

CONCLUSION

1. Hahrie Han, *How Organizations Develop Activists: Civic Associations and Leadership in the 21st Century* (Oxford: Oxford University Press, 2014).

2. Theda Skocpol, *Diminished Democracy: From Membership to Management in American Civic Life* (Norman: University of Oklahoma Press, 2003).

3. Steven Schier, *By Invitation Only: The Rise of Exclusive Politics in the United States* (Pittsburgh: University of Pittsburgh Press, 2000).

4. Daniel Schlozman and Sam Rosenfeld, "The Hollow Parties," in Can America Govern Itself?, ed. Frances E. Lee and Nolan McCarty (Cambridge: Cambridge University Press, 2019), 120–52, summary at https://doi.org/10.1017/9781108667357.006; Ryan D. Enos, Anthony Fowler, and Lynn Vavreck, "Increasing Inequality: The Effect of GOTV Mobilization on the Composition of the Electorate," *Journal of Politics* 76, no. 1 (2014): 273–88.

5. Elizabeth McKenna, Hahrie Han, and Jeremy Bird, *Groundbreakers: How Obama's 2.2 Million Volunteers Transformed Campaigning in America* (New York: Oxford University Press, 2015).

6. Schlozman and Rosenfeld, "The Hollow Parties"; Daniel Schlozman, "The Lists Told Us Otherwise," *N+1*, Dec. 24, 2016, https://nplusonemag.com/online-only/online-only/the-lists-told-us-otherwise.

7. It could be argued that the insurrection must have been the result of organizing of some sort, and it was certainly inspired by Trump, but it doesn't seem like his campaign or the politicos involved were the driving force.

8. Daniel Laurison, "The Willingness to State an Opinion: Inequality, Don't Know Responses, and Political Participation," *Sociological Forum* 30, no. 4 (Dec. 2015): 925–48, https://doi.org/10.1111/socf.12202.

9. My analysis of the American National Election Survey, "2020 Time Series Study," American National Election Studies, https://electionstudies.org/data-center /2020-time-series-study.

10. Nina Eliasoph, "'Close to Home': The Work of Avoiding Politics," *Theory and Society* 26, no. 5 (1997): 605–47.

11. Doug McAdam and Karina Kloos, *Deeply Divided: Racial Politics and Social Movements in Postwar America* (Oxford: Oxford University Press, 2016).

12. James N. Druckman et al., "(Mis-)Estimating Affective Polarization," *Journal of Politics* 83, no. 3 (June 2021), https://doi.org/10.1086/715603.

13. Zoltan L. Hajnal, *Dangerously Divided: How Race and Class Shape Winning and Losing in American Politics* (Cambridge, UK: Cambridge University Press, 2020).

14. Brian F. Schaffner, Matthew Macwilliams, and Tatishe Nteta, "Understanding White Polarization in the 2016 Vote for President: The Sobering Role of Racism and Sexism," *Political Science Quarterly* 133, no. 1 (2018): 9–34, https://doi .org/10.1002/polq.12737.

15. See, for example, comments of the Republican pollster Whit Ayres as quoted in Greg Sargent, *An Uncivil War: Taking Back Our Democracy in an Age of Trumpian Disinformation and Thunderdome Politics* (New York: Custom House, 2018); Katherine J. Cramer, *The Politics of Resentment: Rural Consciousness in Wisconsin and the Rise of Scott Walker* (Chicago: University of Chicago Press, 2016); Jennifer Sherman, *Those Who Work, Those Who Don't: Poverty, Morality, and Family in Rural America* (St. Paul: University of Minnesota Press, 2009).

16. Pierre Bourdieu, "Political Representation: Elements for a Theory of the Political Field," *Language and Symbolic Power*, trans. John B. Thompson, Gino Raymond, and Matthew Adamson (Cambridge, MA: Harvard University Press, 1991), 171–202. Bourdieu writes, "The political field is the site in which, through the competition between the agents involved in it, political products, issues, programmes, analyses, commentaries, concepts and events are created—products between which ordinary citizens, reduced to the status of 'consumers,' have to choose, thereby running a risk of misunderstanding that is all the greater the further they are from the place of production" (172). See also Loïc Wacquant, "Pointers on Pierre Bourdieu and Democratic Politics," *Constellations* 11, no. 1 (2004): 3–15; and Loïc Wacquant, "From Ruling Class to Field of Power: An Interview with Pierre Bourdieu on La Noblesse d'Etat," *Theory, Culture & Society* 10, no. 3 (1993): 19.

17. One important exception, despite its title, is Jason Johnson, *Political Consultants and Campaigns: One Day to Sell* (New York: Routledge, 2011).

18. Karl Evers-Hillstrom, "Most Expensive Ever: 2020 Election Cost $14.4 Billion," *OpenSecrets News* (blog), Feb. 11, 2021, https://www.opensecrets.org/news /2021/02/2020-cycle-cost-14p4-billion-doubling-16.

19. A recent study showed little return for corporations whose PACs contributed to Senate races. See Anthony Fowler, Haritz Garro, and Jörg L. Spenkuch, "Quid Pro Quo? Corporate Returns to Campaign Contributions," *Journal of Politics* 82, no. 3 (July 2020): 844–58, https://doi.org/10.1086/707307. But there is evidence that politicians are more likely to meet with people they believe are donors.

See Joshua L. Kalla and David E. Broockman, "Campaign Contributions Facilitate Access to Congressional Officials: A Randomized Field Experiment," *American Journal of Political Science* 60, no. 3 (2016): 545–58, https://doi.org/10.1111/ajps .12180.

20. Martin Gilens, "Inequality and Democratic Responsiveness," *Public Opinion Quarterly* 69, no. 5, Special Issue (2005): 778–96, https://doi.org/10.1093/poq/ nfi058; Larry M. Bartels, *Unequal Democracy: The Political Economy of the New Gilded Age* (Princeton, NJ: Princeton University Press, 2008); Kay Lehman Schlozman, Henry E. Brady, and Sidney Verba, *Unequal and Unrepresented: Political Inequality and the People's Voice in the New Gilded Age* (Princeton, NJ: Princeton University Press, 2018).

21. Thomas Piketty, *Capital in the Twenty-First Century* (Cambridge, MA: Harvard University Press, 2014).

22. Jamila Michener, *Fragmented Democracy: Medicaid, Federalism, and Unequal Politics* (New York: Cambridge University Press, 2018).

23. Eliasoph, "'Close to Home.'"

24. Betsy Leondar-Wright, *Missing Class: Strengthening Social Movement Groups by Seeing Class Cultures* (Ithaca, NY: Cornell University Press, 2014); Lisa García Bedolla and Melissa R. Michelson, *Mobilizing Inclusion: Transforming the Electorate Through Get-Out-the-Vote Campaigns* (New Haven, CT: Yale University Press, 2012).

25. Peter K. Enns, Paul M. Kellstedt, and Gregory E. McAvoy, "The Consequences of Partisanship in Economic Perceptions," *Public Opinion Quarterly* 76, no. 2 (July 2012): 287–310, https://doi.org/10.1093/poq/nfs016.

26. Enns, Kellstedt, and McAvoy, "The Consequences of Partisanship in Economic Perceptions," 287–310; Katherine Clayton et al., "Elite Rhetoric Can Undermine Democratic Norms," *Proceedings of the National Academy of Sciences* 118, no. 23 (June 2021), https://doi.org/10.1073/pnas.2024125118.

27. Liz Hamel, Ashley Kirzinger, Cailey Muñana, Lunna Lopes, Audrey Kearney, and Mollyann Brodie, "5 Charts About Public Opinion on the Affordable Care Act and the Supreme Court," Kaiser Family Foundation, Dec. 18, 2020, https:// www.kff.org/health-reform/poll-finding/5-charts-about-public-opinion-on-the -affordable-care-act-and-the-supreme-court/.

28. Lane Kenworthy, "America's Social Democratic Future: The Arc of Policy Is Long but Bends Toward Justice," *Foreign Affairs* 93 (2014): 1–100; Lane Kenworthy, *Social Democratic America* (Oxford: Oxford University Press, 2014).

29. See, for example, Jürgen Habermas, Thomas Burger, and Frederick G. Lawrence, *The Structural Transformation of the Public Sphere: An Inquiry into a Category of Bourgeois Society* (Cambridge, MA: MIT Press, 1989).

30. Michael Young, *The Rise of the Meritocracy*, 2nd ed. (New Brunswick, NJ: Routledge, 1994); Michael Young, "Down with Meritocracy," *Guardian*, June 29, 2001, http://www.theguardian.com/politics/2001/jun/29/comment.

31. Dana R. Fisher, "The Pro-Trump Riots at the Capitol May Be a Startling Preview of a New Political Reality," *Business Insider*, Jan. 10, 2021, https:// www.businessinsider.com/trump-capitol-building-riots-violence-republicans -inauguration-biden-preview-2021-1; Brennan Center for Justice, "Voting Laws Roundup: October 2021," Oct. 4, 2021, https://www.brennancenter.org/our-work /research-reports/voting-laws-roundup-october-2021.

32. Dana R. Fisher, *American Resistance: From the Women's March to the Blue Wave* (New York: Columbia University Press, 2019); Leah Greenberg and Ezra Levin, *We Are Indivisible: A Blueprint for Democracy After Trump* (New York: Atria/One Signal, 2019).

33. Eitan Hersh, *Politics Is for Power: How to Move Beyond Political Hobbyism, Take Action, and Make Real Change* (New York: Scribner, 2020).

34. Matthew Feinberg and Robb Willer, "From Gulf to Bridge: When Do Moral Arguments Facilitate Political Influence?," *Personality and Social Psychology Bulletin* 41, no. 12 (Oct. 2015): 1665–81, https://doi.org/10.1177/0146167215607842; Andy Kroll, "The Best Way to Beat Trumpism? Talk Less, Listen More," *Rolling Stone*, Sept. 15, 2020, https://www.rollingstone.com/politics/politics-news/2020 -presidential-campaign-tactic-deep-canvassing-1059531; David Broockman and Joshua Kalla, "Durably Reducing Transphobia: A Field Experiment on Door-to-Door Canvassing," *Science* 352, no. 6282 (Apr. 8, 2016): 220–24, https://doi.org /10.1126/science.aad9713.

INDEX

ABOUT THE AUTHOR

D aniel Laurison is an associate professor of sociology at Swarthmore
College, the associate editor of the *British Journal of Sociology*, and a
2021–2022 Carnegie Fellow. He received his PhD in sociology from the
University of California at Berkeley, then had a postdoctoral appointment
in the Sociology Department at the London School of Economics. At
Swarthmore he teaches classes on social science research methods, data
visualization, how class matters in everyday life, and US politics and elections. In addition to his work on campaign professionals, he researches
and writes on social class and political inequalities. He is interested most
broadly in how the world looks different to people in different social positions and how those differences in judgment, expectations, and interpretations reproduce political, economic, and racial inequality. His work has
been published in the *American Sociological Review*, the *British Journal of
Sociology*, *Sociological Perspectives*, and *American Behavioral Scientist*. His previous book was *The Class Ceiling: Why It Pays to Be Privileged* (coauthored
with Sam Friedman). He lives in West Philadelphia with his family.